D0096539

BUILDING EFFECTIVE MINISTRY

BUILDING EFFECTIVE MINISTRY

THEORY AND PRACTICE IN THE LOCAL CHURCH

EDITED BY CARL S. DUDLEY

Harper & Row, Publishers, San Francisco
Cambridge, Hagerstown, New York, Philadelphia
London, Mexico City, São Paulo, Sydney

 For information address Harper & Row, Publishers, Inc., 10 East 53rd Street, New York, NY 10022. Published simultaneously in Canada by Fitzhenry & Whiteside, Limited, Toronto.

FIRST EDITION

Designer: Jim Mennick

Library of Congress Cataloging in Publication Data

Main entry under title:
BUILDING EFFECTIVE MINISTRY.

Bibliography: p. 246
Includes index.
1. Parishes—Addresses, essays, lectures. 2. Theology, Practical—Addresses, essays, lectures. I. Dudley, Carl S.
BV700.B84 1983 254 82-48411
ISBN 0-06-062102-8

83 84 85 86 87 10 9 8 7 6 5 4 3 2 1

Contents

III. FROM THEORY TO PARISH: MULTIDISCIPLINARY APPROACHES TO EFFECTIVE MINISTRY

IV. OVERVIEWS

Contributors

JAMES DESMOND ANDERSON is dean of Program at the Cathedral College of the Laity in Washington, D.C., author of *To Come Alive,* and co-author of *The Management of Ministry.* He has been a consultant for various denominations, including work in Europe and South America, and served as the first president for the board of Alban Institute.

DON S. BROWNING is widely appreciated for his integrative approach to practical theology through many articles and such well-known books as *Generative Man* and *The Moral Context of Pastoral Care.* He is Alexander Campbell Professor of Religion and Psychological Studies of the Divinity School and dean of the Disciples Divinity House, University of Chicago.

JACKSON W. CARROLL, as director of the Center for Social and Religious Research of Hartford Seminary, has stimulated and written research on a wide range of critical issues facing the church, including his recent co-authored studies, *Religion in America: 1950 to the Present, Too Many Pastors: The Clergy Job Market,* and *Women of the Cloth.*

CARL S. DUDLEY is professor of Church and Community at McCormick Theological Seminary and director of the Midwest Center for Congregational Ministries. He has specialized in the study of congregations, including small churches, church growth, and churches in changing communities, and has published *Making the Small Church Effective* and *Where Have All Our People Gone?*

ALICE FRAZER EVANS is well known for her development of educational case studies from actual situations. She has published frequently through Harvard University's Intercollegiate Case Clearing House, contributed to many case study books, and co-authored *Introduction to Christianity: A Case Method Approach* and *Casebook for Christian Living.* She is executive director of the Association for Case Teaching.

H. BARRY EVANS is director of Program, College of Preachers, at Washington Cathedral. He coordinates a program on the Authority of the Church in Society, sponsored by the College in association with The Grubb Institute of Behavioural Studies, London, England. He is a frequent consultant for congregations, advisor to clergy in programs of study, and general editor of *Homiletic* magazine.

ROBERT A. EVANS is founding president of the Association for Case Teaching and general editor for the Harper & Row series *Experience and Reflection: Theological Casebooks.* Dr. Evans is author of a dozen books, most recently *Human Rights: A Dialogue Between The First and Third Worlds*, and the executive director of Plowshares Institute, an agency for world peace and justice.

JAMES F. HOPEWELL began his ministry as a missionary priest of the Episcopal Church in Liberia and then served for a decade as director of the Theological Education Fund for the World Council of Churches. Dr. Hopewell, who has specialized in world religions and cross-cultural communication, is professor of Religion and the Church, and director of the Rollins Center for Church Ministries, Candler School of Theology, Emory University.

JOSEPH C. HOUGH, JR. is dean of the faculty and professor of Christian Ethics at the School of Theology, Claremont, California. Author of *Black Power and White Protestants,* he is best known for his contributions to Christian ethics in the areas of racism, sexual oppression, world hunger, and ecology, and for his advocacy of reform in theological education.

H. NEWTON MALONY is professor of Psychology in the Graduate School of Psychology of Fuller Theological Seminary. Dr. Malony is also director of the Programs of Integration in Psychology and Theology, and director of the Church Consultation Service. He has published numerous articles and books, including *Understanding Your Faith* and *Living the Answers.*

WILLIAM MCKINNEY is secretary for research and evaluation with the United Church Board for Homeland Ministries in New York and president-elect of the Religious Research Association. He is co-author of two forthcoming books: *The Varieties of Religious Presence* (with Jackson W. Carroll and David A. Roozen) and a reconsideration of the social sources of American denominationalism (with Wade Clark Roof).

LOREN B. MEAD is founder and executive director of the Alban Institute in Washington, D.C. Formerly a pastor and teacher and director of Project Test Pattern, he is author of *New Hope for Congregations*. He is best known for creative research and consulting with clergy and congregations at the critical points of ministry and for his insightful column, "From Where I Sit," published regularly in *Action Information*.

DAVID S. PACINI has served in various positions, from Harvard University tutor to assistant to the president of Colgate University to senior consulting psychologist in a detoxification center. Presently he is co-chairperson for the 1982–83 Emory University Symposium "Rethinking Human Rights" and assistant professor of Historical Theology, Candler School of Theology, Emory University.

BRUCE REED studied architecture and theology in Australia before moving to England after World War II. In 1957 he founded the Grubb Institute of Behavioural Studies for applied social science research with consulting relationships to industry, educational and penal institutions, social service agencies, and churches. He introduced the oscillation theory of religious experience with the publication of *The Dynamics of Religion* in 1978.

WADE CLARK ROOF, with the publication of *Community and Commitment* in 1974, demonstrated the relationship between particular community lifestyles and the patterns of growth in denominations with corresponding values. He is professor of Sociology, University of Massachusetts, Amherst, and associate editor of both *Review of Religious Research* and *Social Forces*.

LYLE E. SCHALLER, more than any other single individual, has shaped the field of church consulting during the past twenty years. Annually he works with about 150 congregations of twenty denominations in thirty states and still finds time to serve as resource person to workshops, pastors' schools, and training programs. He has authored more than four hundred articles and a score of books, most recently, *The Small Church Is Different* and *Growing Plans.*

Barbara G. Wheeler has specialized in continuing education for clergy and theological education for laity, with an emphasis on evaluation and program development. She has served as consultant in the Religion Division of the Lilly Endowment and evaluator for such places as the Harvard Divinity School and the National Institute for Campus Ministries. Ms. Wheeler is president of Auburn Theological Seminary in New York City.

Melvin D. Williams is a cultural anthropologist who has applied ethnography to the study of religion in the study of a church, *Community in a Black Pentecostal Church,* and of a community, *On the Street Where I Lived.* As professor of Sociology and Anthropology and director of Africana Studies and Research Center, Purdue University, he is finishing a new book, *Black Churches in West Middletown, U.S.A.*

Preface

The importance of the local church is often overlooked in the public press. In their reporting on religion, the mass media seem preoccupied with the actions of extremists, trends reflected in the public opinion polls, and statements by leaders and national religious assemblies. But the majority of people in the United States and Canada have chosen to relate themselves to the Christian faith through local congregations. Their faith is not found in extreme behavior, opinion polls, or pronouncements about religion. They associate believing with the local church and community pastor, with weddings, funerals, and personal crises, with Sunday school and neighborhood church activities.

Church members support more than 330,000 local congregations, which are found in every segment of society. There are more churches than schools, more church members than people who belong to any other voluntary association, and more financial support for churches than for all other philanthropic causes combined. Dire predictions of an earlier decade to the contrary, congregations of believers have retained their strength in a changing world. Although the ministry of the church takes on many essential forms, the body of Christ is most often associated with the outreach and caring of the local congregation.

This book celebrates the importance of the local church. It is based on two convictions. First, congregations yield unanticipated riches when taken as worthy objects of serious study. Second, the accumulation of several disciplines is necessary to fathom the diverse and complex interaction that characterizes the local church.

For many people, the beauty of a fresh look at congregations provides its own reward. The congregation appears to have endless resources in its history and in the intricate relationships and diverse perspectives of those who are committed to it. The congregation is always more than we expect because it has roots and resources beyond our understanding. The congregation is a complex gift of God.

Reflecting the fact that pastors and lay leaders alike have found the study of the congregation to be both challenging and fun, this book is written around a case study. In Part I the "case" of Wiltshire Church is presented. It is a factual account of a particular moment in the life of an actual church, although the names and places have been changed. A leading figure in the congregation tells his story, and further information is provided in background materials. This is not a model of perfection, but a congregation typical of many others, with a memorable history, identifiable resources, uncertain leadership, and recognizable problems. Given this base of information, you are invited to join with others in exploring the problems and possibilities for the people of Wiltshire Church.

The rest of the book is an exploration of insights based on studies of the Wiltshire Church case by authors who have had extensive experience working with congregations. Nine selected approaches are divided between two sections, Parts II and III, reflecting the distinction between those who seek to apply a particular discipline and those who focus primarily on the resolution of congregational problems. Part II consists of chapters written from the vantage point of disciplines that bring a recognized theoretical orientation to the study of congregations: psychology, anthropology, sociology, literary symbolism, and theology. These approaches provide the building blocks from which multidisciplinary studies are constructed. Part III includes contributions from church-related consultants who employ several disciplines in working with congregations. They emphasize the necessity for a pragmatic and eclectic approach to respond to whatever problems and needs they find.

Part IV presents three efforts to assimilate the various approaches: first, through the practice of ministry; second, through the rubrics of practical theology; and finally, through contributions that congregational studies might make to the issues of contemporary church life.

The purpose of this book is to provide new routes into the social and spiritual dynamics of the local church. Renewed appreciation for the congregation should release new energy among the membership to challenge and enliven the whole Body of Christ. Here we see hope for clergy and church members working together to build more effective ministry in and through our congregations.

The labor and vision of many people are invested here. It is one expression of a continuing study of different approaches to working with congregations that has been under the direction of a Committee for Congregational Studies composed of Jackson W. Carroll, James F. Hopewell, Loren B. Mead, Barbara G. Wheeler, and myself. We especially appreciate the catalytic participation of Robert W. Lynn of Lilly Endowment and the support that made possible several interdisciplinary gatherings during the two years of preparation. We recognize with appreciation the extensive and creative work of the contributors who prepared and tested several drafts of each chapter in dialogue with representatives of several approaches. We received particularly valuable insights from more than three hundred pastors, executives, consultants, and other church leaders who met for a three-day conference in Atlanta, Georgia, reviewing the content of this volume and helping to shape it for publication. Several other people made extensive contributions, especially Elizabeth Whipple of the Rollins Center for Church Ministries, and Sue Cossey Armendariz, who served as research assistant and typist for the final draft. At the center of our work we want to thank the people of "Wiltshire Church," and the thousands of congregations like it, who have shared their lives in a way that all of us may learn to be more effective servants of our Lord.

CARL S. DUDLEY

I

A CHURCH IN TRANSITION

1. The Case of Wiltshire Church: A Narrative

ALICE FRAZER EVANS and ROBERT A. EVANS

The case study in this chapter and in Chapter 2 is the true account of a series of events in the life of a specific congregation. However, the names of persons and places involved have been disguised to protect the privacy of those who shared their story.*

To the pastors, lay leaders, and members of the congregation of "Wiltshire Church" we extend our deep appreciation for their willingness to share their visions for the church, but also to share their problems and personal struggles. Their ability to risk, to be vulnerable, should be seen as a gift to the wider church.

Working closely with the researchers who have contributed chapters to this volume, the case writers initially identified a mainline congregation that showed signs of basic health but was dealing with significant problems. Wiltshire Church became the object of a four-month intensive field study in the winter and spring of 1981. We conducted more than sixty hours of taped in-depth interviews with church staff, lay leaders, congregational groups, judicatory executives, and town officials. Maps, newspaper articles, census data, real estate brochures, historical books and articles, and local photographs were gathered. We attended town meetings as well as church board meetings, retreats, church school classes, seminars, and Sunday worship. Official church documents gathered included conference records, annual reports, personal letters, announcements, bulletins, newsletters, and sermons. A number of question-

* The case and background statement were prepared as a basis for discussion rather than to illustrate either effective or ineffective handling of the situation. They are drawn from material available through the Association of Theological Schools, copyright © 1982 by the Case Study Institute.

naires were also distributed to the staff and congregation as a whole. Some of these we designed; others were specifically requested by the researchers. Though not all of the researchers had the opportunity to visit the congregation, each had access to all of these data.

When we refer to a "case," we mean a "slice of life"—a factual account of an event or series of events that climaxes in a decision of import. The decision must be one about which reasonable people would disagree. As a check on the objectivity of conflicting viewpoints, the final case was read and released by the pastor and selected lay leaders of the Wiltshire congregation. Their additional suggestions were absorbed into the narrative of Alan Hyatt and the background statement.

Subsequent chapters of this book use this case as a common focus to model their distinctive approaches to the local church. As you read the case, we urge you also to "enter" Wiltshire Church during this period of its life. We suggest a structured process to fix the case in your mind and to provide comparisons with the approaches in other chapters. First, you might want to list the important persons, the characters in the story, and note information contributed by each. Second, a time line of the story might be helpful, listing dates and significant events in the life of the congregation. Third, and most important, you might make a priority list of the forces and factors that contribute to the present problems of the congregation. Finally, you may wish to consider specific recommendations for Reverend Carlson, Mr. Hyatt, the administrative board, or even the bishop. The reader who has written a perspective on the issues of Wiltshire Church prior to working with subsequent chapters will have a base that may be affirmed, expanded, or challenged by each of the later approaches.

An additional consequence of entering the case through personal study is to experience the potential use of the case as an instrument of education and consultation. As a relatively nonthreatening instrument for reflection and discussion, cases like Wiltshire can allow congregations to gain objectivity about their situation and insights about themselves. Although this case is written as if it were a Methodist church, the prominent factors are not at all unique to the Methodist denomination. Lyle Schaller notes in his chapter that the Wiltshire Church should have been named Legion, "for there are many churches that resemble this one very closely." As you draw out the "universal" elements evident in Wiltshire, you may be better equipped to move from the specific approach of each chapter to the more general principles that concern congregations everywhere.

ALAN HYATT shook his head and smiled to himself as he hung up the phone. This was the second call he'd had tonight from other members of the administrative board of the Wiltshire Methodist Church. How naive and eager he'd been to accept one of the five annual openings on the fifteen-member church board. Now only three months into his three-year term, he was faced with voting for or against a building plan. Though the plan had initially seemed very straightforward, Alan was aware that the vote was much more complex than he had ever imagined. Alan now saw a string of accumulated and unresolved problems. These ranged from housing for the senior pastor and staff conflicts to divisions among board members and grumbling about "no spirituality" and "too-weak lay leadership." Most disturbing to Alan was the undercurrent of rumors that was tearing at the heart of the congregation.

Alan opened his study door, called to his teenage son and daughter upstairs to turn down their competing stereo sets, went into the kitchen to pour another cup of hot coffee, then retreated again to his desk where he had been studying the minutes of the two previous church board meetings. As he sought to put things into perspective, Alan turned his thoughts to the town of Wiltshire. He had become increasingly intrigued with the idea that the history not only of the congregation but of the town of Wiltshire was relevant to the issues the church was now facing.

Company Town—Company Church

Wiltshire, a historic Massachusetts town, was founded in the late 1600s and is almost as old as Springfield, some sixteen miles away. At one point in its history Wiltshire's central employer was the Adams Company, a textile firm that had moved to the community from England in the 1800s. It was Alan's understanding that the company had had two primary operating principles: one was a strong paternalism that dictated hiring workers for low wages but "took care of them." This was evidenced by more than two hundred small mill-type wooden houses still in town built originally for Adams's workers. The other principle was adherence to primogeniture. In each generation the eldest son or son-in-law gained operating control of the company. Other family members were also in significant administrative roles.

It was at this point that the history of the town and that of the Methodist church merged. Alan could hear Sidney Carlson, the senior pastor of his church, retelling the story. "In 1836 a Methodist circuit rider preached revival services in Wiltshire. He converted Joseph Adams, one of those early Adams Company owners. In 1840 that converted man, the individual Joseph Adams, built the first Methodist church. It was a gift and cost him three thousand dollars. Then in 1907 one of Adams's descendants, Harold Blakely, and his wife, Sophia, made a grand tour of England. They worshiped one Sunday in a quaint historic church with which Sophia fell madly in love. When they returned to Wiltshire they hired an architect to go to England and draw up plans to reproduce the building in Wiltshire. It was completed in 1909. Harold Blakely paid for the whole thing—fifty thousand dollars. Parishioners were not involved. The only significant difference was that, rather than the gray English fieldstone, the church's exterior was constructed out of the same New England sandstone as that of the main Adams Company buildings."

Alan Hyatt had also heard the Methodist district superintendent refer to it as "a big, lovely old church standing in the middle of town." He continued, "If you hadn't known it, you would assume it to be an Anglican church out of the 1700s. Most often our Methodist presence in this part of the country has been a struggling wooden church on the edge of town."

Alan Hyatt had learned from Sid Carlson additional historical facts that had fascinated him. For this reason Alan had saved the notes on Sid's presentation at the "new members seminar" he had attended just four years ago. In 1950 Ralph Adams, a descendant of Harold Blakely, paid for the construction of the fellowship hall.

Alan's notes on Sid's comments continued, "Adams challenged the congregation to match his gift, and if you want a visual picture of the mentality of the Adams Company employees, look at the two structures. Fellowship Hall, built by Adams, has cut stone, leaded glass, and oak wainscoting. The matching Sunday school wing is the cheapest form of cinder block and industrial sash."

Alan knew Adams was chairman of the church administrative board for thirty-five years. He had heard Sid say that the church pattern, before he came, was for the trustees to "meet in the Adams home on High Ridge once a year in November, just before Adams and his wife departed for four months in Florida. The officers would add up the projected disbursements, and Ralph would write out a check for the deficit—approximately five thousand dollars a year—to balance the church budget. The last year Ralph did this was 1969, when the budget was thirty-nine thousand dollars. He died that fall of a sudden heart attack. Within six weeks three other board members died. The church was in trauma."

Sid Carlson Appointed to Wiltshire

It was at this point, Alan knew, that the bishop notified Sid, who had had success with helping other congregations grow, that he was considering sending Sid to Wiltshire. Alan recalled Sid's story of first coming to Wiltshire in a February snowstorm to "check out" the town. He had gone to the town clerk and gathered a tremendous amount of information by introducing himself as a Mr. Mueller, representing a corporation considering moving to Wiltshire. He then went to the big Congregational church at the other end of town that would be his "major competition." He asked for directions to the high school and was given a grand tour of the church building and a good sketch of their program.

Sid found a town that had more than quadrupled in population in twenty years. In 1950 it was a town of 4,500. By 1960 it was 10,000, and by 1970 the population had jumped to 18,000. Once tied to farming or employment in the Adams Company, Wiltshire residents by 1970 were predominantly young upper-middle-class families whose sources of income were Springfield-based businesses and professions. Though other churches in town were growing, this tremendous growth in population was not only *not* reflected in the Methodist church, the records indicated net loss in membership between 1960 and 1970. In Sid's opinion too many of the previous pastors had been "older men, ready for retirement, whose basic duties were to preach on Sunday morning, visit the sick, and bury the dead."

When Sid, his wife, and two daughters moved to Wiltshire Church in June of 1970, he immediately made several changes. The listed membership was over 700, but Sid found a regular Sunday worship attendance of only 140. These were divided into two services in a sanctuary that could seat 270 people. He moved to one service the week after his arrival. Both the longtime secretary and the choir director left within four months.

Sid had told Alan that the only significant "uprising" came from the choir. Sid had learned that about twenty choir members, spouses, and friends were meeting to consider petitioning the bishop to have Sid removed. Sid drove over to the meeting, walked in, and offered to dial the bishop's number for them. The group dissolved.

At the first annual meeting the following January, Sid made additional changes. At this meeting, which lasted five hours, Sid cleared the rolls of 221 out-of-town or "lost" members. Each "removal" necessitated a congregational vote. The official church roll then went from 751 to 530 members. Alan also remembered Sid telling him that when he came to Wiltshire he found an administrative board of fifty-five members, most of whom had served for countless years. At this same annual meeting Sid challenged the entire administrative board literally to "vote itself out of existence" by adopting two new administrative principles: that no one would be in a job for more than three years, and that no one would have more than one job at a time. Since church discipline made no contrary provisions, these decisions were retroactive and passed by majority vote at the annual meeting. Alan smiled as he recalled Sid telling the story. "My attitude was that I was going to push for what I thought was correct—and if people didn't like it, I expected them to push back. And if they didn't push back they should shut up." Sid attributed his successful intervention to his own style of "pure brass," the strong support of his bishop, and the awareness of lay members that "changes needed to be made." After the positive vote Sid worked with the newly elected nominating committee to select a slate of fifteen members for the administrative board.

Alan recalled another major change that Sid brought about during his first year. This was, in Sid's words, "to get the church into debt." Sid had found the church with a $400,000 portfolio of stocks and bonds on which the church was depending for a substantial part of its income. He also found many members contributing an average of twenty-five cents a week. In the spring of 1971, with Sid's urging, a called congregational meeting voted to renovate the church building, completely rewire it, and bring the church into compliance with the fire code. The following year the parsonage, built in 1790 with additions in 1831 and 1870, was gutted and rebuilt with a design to provide adjunct meeting space and a possible apartment for an associate minister. The renovation work then tied up the endowment income for ten years in repayment of a bank loan.

Growth in Wiltshire Church

Over the next few years Wiltshire Church grew substantially, averaging nearly a hundred new members a year. With transfers out of the community, the net gain was about sixty members annually. Alan attributed the bulk of this growth to Sid's influence. Sid had once discussed with Alan the basic concepts that shaped his ministry in Wiltshire; much of his thinking was based on his analysis of the community. He saw Wiltshire as "a highly transient community" with as much as one-fifth turnover in population in some years. It was also a highly select group of people, most between 35 and 50 years of age, with relatively few older people. They were "for the most part upwardly mobile middle-class executives" moving to the suburbs to find a place to retreat, with good schools for the children.

Based on this analysis, Sid placed high emphasis on a strong church school, on youth work, and on the Sunday morning worship service. He saw the key components of worship as being an excellent music program and a sermon that addressed relevant contemporary issues and met, in some ways, the needs of the congregation. Sid saw "highly transient, articulate, intelligent" people, but "folk who are not biblically literate, people who wish that they could believe the message of the Christian church but really find this difficult to do, people who are disillusioned with the American dream of the two-car garage and the house in the country—divorce—kids drinking and using pot—job conflicts—the plumbing leaking and your husband in San Francisco—the family needs as monumental. I look upon myself on Sunday mornings as addressing a congregation of wistful hearts. I am not preaching to the saints, many of whom sit in our church; I am basically addressing a secular, agnostic congregation of people who are drawn to the church because they find themselves with children and suddenly begin to sense that they want to give their kids some kind of background. This leads to our emphasis on church school and directly informs both my subject matter and the manner in which that subject matter is preached."

As Alan thought of the congregation, he agreed that a substantial number of those who became members had been attracted by both the church school and Sid's sermons. Alan had been a nominal Christian a few years ago—seldom attending church until the family moved to Wiltshire. He and his wife had brought their children to the church to Sunday school. Sid's sermons and Tom Forbes's music program had kept him coming. Alan also felt that Sid's unorthodox style had appealed to him—clearly not your typical minister. Sid certainly wasn't averse to tossing in a few four-letter words, and he would often be seen in town in tennis shorts with a racket slung over his shoulder. Alan found Sid to be a man "who knew how to take charge of a situation in the best corporate sense." Alan also agreed with his wife's description of Sid as one who "could charm your socks off." This had certainly been true when Sid called on them the week following their first visit to the church. Equally impressive, Sid didn't forget who they were. Alan had heard from other people that Sid was also a real "rock" for people at times of personal crisis.

Recent Changes

In the four years since Alan and his family had lived in Wiltshire, Alan felt there had been some changes both in the town and in the congregation. Between 1975 and 1980, the population of Wiltshire had only increased from about 21,000 to 22,400, not the dramatic jump of previous years. In those same years, property values had skyrocketed. One friend in the church who had bought a home for sixty thousand dollars in 1976 sold it for over a hundred thousand in 1980. On top of that, interest rates had gone from 8.5 to 16 percent. Alan found fewer families moving in and out of Wiltshire. Several, like himself, had been transferred to executive positions in main offices in Springfield and would stay there. From observations made by longtime residents, Alan also learned that the current "commuter" residents were assuming a stronger role in local issues. A few months earlier, resistance from the town council and the zoning commission, in response to a vocal landowner coalition, had led the Adams Company to withdraw a zoning change proposal. The company had planned to develop a large wooded tract of company-owned land for multifamily units. In the past the council had had the reputation of "rubber-stamping" Adams proposals.

Alan wondered how these changes were affecting the congregation. He remembered talking to Beth Wilbanks, who had served on the church board from 1972 through 1974. Beth commented that during her tenure there was an "exciting upward movement" in the church. "We moved from a dwindling, elderly congregation to a young, vibrant, denominationally diverse membership. We had a good thing going, and we were eager to follow Sid's strong lead. In 1974 we needed to go from one Sunday service to the two we have now; we were simply too crowded. We established neighborhood parish groups to maintain a feeling of closeness. In 1974 our couples club had over fifty members. Now both of these have fizzled out and no longer meet at all. We seem so big with eleven hundred members, I feel Sid is the only one who knows everybody."

Alan also reflected about a change he had seen in Sid. Though it was hard to define, this had been confirmed by other friends who had known Sid much longer. In 1978 Sid turned 50. At the time, members of the church gave him a party and a check for a thousand dollars. A smaller group of friends gave him a rocking chair. About this same time he entered the doctor of ministry program at a theological seminary. The church, through a special grant, gave Sid the funds to cover the cost of travel and tuition. In Sid's words, he entered the program "to keep the grey matter active." Alan had heard friends say that Sid had become much more anxious about retirement and that he had even shared privately that he was considering a nonclergy profession.

Maybe he was closer to the center of things now that he was on the board, but Alan was also aware of expressions of frustration in the congregation he had not heard before. Joyce Henry was a good example—a solid, devout Methodist who taught in the Sunday school. Not long ago Joyce had laughingly commented that she had been able to adjust to being served wine rather than grape juice at Communion, but it really distressed her that this was the only church in the district with no group of United Methodist Women (UMW). The only thing close was one remaining circle composed mostly of elderly women. "Maybe that's just a sign of the times with so many women working. However," Joyce added, "I think Sid is really turned off by Methodism; he sees it as bureaucratic and cumbersome. Sid even said from the pulpit that he never stays more than one day at the week-long annual conference meeting with the bishop. We're the largest church in our district, but no one in the church serves on any of the regular conference committees. We pay our annual conference apportionment, but that's about all."

In considering the other disgruntled comments made lately, Alan thought about Jill and Hank Edwards, who, according to the church "grapevine," were no longer attending Wiltshire Church. Their primary critique was that Sid simply was not "spiritual" enough. He "never opens meetings with prayer," and on Sunday morning he "gives an excellent speech" but one Jill says she could hear at the Junior Women's Club. "We've had to form our own group outside the church for fellowship and support. There's not even any Sunday adult education." Jill added that this is a "country club" church where people are "all on the surface."

Alan realized that the Edwards were representative of several other members who had not left the church, though he was not sure how many. At the time, however, he had replied that "a pastor can't please everyone. Sid attracts a wide diversity of folk and the church can't change to please everyone."

Alan's mind flipped back to one of the phone calls he'd had this evening—from Bill Porter, a member of the social action committee. "This blasted building of Sid's has got to be the last straw." Bill had sounded as exasperated as Alan had ever heard him. "What are we doing spending two hundred thousand dollars on ourselves?! When you look at the tremendous unrealized potential in our church, all of the possible clout we could have, and so little of it realized. We've got people who are leaders, persuaders of people, spenders of millions—literally—and people who work with state and federal government. This is a young, energetic congregation. I know that some people—maybe a lot of people—join Wiltshire Church because it's the 'in' place. Because we're a large church, some folks may just want to get lost. But I'm convinced there are people who want and need more out of the church.

"We averaged thirty-five to forty people at the Lenten series that highlighted social concerns. For an evening program that was pretty high attendance. Well, we're not keeping on Stew Collins, our part-time associate pastor who organized the series, and he's been one person who has really expressed some interest in outreach. It was Stew who opened my eyes to the fact that, though we appear to give 6.6 percent of our $155,000 budget directly to mission and social action, last year we actually gave less than half that amount. Even our weekly dinner-in-a-dish hot meal program for the elderly primarily serves our own members. I know that Sid doesn't give priority to social action concerns, but it's surely not because he's not willing publicly to tackle difficult or controversial issues. I remember his announcement from the pulpit a couple of years ago that he was getting psychiatric help. A lot of people really appreciated that. He even announced to the congregation when he failed his first set of doctor of ministry exams. I've never known anyone that gutsy. Why can't some of this courage be directed to motivate folk?"

Alan had responded, "Look, Bill, you can't mold Sid to your expectations. In the past Sid was instrumental in establishing a housing project for the elderly, in developing a program to bring promising black ghetto kids into our school system, and in opening our facilities to the Jewish community before there was a synagogue in Wiltshire. For years he worked as a volunteer ambulance driver, and he now serves on the board of directors for the Springfield Catholic Family Services. He just doesn't preach about those things on Sundays. That's why we have you on outreach—to motivate folks if you see it that way." Bill's answer had been, "It's hard to do it alone. I don't even feel I can publicly voice my concerns without appearing in opposition to Sid personally."

Administrative Board Retreat

In rethinking the phone conversation, Alan realized that Bill had initially called about the building plan—but this building thing had been around for over three years. It seemed that recently everything was coming to a head. He remembered his own frustration at his first administrative board retreat three weeks ago. Stew Collins, the associate pastor, had urged them to spend time on describing who they were and then work on goal setting. When they broke up into small groups to discuss their image, Alan heard comments about "professional-centered church" and "the best show in town." Alan felt the lay leader pretty well summed up the gist of their discussion:

> I hear us saying we are a community of individuals who profess a belief in Christ, who have a limited or nominal belief in his teachings and the extension of his work, and who pose very limited responsibilities on becoming part of our group. . . . Our primary focus is concerning ourselves with the needs of the community of which we are a part.

Fred Bates, the chairman of the board, asked, "How comfortable are we with this profile?" Alan heard a chorus of responses, both positive and negative. As Fred began to push for focus and goals, Alan heard expressions of confusion. "What are we doing?" "How can we decide who we are in an hour?" "What do we need to work on?" "Let's identify the holes in our total program."

At this point Sid, who had been sitting at the edge of the group and had not entered the conversation that morning, stepped in with some clear needs for staffing in terms of music, visitation of the elderly, and youth work. Sharon Giles was solid as part-time superintendent of the large K–6 elementary church school program. But the part-time, retired minister of visitation had resigned due to poor health. They would lose in June both Stew Collins, who was going to his own church, and the seminary assistant who had led the youth groups and youth choir. Most of the rest of the morning was spent on staffing questions.

After lunch the building issue was raised. There were clear comments about the need for additional Sunday school space and the responsibility for more adequate insulation in the building. However, there were also expressions of concern about raising money in the current economy or in a congregation where the average pledge was low. Sid's response was strong. "I am utterly convinced we can do this. I've done it before. Our finances are down right now, but this is due to some personal conflicts that will pass." One board member added, "We can rally everyone around the building issue." The only clear decision Alan felt coming out of the retreat was an agreement to vote on the building plan at their regularly scheduled meeting next month.

After the retreat, Alan and Jeff Oates, in his third year on the board, went over to Harry's Pub, a comfortable little place not far from the church. Alan had told Jeff that he was aware of the tension between Fred Bates and Sid, and that he had felt a real feeling of discomfort between several board members. "What's at the bottom of all this?"

Pastoral Housing Proposal

Jeff said he believed that most of it stemmed from early last fall when a proposal for housing for Sid had come before the board. "I guess it all got started when Sid let it be known the previous spring that he'd had a couple of enticing offers to go elsewhere. Lucie Owens, one of Sid's avid devotees, told me she and a few others were deeply concerned, convinced the church would suffer if Sid left. They were determined to keep him here. Lucie's brother is a pastor and had told her how important owning his own home was. Now when the group approached Fred Bates and the district superintendent, it was told, 'This is just not done in our conference'; 'The bishop disapproves'; and 'A church would have to assume complete responsibility for such a move.' Undaunted, the ad hoc group proceeded with the investigation, consulted tax experts, and worked out a definite proposal. They then requested time on the agenda to present all this to the administrative board. I must admit I saw their rationale; taxwise it made a lot of sense. Sid is now 53. He is deeply worried about retirement; in this conference retirement benefits are paltry, and he's still paying for kids in college. We would solicit funds to help Sid with the down payment. Then part of his present salary would be applied to housing to cover utilities and begin to build up equity for retirement.

"He and Connie also live a fishbowl existence right next to the church. On off hours any calls to the church ring in the parsonage. Because he is so responsive to people, Sid is virtually on call twenty-four hours a day. Lately I've been particularly aware of the pressure he is under. Now, by conference regulations, a minister must live in the parsonage, but we could hire and house a full-time associate here—which we need and haven't been able to afford—and we could also utilize large areas of the parsonage for additional church school space, which would mean we could scrap the building plan. I feel that Sid was extremely pleased with the whole idea.

"Now when this whole thing outlining a specific house, mortgage payments—the whole bit—was presented to the board, many were hearing it for the first time. Fred Bates was even out of town, as he had been for several of our meetings last year. Sid was not present for the discussion, though he must have gotten it word-for-word later on. There were some, like myself, who thought the housing idea made sense. Questions by some, however, were strong. 'We're considering a building campaign and would be approving this housing group to approach the same people for Sid's down payment that have been selected as major contributors.' 'Does this mean we're tied to Sid for the next ten years?' 'What happens if Sid dies?' 'Isn't the bishop opposed to this?' 'Have we looked into annuties for Sid?' 'I thought that big raise we gave Sid last year was for retirement resources.' 'Is this a personal gift for Sid or would it apply to a future pastor?'

"Marilyn Davis was one of the more outspoken opponents of the housing proposal. Her husband had been approached for funds before the issue ever reached the board. Marilyn indicated that this kind of extraboard process 'would lead to anarchy.' She continued, 'This proposal also isn't honest. It says Sid earns twenty thousand dollars. That's the highest salary in our district. But with all of the hidden benefits, he's making close to forty thousand. Then Connie works full-time, which gives them a substantial combined salary. Now I'm certainly not advocating that a minister has to take a vow of poverty, but we've got to act responsibly for the whole church.' The housing issue was tabled for further study."

Jeff Oates continued by telling Alan that Sid was "deeply distressed." "I hadn't realized how important it was to him. He felt that after giving his heart and soul to the congregation for ten years, the first time he asks for something for himself, he's slapped down. In Sid's words, 'All this support is only a veneer. They don't give a goddamn about me.'

"Not long after, in a public meeting, Sid sharply criticized Marilyn Davis, whom he had 'once considered a close personal friend.' After this," Jeff continued, "all hell broke loose. Marilyn is in the choir and chairs the music committee. The organist, Tom Forbes, went to Sid, charging Sid was publicly attacking Marilyn, and said he would resign unless Sid publicly apologized to her. Then Fred Bates came on the scene and wrote a letter to all board members canceling further discussions of the housing issue. He also called an ad hoc board meeting at his own home, excluded Sid, and proceeded to share a significant number of complaints he had received about Sid during his term as head of the board."

Tensions Increase

Jeff paused. "I must add that Fred is a long-standing member here, over twenty-eight years. He was on the board that voted itself out when Sid first came. Now I'm not sure what all of the issues were, but it was clear that Fred was deeply concerned about Sid's leadership. In the midst of this meeting, the six-member pastor-parish relations committee (PPRC) said Fred was out of line to have called the meeting and that they should be handling such complaints, not the whole board. The meeting broke up, and I know that Sid and Tom met with the PPRC the next week, but no one else on the board seems to know what was decided. Not too much later, Marilyn Davis resigned from the board.

"Now, Alan, if you detected the tension between Fred and Sid, that background may help clarify things. The fact that you didn't know about all this hoopla adds weight to my conviction that the majority of folk out there on Sunday morning don't know anything about it. Some of the board feel we're better off to bury the whole thing and let the malcontents drift away.

"You also said you experienced a feeling of discomfort between board members. My analysis deals with style. Three years ago, to reflect the size of the congregation, we increased the size of our nominating committee from six to nine members. Not only is our larger congregation more diverse, the same is now true of the board. I think we've got more vocal, independent board members than in the past, but I also think this is threatening to people. Now the present style of dealing with this diversity is to put folks down. Did you see some of the raised eyebrows and grins when Jill Edwards's name was mentioned? We're meeting controversy with contempt, not dialogue. I hate to say it, but I feel we may be taking our cue from Sid. I even had one board member tell me she had wanted to speak out for Marilyn Davis before she resigned, but that 'Sid knows so much about me, my story would be all over the church if I did.' Now I've known Sid to break confidences in the past, but I certainly never saw things in this kind of light. I've always felt his strengths far outweighed his weaknesses. But I agree that right now he's under too much pressure without enough help. That's where the whole staff thing we talked about this morning comes in. Now after hearing Sid's questions about the music program, I think he feels it needs some re-organization. With the tension between Sid and Tom, I wouldn't be surprised if Tom resigned as organist on top of everything else."

The retreat and Alan's conversation with Jeff Oates had been three weeks ago. In the interim, Alan had heard that Tom was going to submit his resignation as organist and choir director. Alan knew what a close-knit community that thirty-five member choir had become. He anticipated some real expressions of anger if the rumor were true.

Building Proposal

Alan took another sip of coffee and frowned. It was stone cold. He spread out on his desk the building proposal and looked at the list he had made of pros and cons. It was clear they needed more space. Every room in the education wing was full on Sunday morning, and due to poor construction, the rooms were cold and drafty in the winter. The church rented space a block away for grades 7–12, which Alan felt was adequate but seemed to separate the older kids from the life of the congregation. The only possible room for adult education would be the pastor's study, and this was the only place Sid had to take a breather or meet privately with someone between services. Administrative and office space in general were not efficient. There were also no access ramps for the handicapped into the church, into either the main sanctuary or the church school wing. Emergency exits in the event of a fire were probably also inadequate. Insulation in the whole wing was extremely poor, and heating costs continued to escalate. They ought to build now before the cost of oil and building materials got any higher.

On the other hand, Alan felt the present parsonage could offer additional space if they worked out the pastoral housing thing in the future. Then again, if Sid weren't there as pastor, was there any way they could anticipate the same numbers in the church school? The K–6 superintendent was clear: "On Sundays when Sid doesn't preach, our attendance figures are significantly lower." Population growth in Wiltshire was leveling off. Wiltshire public schools were now averaging an annual drop of two hundred children. So far the Methodist church school attendance records were against the trend. Alan was also uncertain about voting for a campaign while things were so uneasy in the church. The board's ambivalence was evident to Alan as he looked over the past minutes. Last March they had voted for renovation of one area then rescinded this at the next meeting. Then another committee was formed to present this new plan for additional space. Maybe Jeff Oates was right. They ought to get an outside professional church consultant before proceeding with either new staff or the building thing.

Alan leaned back in his chair and thought about Sid's role in the whole situation. Beth Wilbanks had shared with him an image that seemed helpful. "I see Sid clearly as the dominant figure in this congregation. There is a broad range of groups, some of whom have complaints. Sometimes board members don't carry through on their responsibilities, but because of his visibility, Sid gets the blame. He's like a maypole with all of these colored ribbons attached. Every issue that comes up adds another ribbon to wind tighter around him." Alan felt that in the past ten years the lay leadership had not assumed a strong enough role. He wondered how the board could begin to work as a team to take some of the pressure off Sid.

Just then the phone rang. It was Jeff Oates. "Alan, I hear Fred Bates is resigning as chairman of the administrative board. Since you're new on the board, we'll be looking to you for a fresh perspective and some solid leadership to break through this morass. I'll be glad to help in any way I can. Do you think it's time to look into hiring that consultant?"

2. The Case of Wiltshire Church: Background

ALICE FRAZER EVANS and ROBERT A. EVANS

The Setting

Wiltshire is a historic community located on the site of a former Indian village in western Massachusetts. Although it was first settled by Europeans in the late 1600s as a farming community, its early growth related to a local textile firm. In the past two decades Wiltshire has doubled in population (from 10,000 to over 21,000) due to expansion from nearby Springfield, Massachusetts.

The mayor describes Wiltshire as "a typical suburban community," lodged between two sets of ridges that divide it from Springfield and from other surrounding communities. She suggests that many people believe that it has a "Shangri-la atmosphere [that] gives the town a positive sense of identification, but also a sense of isolation and values to be protected."

The mayor based her philosophical reflections on patterns and cycles that she associated with the writings of Santayana and the Durants. She felt there was a quest for privacy among the citizens of Wiltshire. "In an outgoing, aggressive, and competitive culture, there is a basic reserve," she asserted. The attraction of Wiltshire was "the ability to live in a suburban community and yet have . . . your own island. You can not only get in between the ridges every night, you then go and get in between the birches and the elms. You really can isolate yourself . . . whether for positive or negative reasons is for someone else to determine. In my own case, it has been positive. I can go at a rapid pace as long as I have a period of time to restore that energy."

Most of the residents of Wiltshire are white, middle class. The figures from the 1980 census show the population: white, 20,683 (97.7 percent); black, 183 (0.9 percent); and other, 295 (1.4 percent). Most of the residents in Wiltshire, including the blacks, have upper management jobs or are corporate executives, according to the mayor. A high percentage of the community is professionally employed, and an increasing number of the women are finding employment outside the home.

To conserve the Wiltshire "quality of life in a rural setting," an advocacy group has been formed called the Wiltshire Conservation Committee. A recent article in the *Springfield Times* described the town as having a "drawbridge mentality." The mayor cites an attitude among some citizens: "There is an attitude in some quarters that we worked hard to get here and anyone else who wants to be here can also work to get here. On the other side of the issue [are] the three-hundred-year residents, the descendants of the original residents, who are saying to the new people, 'We made room for you and we think you should take an example from us and make room for others.'" In the spring of 1981, the largest town meeting in the history of Wiltshire voted overwhelmingly to sell a parcel of town land to a large company for its corporate headquarters. Many residents voiced support based on the need for a wider tax base.

In the past few decades Wiltshire has been a "child-oriented" community, reflected in the middle-aged families who place a high priority on education. One resident indicated that her family had moved to Wiltshire "to buy a school, not a house." Thirty-five percent of the population is under 18 years of age. In the past decade few young married couples moved into the community because of the high cost of housing, and older people often moved to smaller houses or condominiums when their children left home. This pattern may be changing. There is a trend for older couples to retain their homes and older children to continue to live with their parents.

Population projections for 1990 suggest a decline for the school age population (from 35 percent to 27 percent) and a proportionate gain in the number of residents over 45 (from 25 percent to 33 percent). It is not clear how this will affect the employment patterns of Wiltshire, since the majority of people are at present employed in other communities, primarily Springfield. In Wiltshire, the Adams Company is the largest employer, with a employment base of about 800. The second largest employer is the town of Wiltshire, which has 637 employees, most of whom are related to the school system.

The Congregational church is the oldest religious institution in Wiltshire, although the Methodists began home worship in the early 1800s. A Baptist church was constructed as early as 1833, and the Roman Catholic church dates from 1850. Lutheran, Presbyterian, and Universalist-Unitarian churches were established within the last century. Most recently, the Wiltshire Valley Jewish Congregation constructed a synagogue in 1972.

The Methodist Church Building

The church is located at the center of the historic and business district of Wiltshire. Within a hundred yards of the church building are located City Hall, the Public Assembly Building, the restored first meeting house, and at least twenty shops and restaurants, including a modern supermarket.

The church sanctuary, fellowship hall, classrooms, and parsonage are located on a relatively small lot at a major intersection, with a parking lot behind the church buildings. The sanctuary is warmly furnished with dominant dark wood tones, exposed wooden beams, and elaborate Tiffany stained glass windows. On Sunday mornings it is regularly three-fourths full at the 9 A.M. service and quite full at the 11 A.M. service. The sanctuary is the largest gathering space in the church buildings, with comfortable seating for 270 adults.

The fellowship hall, adjacent to the sanctuary, is about one-fourth its size. The Sunday school rooms, offices, choir rooms, and kitchen are located on two floors in relatively crowded conditions. Committee meetings are regularly held in the pastor's study, but a gathering there of more than fifteen people seems crowded. The junior and senior high youth classes meet in space across Main Street, rented from an art gallery in the historic area. The church building, which is crowded on Sunday, is relatively empty during the week. It is used by office staff, weekly for scouts and a prayer group, and for other occasional meetings.

Church Membership

Membership in Wiltshire Church comes by transfer of letter or confession of faith. An active visitors calling program is followed by an optional one-session class for membership orientation conducted by the pastor. One lay leader said that there were two explicit expectations for membership: a financial contribution and occasional worship participation. Issues of belief or commitment were generally assumed.

The composition of the congregation is typically middle-aged upper-middle-income white families. Exceptions do not break the pattern: some younger couples, single adults, black families—all seem to share the same basic values and aspirations. Although the black members can frequently trace their Methodist roots to the South, many of the most recent white members of Wiltshire Church have no previous experience with the Methodist church.

Of the 1100 members, the senior pastor lists 800 as active. The average weekly worship attendance is 350. Since a significant number of the membership must travel in their employment, the attendance average appears to represent a larger membership who attend on a "rotating" basis. There is also a strong Sunday church school program for children and youth, with an average attendance of 250. Adult education during the week accommodates another 30 participants. Interviews with lay members suggest that their church activities are focused on Sunday morning, with a few active members involved in leadership functions and special programs during the week. Some of those interviewed identified a group of "old-timers" or "established members" that was estimated at 15 to 25 percent of the congregation and was seen to be less active in recent years.

The total projected church budget for 1981 was $155,000, with $9,000 (6 percent) allocated for mission and benevolence. Given the resources of the congregation, clergy and lay leaders agree that financial contributions to the church are "terrible" and "depressing."

Church Programs and Activities

For most of the year *worship* involves two virtually identical services on Sunday morning, at 9 A.M. and 11 A.M.; during the summer and Christmas holidays a single service is sufficient. Professional leadership is provided by the senior pastor, part-time associate pastor, and organist/choir director. Special music is offered by the church choir, anchored by four professional soloists, which may be supplemented by one of the choirs of children and youth. Communion, served on the first Sunday of each month, takes a different form of worship. The Eucharist is served at the rail, necessitating the communicants to come forward and return to their seats.

Church school is offered during both services of worship. The basic Methodist curriculum, *Christian Studies,* is employed for K–6, under the leadership of a paid part-time program director. As her goal, the director declared, "I want children to leave here feeling they are loved and knowing they can always come here. If we create an atmosphere of caring and love, then we are successful."

Youth program includes a separate Youth Worship Service during the 11 A.M. worship on Sunday morning and activity groups on Sunday evenings. Programs vary from devotional to social interests. The youth groups are known for their annual musical events, such as *Jesus Christ, Superstar,* performed by a combination of youth groups and many young people unrelated to the church. Leadership is provided by a paid part-time youth director and volunteer advisors from the congregation. A number of members view the youth program as outreach to the community by Wiltshire Church.

Administrative board is composed of fifteen members, who serve for a three-year term. Each board member has specific responsibilities for the operation of the church. As a board they meet with the pastor to make policy and implement programs in Wiltshire Church. At present all members of the board are between the ages of 35 and 50. The board is relatively small for a Methodist church of this size.

Adult groups reflect the needs and interests of particular constituents. They at present include two *Bible study* groups meeting biweekly, one with the leadership of the pastor. A *prayer group* of women meets every Wednesday. *Sara Circle* for the older women meets monthly for devotions, sharing, and service. *Women's Sharing Group,* for recently married women, meets monthly for a program and discussion. *Meals on Wheels* is a service group that prepares and delivers about thirty dinners each week to elderly members of the parish. *Adult education* programs, series, and special events are generated as the need is expressed and the leadership is available.

Leadership

Although charitable concerns, especially among individual members, were attended to from 1846 to 1970, there was no discernible pattern of religious presence in the community on behalf of the church as an institution. The structure and leadership of Wiltshire Church was radically altered in June 1970 by the appointment of the present senior pastor. In his view, the pastorate had been a "safe chaplaincy," and the church had been "sitting on its hands for fifty years." With the clear understanding that the bishop expected him "to straighten this place up," the newly appointed pastor dramatized his entry with a series of decisive actions that are widely recounted in congregational interviews. As a result the entire existing administrative board resigned. This placed the official control of the church in the hands of a new board, with the new pastor clearly in charge.

Current lay leaders of the congregation agree that the pastor "filled a leadership vacuum" during his first years in the congregation. The feeling persists among some members that a small group of leaders makes the decisions for the congregation under the direction of the senior pastor. Most members of the administrative board believe that the pastor has been the primary factor in decision making for the church. Yet the current situation is in flux. Some board members have expressed confusion about their responsibilities on the board, and some have commented on the lack of clarity about the goals and direction of the church in the past several months. In the same period of time, several board members have observed an increase in conflict within the congregation. Many board members noted, with a variety of feelings, that the pastor recently had not appeared to function with his usual strong style of leadership. At the time of the annual board retreat, the pastor admitted that he was attempting to withdraw from his usual directive pastoral leadership style "while the board attempts to develop new leadership."

During the course of this study, several changes in church leadership occurred. Resignations were submitted by the chairman of the administrative board, one other board member, and the church treasurer. In his letter of resignation, the chairman of the board raised several "charges" about the senior pastor, and indicated his concern for the quality of life in the congregation. Several staff positions also opened: the part-time associate pastor received a full appointment to another congregation; the interim youth director returned to seminary; and the minister of music resigned.

Methodist Structure and Organization

During the past decade Wiltshire Church functioned as "a village community church," as one member described it. The senior pastor has publicly criticized the Methodist system. When asked why neither he nor lay leaders provide leadership for the conference, the pastor indicated that the meetings were more than two hours away, large, tedious, and unproductive, with debates clouded by "polarized pressure groups." Further, both the pastor and the board expressed unhappiness with the district superintendent for offering "no help whatsoever" on two occasions when they felt they needed the appointment of an assistant pastor.

At the same time, the district superintendent said that, although Wiltshire Church was unique as a Methodist church in its building, administrative structure, and relation to the conference, it was the "strongest church in the district" in terms of growth in members, money, and church school. He noted that it was not numerically the largest church in the district, at least not yet. He further expressed concern about a connectional church built as heavily around the style of the pastor as is Wiltshire Church.

The middle-management mentality of the community is reflected in the mind-set of the membership, who expect professionally competent services from the staff under a directing but noncontrolling board. One leader observed, "We don't know what we want and expect from the church staff, so we hire talent to give it. This results in what appears to be a 'one man show.' " A board member declared that the priority on personal needs often resulted in burdens on the pastor and conflict in the congregation. On the other hand, the pastor and several lay leaders stated that the "quiet majority" of the congregation was satisfied with the present tone and direction of the church.

Observable Themes in Congregational Life

The "best show in town" and the "in" church were frequently used to describe Wiltshire Church by members, visitors, community residents, and even staff. The meaning and specific application of the terms varied with the speaker, but the image was consistent. The First Congregational Church of Wiltshire was viewed as "historic" and "established." But Wiltshire Church was where the action was. No other congregation had such clear and immediate recognition in this way.

When asked about the impact on the community beyond the church, the senior pastor recalled the support of the congregation in the face of opposition by many town residents for the church's purchase of a building to house a program for helping runaway youth. "However," he said, "I look on myself as a minister of this Methodist church, with a minimal interest in impacting major social and economic problems in the community. There is a major question in my mind whether the church ought to be addressing these as a church. We do attempt to reach out through the conference . . . but for the most part that is a very peripheral part of our lifestyle." Over the past ten years, however, the senior pastor has served on numerous community boards and agencies.

The associate pastor agreed with the pastor's analysis of social involvement. After a recent administrative board meeting, called for the purpose of setting goals, he said, "We are the church of Jesus Christ. What does that mean for us? They have a reputation as a country club. . . . I am surprised we don't have some sort of service at . . . the beginning of the season when everybody brings their tennis rackets to church and they bless the damn things."

The associate pastor indicated particular frustration with the administrative board. He believed the leadership was out of touch with those members in the congregation who want to "spend less time and attention on ourselves, and to address the community needs not only of Wiltshire, but of the people in Springfield as well."

Among the membership a significant number had not been active in any congregation prior to membership in Wiltshire Church. The church image was felt to be communicated through the style of the church and the personality of the pastor. There are also a number of people who attend regularly but have not become members. Since the line between church member and constituent is not sharply drawn, these church attenders are listed in the directory of membership, but in different size type.

The relationship between the larger mass of members and the church leadership was not always clear. Among some leaders there were concerns voiced in dramatic terms of "our present problems," "distress," and "the turmoil in the church." For these people, three themes occurred most frequently:

1. The need for *spiritual depth and growth* was expressed. Some people sought help from the worship services, which sometimes seemed to lack "spiritual and theological depth." Others looked for help in Bible study and prayer groups both within and beyond Wiltshire Church.
2. In what had become a "large church" some expressed a need for *nurturing communities.* Some wanted a sense of community in a transient world. Others wanted space where they could "comfortably share problems and seek help."
3. Some indicated their desire for a church to be a vehicle for *service* to the community and beyond. Some people wanted a channel for their own commitment, and others were pushing for the commitment of the congregation as a whole.

Although these issues were frequently mentioned, it is not clear how many people were involved in the "turmoil." Several leaders suggested that such restlessness was limited to "splinter groups" and a "relatively small percentage of the congregation."

Theological Self-Understanding

Both pastors and most lay leaders were unable to define the church's theological self-understanding. The traditional terms, "conservative," "liberal," "fundamentalist," were avoided or rejected. Whenever the interviews pressed the theological question, the response was a description of the needs of the congregation or the community. The senior pastor suggests, "It is difficult to assign a theological category to the bulk of those people because I don't think they think in theological terms. It is alien to their lifestyle."

The theology that appears to be reflected in the worship and life of the congregation is very personal and individualistic. This is typified by the conviction that loneliness, anxiety, or failure can be "lived through," or survived, by virtue of Christian faith. The God proclaimed is "loving Father," who knows how to give good gifts to his children. The Jesus proclaimed is the one who says "come unto me for my yoke is easy and I will give you rest." The Holy Spirit that is summoned is the "comforter" who assures of God's forgiveness and Christ's presence in moments of trial. The world outside the doors of the church is seen as the appropriate arena for one's life actions. Christ is present in and involved in that world through individual Christians. The church provides "sanctuary," as the senior pastor stressed in a recent sermon. It is the place that provides nurture and caring for those who must go out of the sanctuary and do battle in a fundamentally positive and exciting world. Faith in God and participation in the community of the church can provide the strength to live in the midst of the tensions of the world and the socio-economic conditions in which we find ourselves. It is the pattern of Jesus' life and the model of caring among individual Christians that are the resources to which one appeals. The gospel is forgiving and restorative.

Some have said in the community, "If you can't afford to join the Wiltshire Country Club, join Wiltshire Church." This piece of local humor can be variously understood. Some take it as a good-natured compliment, and others are highly offended by the image. Still others take it as a simple statement of fact, that Wiltshire Church offers a significant ministry to its own constituency. There exists a difference of opinion among present staff and members whether the church *should* be more active in the world outside its doors. There is, however, a congruence between the church's self-understanding and the activities it supports.[1]

---

[1] The writers of subsequent chapters of this book are accustomed to developing their analyses in dialogue with the people of the local church. This working relationship provides a test for the accuracy of their insights. More important, by sharing their information, the congregation joins with the researcher-consultant in shaping the result in such a way that it becomes absorbed naturally into the life and work of the church.

Their normal procedure was not possible in this instance. Although they could request information, the contributors could not work personally with the congregation. The written case undoubtedly reflects some of the values and biases of the authors. In addition, the contributors experienced unexpected frustration as they developed their perspectives apart from the congregation. Many authors rediscovered how important to their ministries is the personal contact that they have in working directly with members of congregations they serve.

However, the congregation was very cooperative in providing additional information not normally available in church consultations. As noted in the Preface, the case writers developed far more documentation than could be included in this brief case. Additional information, such as letters and minutes, are sometimes quoted by contributors with appropriate citations. The sociologists were especially active in gathering further information about the community. The theologians were provided with additional data from a survey of the membership and from worship materials. Newton Malony engaged the pastor and a few members in a leadership study, and James Hopewell was provided with an additional survey on the world view of the membership. Even in the absence of extensive personal contact, the members and leadership of Wiltshire Church were outstanding in their cooperation for a common cause.—ED.

II

BASIC BUILDING BLOCKS: THE APPLICATION OF THEORY

SEPARATE disciplines are like primary colors of red, green, and blue. They are not more pure than other approaches, but they provide the basic building blocks of recognized theory that produce a consistent perspective in themselves and combine with others, without losing their integrity, to enrich the picture of the whole. We include five disciplines: psychology, anthropology, literary symbolism, sociology, and theology.

Although *psychology* is frequently associated with studies of individual needs (contributing directly to such fields as pastoral counseling and clergy development), the group consciousness of social psychology has also had an impact on the church. Kurt Lewin and Robert Bales, for example, directly influenced the small-group movement associated with programs promoted by National Training Labs. Organizational psychology, with roots in business and industry, strongly influenced the organizational development program adopted in many denominations. In England the Tavistock and Grubb institutes are widely known for the application of psychological, and even psychiatric, principles toward the understanding of group behavior. The chapter by Barry Evans and Bruce Reed applies the basic principles of dependence, expectancy, and fight-flight to the problems of Wiltshire Church.

As a field method of cultural *anthropology,* ethnography has come of age in recent years as an efficient instrument for congregation studies. Ethnographers do not study the church as if it were only an object, but become participants. Their basic tools are interview and observation. Melvin Williams advocates participant observation, implying that without participation there is no accurate observation; this made his work through the screen of case writers particularly difficult. The ethnographer interviews "informants," not "subjects" or "respondents" as they are called in other social sciences where a priori theories dictate both questions and possible answers. Ethnography seeks to find implicit patterns of behavior and of language that suggest the deep structures of symbolic meaning for that particular church. Because cultural anthropology is primarily concerned with the powerful symbols and social values that bind or divide a congregation (or any subculture), many sensitive pastors and church people may discover that they have been "closet ethnographers" for a long time.

Literary symbolism is related to ethnography through the awareness of the congregation's story. Of all the disciplines represented, seminary graduates have the most training and practice in the importance of literary criticism of the biblical text and use of literary symbols in skills of communication, especially in preaching. James Hopewell applies an old, familiar discipline of literary symbolism to the congregation as a whole. Through the tools of ethnography, the patterns and beliefs of the congregation become his text. Through literary concepts he shows how the congregation's web of meaning is often an unspoken story continuously retold in the actions of the people. Like an ancient myth recounted in the light of the campfire, his analysis is at once mysterious and comforting.

In recent years *sociology* has embraced at least three different traditions of social inquiry: first, the classical empirical approach with an emphasis on population predictability based on age, sex, social class, context, and ecology; second, the institutional orientation based on studies of subsystems and small work groups, using principles of integration, conflict, and exchange to interpret behavior; and third, the concern for culture and value systems, for symbolic interaction and significant reference groups. The three authors in sociology, William McKinney, Jackson Carroll, and Clark Roof, originally prepared three separate analyses of the Wiltshire Church case. Because of their common commitments to empirical data and sound sociological theory, they integrated these into one chapter showing a unified sociological approach—with the strengths of their differences still clearly evident to the discerning reader. Taken as a whole, the chapter provides a brief cross section of contemporary sociology and a protest against the fractured way that sociology is commonly employed.

Theology came first for the church. In the Middle Ages, theology was called queen of the sciences, but more recently it has fallen on hard times. Thinking theologically about the congregation has become so muddled that many pastors seem to have stopped trying. For our project it was difficult to find professional theologians who concentrate on anything as concrete and particular as the local church. We offer two positive approaches.

Theological ethics provides a model of a theologian at work in the parish. With the aid of the social sciences, Joseph Hough develops a fascinating profile of faith in Wiltshire Church. As a second step he uses the Bible and appropriate theological interpreters to expand an ideal of the authentic Body of Christ. Step one is the situation he finds, and step two is the ideal he desires. Like any good pastor, in step three he struggles with the difficult task of reconciling the two images.

In using *philosophical theology,* David Pacini points to a fatal flaw in the metaphors that have been taken for granted in Wiltshire. He then broadens the discussion to challenge the assumptions unquestioned by his colleagues in this book. In his discussion of "breakdown," Pacini reflects a major thrust of contemporary philosophical theology that projects an edge of doubt into the polished veneer of Wiltshire's success and self-sufficiency.

Each of these approaches stands alone as an intense engagement with Wiltshire Church. Although each of the contributors felt limited by the style of research and space for reporting, taken together they represent far more "study" than would be needed in most situations. These disciplines are presented to show their separate insights—the discovery of what they do best and when their approach would be the most appropriate. For the purpose of understanding the particular light that each discipline casts upon the congregation, these chapters are best read separately and digested slowly, to enter into the logic and to discover the results that are possible from each distinctive vision of the church.—ED.

3. The Success and Failure of a Religious Club

A Psychological Approach

H. BARRY EVANS and BRUCE REED

ANALYZING AN INSTITUTION: APPROACH AND CONCEPTS

The objective of our approach is to understand the psychological state of mind of the people of Wiltshire and to formulate hypotheses and interpretations about Wiltshire Church in relation to its environment at particular points in time. Finally, we try to arrive at a statement describing the primary task of Wiltshire Church—its normative function in the community—that could have significance for those involved in its future.

In formulating these working hypotheses, we make a number of assumptions that are derived from a theoretical framework developed by the Grubb Institute of Behavioural Studies, in England, from its study of groups and social systems. A term that describes this framework is *systems psychology.* A brief introduction to it will reveal some of the assumptions behind our analysis of Wiltshire Church.

The concepts of general systems theory are used to describe groups and institutions. The tacit psychology of the Old Testament is a conception referred to by theologians as "corporate personality." The Pauline image of the church as body is a systems notion: "We are members one of another." When viewing an organization systemically, the actions and experiences of individual members reflect not only their unique personal history and orientation toward life but also ideas and images that are held by the group corporately. Thus, when we are observing or being told about the behavior of particular individuals, we consider how this behavior is transmitting hopes, fears, and conflicts that are the property of the larger social system.

In terms of a theoretical model, institutions and organizations can be construed as open task systems of activity. As an open system, an institution can be studied by examining the processes by which it interacts with its environment. Yet, a system can also be identified in certain respects as independent of other systems, so that we can say that it has a boundary that separates it from its environment.

Whenever an input into the system is changed into an output, the process of transformation is called a *task,* which is susceptible to analysis and definition. A task is different from an aim or objective of the system. Whereas an aim refers to what people would like the system to be doing, a task describes what is actually happening. By making this distinction, the realities of the system can be separated from the fantasies held by those both within the system and outside it.

Organizations perform many tasks. But the concept of "primary task" has proved useful in sorting out the priorities among the various tasks performed. The primary task is that one process that keeps the organization existing, viable, and stable.

This brief description of an organizational model can be a useful conceptual framework for understanding systems. But in working directly with the experience of people, it is necessary to develop a language for communicating about their own experience of relatedness to the other persons and social systems that make up their world. To do so, we draw upon W. R. Bion's unconscious "basic assumptions" that influence the behavior of groups.

Bion suggested that in any group it is possible to discern two types of mental activity. The first he called "work-group" activity. This is rational thought directed toward carrying out the task for which the group has been constituted. He referred to the other kind of mental activity as "basic assumption," which is usually unconscious and held in common by all members of the group. This may be seen as directed toward defending the individual against anxieties about the survival of the group. Bion describes three recurring basic assumptions, each of which gives rise to characteristic patterns of relatedness between group members and between leader and members. The three basic assumptions may be summarized as follows:

Dependence. The unconscious assumption that the group's survival depends upon being sustained and protected by an all-powerful, all-knowing leader (who may be a person, present or absent, an institution, or an idea).

Expectancy (Bion's term for this is *Pairing*). The unconscious assumption that the group's survival depends upon producing a new leader (person, institution, or idea) who will deliver the members from their present difficulties. Groups frequently produce pairs of members who are regarded as though they are the potential parents of this new messiah.

Fight-Flight. The unconscious assumption that the group's survival depends upon destroying or evading an enemy (person, institution, or idea) that threatens it.

Both work-group and basic assumption activity include thought, words, actions, intentions, hopes, feelings, beliefs, and attitudes. Work-group activity is overt and can be studied by observation. Basic assumption activity is covert and unconscious and therefore cannot be directly observed but can deduced from other evidence and interpreted in working hypotheses that can then be tested by looking for further evidence and modified accordingly. This describes our approach to analyzing Wiltshire Church in the next section.

These two types of mental activity occur continuously and simultaneously: sometimes basic assumption activity will reinforce work-group activity, sometimes work against it. Whenever persons are involved in task systems, these levels of mental activity will constitute part of the processes being carried out. This will occur particularly where the organization largely focuses on processing information rather than products, such as happens in churches.

Recently, the Institute has attempted to integrate the systems model and the patterns of dependent, expectant, and fight-flight relationships in the following way. Each organization has a dual tendency: to preserve and assert its individuality as an autonomous whole (fight-flight) and to function as an integrated part of a larger whole (dependence). In order to engage with the purposes of the large system, a group must be ready to subordinate its own purposes and depend upon the system, thus construing that world as potentially or actually nurturing and secure. But systems survive and develop, not only through self-assertive and integrative activities, but through reproductive activities (expectancy). Under normal conditions hope is the driving force for work that is intended to bring about its fulfillment.

In analyzing an organization, our approach is to collaborate with its members and attempt to *describe* the realities of the situations rather than to *evaluate* them. If the members of the organization can see their situation in greater depth, then they can decide whether or not they want to change and may also see some way of doing so. We follow this descriptive approach in the present analysis.

WILTSHIRE CHURCH AND ITS ENVIRONMENT: FOUR HYPOTHESES

We consider evidence about Wiltshire Church in three stages in its history: prior to 1970, in the early 1970s, and at the time of the research (1981). The analysis of evidence leads to the formulation of hypothetical statements about the church in relation to its environment.

Prior to 1970

In 1840 Joseph Adams paid for the construction of the first Methodist church building. The present building, completed in 1909, was given by Harold Blakely, a descendent of Joseph Adams. It was modeled after an Anglican church he had seen in England, except that the material was the same sandstone used in the Adams Company buildings. The chairman of the church's board of trustees for thirty-five years, until his death in 1969, was the head of the Adams Company. He personally made up the church's deficit each year. The church was described as the "company church" in a "company town" and the previous pastorates as a "safe chaplaincy." This information leads us to Hypothesis 1:

Wiltshire Church was developed as a "private chapel" of the Adams Company in order to establish a dependent relation between the company and the congregation (the employees).

That the church was private can be seen from an observation made by the researchers: "While charitable concerns, especially among individual members, were attended to from 1846 to 1970, there was no discernible pattern of active religious presence [in the community] on behalf of the church as an institution or of the pastor." Though the church was ostensibly part of the Methodist denomination, it appears to have been more a private chapel than a representative of a major Christian denomination in the community.

For more than a century Wiltshire Church was dominated by managers of the Adams Company. This had the effect of controlling their employees, even though it might have been unconscious.

The weakening effect of this paternalism was made evident when one of the Adamses built the fellowship hall in 1950 and challenged the congregation to match his gift. The present pastor comments, "If you want a visual picture of the mentality of the Adams Company employees, look at the two structures. Fellowship Hall, built by Adams, has cut stone, leaded glass, and oak wainscoting. The matching Sunday school wing is the cheapest form of cinder block and industrial sash."

By the 1960s a new kind of resident began to appear in Wiltshire, whose business interests were outside the town and therefore differed radically from the time when the majority of the residents were employees of the Adams Company. Some of these new residents joined existing congregations or founded new ones, but there was a substantial proportion whose needs could not be met by churches with strong cultural, ethnic, or denominational identities, such as the Roman Catholic, Jewish, or Lutheran congregations.

By now the influence of the Adams family in the town had waned, and its domination of the Methodist church ended with the death of Ralph Adams, the chairman of the church administrative board, in 1969.

At the same time the last of the Adams "chaplains" also departed.

In the Early 1970s

The situation can be characterized as a town with residents looking for somewhere to go to church and a church looking for people to come to it. From 1950 to 1970 the town quadrupled in population. "Wiltshire residents by 1970 were predominantly young, upper-middle-class families whose sources of income were Springfield-based businesses and professions." These young executives and their families were looking for something different from Wiltshire than the older residents. For them it represented relaxation rather than work, a place where they could enjoy themselves. Their heavy emphasis upon children represented an investment for the future. Wiltshire residents joke about "buying a school not a house." The town was referred to as "child-oriented"; 35 percent of the population was under 18.

The overall picture is that of young executives looking to the future. They have fought their way into an ideal community, and they are providing their children with good schools; so the prospect is full of hope. With so many like-minded people, it would be natural for them to seek out a means by which these hopes could be reinforced.

In some respects, Wiltshire Church appeared to be the last place that they would wish to go. Among the other churches it was a poor performer. For example, between 1960 and 1970 the Presbyterian, Episcopal, and Roman Catholic churches increased their memberships between 31 and 44 percent, whereas Wiltshire Church had a net loss of members.

About this time a new minister, the Reverend Sid Carlson, was appointed. He "had had success with helping other congregations grow." He had the clear understanding that "the bishop expected him to straighten this place up." From his vitae we know that in his three previous pastorates he had achieved remarkable changes in short periods of time. His background suggests the kind of person who is a go-getter, a troubleshooter, who has the ability to size up a situation and take rapid action to capitalize upon it. He possessed many of the same characteristics as the new executives on the church's doorstep. He was seen as "a man 'who knew how to take charge of a situation *in the best corporate sense*'" (our emphasis). Like a good businessman, he "checked out" the town before he decided to take the assignment; he discovered that the Congregational church would be his "major competition." Within the first year after taking the assignment as pastor, he convinced the administrative board to dissolve itself. He cleaned the rolls of lapsed members. He fired the secretary and the choir director and dealt decisively with an uprising of the choir. These are assertive behaviors that businessmen could understand and admire.

These circumstances provided the potential for a powerful mixture. And it soon came. Once Sid Carlson began his ministry the new residents poured in over the threshold. Now the position of Wiltshire Church in relation to the other churches was reversed. In the decade between 1970 and 1980, when the population increased 21 percent, all the Protestant churches declined in membership except the Methodist church, which increased 69 percent!

We therefore offer Hypothesis 2, concerning the state of the church at this time:

> **Wiltshire Methodist Church had become an exciting place, where the needs and hopes of the young executive families could be fostered through a pairing between them and the new pastor.**

From our understanding of psychological behavior, it is not surprising that there should be a dynamic pairing relationship between congregation and pastor. In a community or organization where a previous leader has been looked up to and admired and then fails—that is, the dependent relationship has lost credibility—the leader is frequently replaced by a new relationship of pairing. The pairing symbolizes the idea that if only the pair can get together, they can create a new leader. This new leader would be a "messiah," arousing expectancy and giving them hope. We therefore suggest that the town of Wiltshire, which in the past had depended on the Adams Company, was now looking for a new form of leadership. They now found it, not in a person or in an institution, but in an idea: hope. Symbolically, the new executives and Sid Carlson were a reincarnation of the original Adams family.

Many of the feelings of the congregation, as one of the pair, were expressed through the administrative board, for it was one of the first things Sid Carlson rejuvenated and it was through it he exercised his power. Their response to his ministry provides important evidence as to the state of the church.

Another important factor was the church building. If the church had been a modest wooden structure like most of the other Methodist churches in that locality, it is less likely that the new residents would have been attracted by Sid Carlson, however dynamic he had been. The architectural copy of an old stone English church gave it the desirable image of being more established than it was and thus lent an air of respectability, status, and prosperity to fit the self-image of the executives.

During the 1970s the church continued to grow in its attractions. "'The best show in town' and 'in' church were frequently used to describe Wiltshire Church by members, visitors, community residents, and even staff." Interviews with laypersons at all levels of involvement reflected the attraction of Wiltshire Church: "provocative preaching, excellent music, and an emphasis on church school and youth work."

The minister lacked interest in broader connections with the denomination as well as the wider social-political scene (though in previous pastorates he was active in both). One member said, "I think Sid is really turned off by Methodism; he sees it as bureaucratic and cumbersome." Carlson said of himself, "I look on myself as a minister of this Methodist church with a minimal interest in impacting major social and economic problems in the community . . . for the most part that is a very peripheral part of our lifestyle."

We see here that not only has the church gathered together from the community a particular type of person, it has also reached the stage of drawing a boundary around itself, separating itself from community and denominational obligations and focusing on its own inward needs and interests. This gives rise to Hypothesis 3:

Wiltshire Methodist Church had become a club that existed to cater to the needs of its members.

A club can be defined as "an association of persons meeting periodically at some house of entertainment for social intercourse."[1] The church had the characteristics of a club whose regular meetings were on Sunday mornings, with very little activity by members of the congregation in functions and special programs during the week and with little interest outside itself. "The total projected church budget for 1981 was $155,000, with $9,000 (6 percent) allocated for mission and benevolence. Given the resources of the congregation, clergy and lay leaders agree that the financial contributions to the church are 'terrible' and 'depressing.'"

As a club, Wiltshire Church was not demanding of its members regarding their financial support. Neither did it demand a high level of commitment in other directions: "One lay leader said that there were two explicit expectations for membership: a financial contribution and occasional worship participation. Issues of belief or commitment were generally assumed." These slack obligations are evidence that there was something unrealistic about the hope generated by the pairing relationship of Sid Carlson and the church membership. If the hope had been taken seriously, efforts would have been made by the congregation to develop the church's activities in order to build it up as a community that could provide a much more secure base for confidence in the future.

But here was evidence of the pastor's insight into the businessmen's hearts. They wanted a place to isolate themselves. This was what Wiltshire offered. As the mayor said of herself: "I can go at a rapid pace as long as I have a period of time to restore that energy." So Carlson offered his congregation a private club where they could come and go as they liked without too much interference in "their quest for privacy." It cannot escape our notice that there was a strange similarity developing between this private club and Adams's private chapel.

Such clubs are not expected to act corporately in society, but their members could be encouraged to act individually. Carlson therefore turned his exhortation toward the members of the con-

[1] *Shorter Oxford Dictionary.*

gregation, calling the church "the place that provides nurture and caring for those who must go out of the sanctuary and do battle in a fundamentally positive and exciting world. Yet it is a world filled with tension, threats, and distractions to the love of God and neighbors to which we are all called." But though individual members of the church had responsible positions in the world and the community, it appeared that the pastor's challenge had little practical effect. The researchers reported that the mayor was discouraged by what she saw as "inability of people to transfer their religious beliefs . . . and apply them to day-to-day pragmatic decisions required by government." Speaking from personal experience in working at this issue of lay witness in the world, we can say that it demands considerable spiritual insight and understanding of theological issues, elements that appeared to be lacking from the pastor's "good sermons," according to some of his hearers.

At the Time of the Research

"Between 1975 and 1980 the population of Wiltshire had only increased from about 21,000 to 22,400, not the dramatic jump of previous years. In those same years property values had skyrocketed . . . interest rates had gone from 8.5 to 16 percent. Alan [from whose point of view the case study is written] found fewer families moving in and out of Wiltshire. Several, like himself, had been transferred to executive positions in main offices in Springfield and would stay there. From observations made by longtime residents, Alan also learned that current 'commuter' residents were assuming a stronger role in local issues."

This is a picture of a community that is beginning to settle down. The businessmen were no longer young; they were becoming more settled in their work, and there was less need for a retreat. Moreover, their children were growing up and making their own lives. There was less intensity of hope; in fact, by this time hope might even be replaced by anxiety about the future for children going into the uncertain world. With this change in the mood of the town from expectation to a search for more dependability, what would be the effect on the church that had apparently mirrored the prevailing state of mind of its inhabitants?

Wiltshire Church is changing, too. Members of the congregation are seeking spiritual growth, theological depth, and a nurturing community, and offering service to the community and beyond. But the associate pastor "believed the leadership was out of touch with those members in the congregation who want to 'spend less time and attention on ourselves,' and to address the community not only of Wiltshire but of the people in Springfield as well."

The pastor himself is changing his behavior. "The senior pastor admitted that he was attempting to withdraw from his usual directive pastoral leadership style." About the same time he began to study for a doctor of ministry degree and, more significantly, began to worry about retirement, having turned 50. Sid Carlson is beginning to realize that he is no longer needed as the charismatic to pair with the congregation to generate hope for the future. For the congregation, the "future" has already come. The members have settled down, while he is left up in the air, feeling increasingly hopeless. There is something sad about his belated search for security, for instead of seeking it through the church, he looks elsewhere. He puts himself under psychiatric care; he considers a nonclergy profession and precipitates a crisis in the administrative board when he asks them to help him buy a house away from the church building. Personally, he is wanting his own form of "privacy," but the church that earlier provided it for its members cannot now provide it for him.

This analysis leads to the formulation of Hypotheses 4, about the church at the time of the study:

> **Wiltshire Church is in a state of collusion between the pastor and congregation about the myth of success.**

It is important to remember that much of the material from the case study and the background statement that we have used as evidence for the past of Wiltshire Church was also given to the researchers as descriptions of the present. Although the situation of the church has altered since 1970 along the lines we have indicated, there appear to be members of the congregation who hold the same opinions about the pastor and the effectiveness of his ministry as they held in the early 1970s. Also, those members who are openly criticizing his ministry today would probably have held the same opinion since the beginning of his ministry.

The divisions in the church under Sid Carlson are not of recent origin. Yet, the persistence of the myth of the "best show in town" and the judgment of the pastor and several lay leaders "that the 'quiet majority' of the congregation was satisfied with the present tone and direction of the church" indicate that the internal conflicts of the congregation were having little effect on the reputation of Wiltshire Church. What is even more worthy of notice is that the critics of the lack of spiritual depth of the pastor have still remained to worship with him. Despite their own feelings, therefore, they have contributed to the story of success. There is surprisingly little data about people leaving the church, even after the conflicts in the administrative board as a result of Sid Carlson's outburst on feeling let down over the housing issue: "They don't give a goddamn about me."

At this present time there is chaos and confusion and lack of direction. Yet, there remains a wish to go on as before. The associate pastor, who became a spokesman for a good proportion of the congregation, is held to his limited contract by board members who probably would admit the truth of what he said and who were criticizing Sid Carlson's conduct among themselves. Carlson had stayed well beyond the length of the normal Methodist pastorate, and no mention is made about any intention to leave in the research reports.

This line of reasoning leads to our hypothesis about collusion. We do not suggest that it is conscious but that unconsciously both Carlson and the congregation cannot face the realities being presented to them, because to do so would force them to revise their beliefs about the value of what had been done in the preceding years. Yet, to deny this unconsciously requires constant effort and energy. As a result, the stress has become too great for key members of the church and of the administrative board, and they have resigned. Such actions seem to be the only way the pairing relationship can ultimately be broken.

There are some indications that an undercurrent mood of the congregation is veering away from pairing with Sid Carlson to looking for a pastor who will take seriously their human condition of frailty instead of trying to build on their search for success as

Carlson did. The associate pastor during his brief stay in 1980–81 became a kind of litmus paper signifying this trend on the part of the congregation.

AN INTERPRETATION OF THE ANALYSIS: THE PRIMARY TASK

In this section we consider evidence from the study again in the light of the foregoing analysis and attempt to state a primary task that has persisted in Wiltshire Church throughout its history. This leads us to some concluding comments about functional religion in society.

Wiltshire Church was used by the Adams family as a way of reinforcing its relations with its employees. It created a dependent environment whereby it could meet the emotional needs of the employees and at the same time provide emotional satisfaction for the Adams family in meeting these needs. The gift of the new stone church could be seen, on the one hand, as a nice church for the congregation and, on the other hand, as a memorial to the Adams family. Since the Adams factory was the largest employer in Wiltshire, it could be said that Wiltshire Church became a focal point for meeting the day-to-day human needs of many people of the town.

As time went on, the significance and power of the Adams Company diminished, and the church correspondingly diminished in its influence. Its pastors were older men. The church seemed almost at the point of collapse when the company's influence came to an end in 1969 with the death of the last Adams's trustees.

Because the people of Wiltshire no longer needed to use Wiltshire Church for its original purpose, the church was ready for a new phase of life. It was reconstituted to meet the needs of a particular section of the population that symbolized and represented the town's Shangri-la mentality. This time the emotional needs were not so much for dependence on some munificient provider but for expectancy, some hope for the future. In place of the dependent relationship between the congregation and the Adams family, there was a pairing relationship between the new pastor and the new members of the congregation. This expectancy found additional focus in the attention paid to children as the symbolic hope for the future. Because the expectancy was founded on a fantasy (the "idea" of hope, never to be realized), it was bound to fail.

We can now define the *primary task* of Wiltshire Church, which seems to characterize it from its foundation to the present: *To meet the emotional needs of its current congregation insofar as these reflect the dominant needs of the town of Wiltshire.* By "emotional needs" we refer to those feelings that people long to experience in order to have a sense of well-being in relation to their environment. When there are changes in the environment, the pattern of emotional needs will alter—hence the shift from "dependent" relationships to "expectancy" relationships in Wiltshire Church. By "dominant needs" we are using shorthand to suggest that during the period under discussion, there were people in Wiltshire who epitomized a social condition prevailing in the town as a whole and that they had a common pattern of emotional needs.

The evidence that Wiltshire Church was carrying out some function on behalf of the town is implied in its description as "a village community church." While being neither the oldest nor the most established church in Wiltshire, it was nevertheless seen in a special way. Rather than being firm in its denominational character, it was a church that took on the color of its surroundings.

The conditions that made Wiltshire Church susceptible to this function in the town can be related to a character trait that had been present throughout its history. It was a church founded by bosses for their workers. The building was out of character, pseudomedieval English church architecture. Its government remained in the hands of the Adams family, who took responsibility for its financial state and continued to patronize it. The new pastor used devious means to assess the town and church before he accepted the position. It was called a Methodist church, but it did not behave like one. As far as Wiltshire was concerned, it was like a country club; yet it wasn't one. The church gave support to the idea of Shangri-la, which was a fiction.

From this it appears there was a flaw running through the church and its history. Wiltshire Church possessed a quality that made it susceptible to being exploited, as distinct from struggling to maintain its authenticity as a church. Alongside this, however, it is important to note the evidence that shows that a minority of the congregation persisted in seeking that authenticity.

Wiltshire Church's reflecting the social and cultural conditions of Wiltshire helped to create a pseudofunctional religion. We define functional religion as that activity whereby men and women withdraw from the stress and strain of working, social, and family life to meet in the presence of God to celebrate his holiness, his power, and his love. Functional religion also implies a form of spirituality and worship that enables worshipers to question the values they usually take for granted in their daily life, so they can go out not only renewed in spirit but in a mood to question and challenge the prevailing values and assumptions of the world in which they live. Thus, there is a constant process of withdrawal and re-entry, characterized by acceptance of vulnerability, openness to change, and willingness to challenge.

At first sight, Carlson's statement that the church is "the place that provides nurture and caring for those who must go out of the sanctuary and do battle in a fundamentally positive and exciting world" seems to describe this sequence. But closer reading of the total case indicates that because the church was meeting the "presenting needs" of its congregation, it was not in a position to cause the members to question their fundamental values, hence the pseudofunctional activity. Instead of challenging the world of work, the church members went along with it; and the clergy simply tried to enable the congregation to deal with its ill effects.

We would make a sharp division between two ways of construing the human condition. One is to see humans as having *needs*—physical needs, social needs, economic needs, cultural needs. Consequently, institutions and agencies like families, government, businesses, schools, hospitals, and theaters evolve to satisfy those needs. To the extent that institutions can discern those needs and gather the resources to meet them, they are likely to be welcomed and successful. This is the way we have described the actual functioning of Wiltshire Church—bearing in mind that it is in no way peculiar compared with many other churches.

The other way to describe the human condition is to try to understand what it is about humans that causes them to have needs. If we say, for example, that a man needs food, we are implying that he is hungry. As we interact with our environment, we are constantly reacting to what is available that we think, rightly or wrongly, could satisfy a real or imagined inner state. But probably less frequently, we turn inward and try to understand the fact that we are contingent beings. As living organisms we depend on our environment for life—that is, we are always *in need.* This inward reflection in order to understand the actual relations between ourselves and our contexts is primary, and consequently the identification and pursuit of things to satisfy us is secondary. Functional religion in our opinion is that activity that provides the space and symbols to further the exploration of the nature of these primary relations.

Churches seeking to be functional in this manner will therefore inevitably question the personal and social values of their members. But churches setting out to meet the needs of their members will be more prone to respond to those needs as they reflect and reinforce, rather than challenge, the prevailing values of the society from which the congregation comes. Wiltshire Church is in this latter category. Evidence for the power of assimilation to surrounding social values is seen when Sid Carlson indicated that he wanted to copy the way of life of some of his successful church members and give up his pastoral ministry to achieve it.

The Christian gospel indicates that the priority for human beings, whatever their state, is to perceive their relations with their context in terms of God, and to accept the love of God as offered in Jesus Christ. This can be represented as human beings *in need* responding to God, rather than God being expected to respond to human beings presenting their *needs.* The promised outcome of the gospel is that those who get this right will become God's servants to those who are helpless and incapable because of their lack of food, health, justice, and freedom. It was the failure to follow these priorities that kept the members of Wiltshire Church from turning outward to the needs of the disadvantaged in their own and in other communities.

SUGGESTIONS FOR RELATED READING

Bion, W. R. *Experiences in Groups.* New York: Basic Books, 1961.
Bion, a British psychoanalyst, developed innovative theories about group behavior that have influenced the work of the Tavistock Institute and The Grubb Institute. This book elucidates his theories and the experiences that informed them.

Boisen, Anton T. *Religion in Crisis and Custom: A Sociological and Psychological Study.* Westport, Conn.: Greenwood Press, 1973.
Boisen traces the recurrent social process in religion from institutionalization (custom), to re-organization involving a new religious movement (crisis), to institutionalization again.

Group Relations Reader. Edited by Arthur D. Colman and W. Harold Bexton. Sausalito, Calif.: GREX, 1975.
Reprints and original papers collected under the auspices of the A. K. Rice Institute, the American counterpart of the Tavistock Institute in England. The articles deal with both theory and practice related to group relations. Of particular importance is Isabel E. P. Menzies, "A Case-Study in the Functioning of Social Systems as a Defense Against Anxiety."

Miller, E. J., and Rice, A. K. *System of Organizations.* London: Tavistock Publications, 1967.
Miller and Rice put forth a theory of task systems based upon their consultation and research. The book contains both theory and case studies.

Reed, Bruce. *The Dynamics of Religion: Process and Movement in Christian Churches.* London: Darton, Longman & Todd, 1978.
A study of the nature of religion as a social phenomenon, based upon the work of The Grubb Institute. The book develops the "oscillation" theory of religion and examines the implications of this theory for the organized church.

4. The Conflict of Corporate Church and Spiritual Community

An Ethnographic Analysis

MELVIN D. WILLIAMS

The Approach

An ethnographic analysis of a congregation is an application of anthropology as a method of understanding the culture of the congregation. Stated briefly, the anthropological approach assumes that every congregation has its own distinctive pattern of meaning that can be discovered by the two basic methods of ethnography: participant observation and the ethnographic interview.[1] The ethnographer endeavors to understand the behaviors, customs, interactions, social networks, feelings, and artifacts of the congregation and to determine what these signify to its members.

The selection of informants from the congregation is crucial for the quality of the final report. Rooted in the culture of the congregation, informants are the experts on the language and symbols of the community being studied. Unfortunately, some members are spontaneous conflict generators, who use any conversation or interview to create disturbances. But there are members in most congregations who enjoy their knowledge of their church and its members and are anxious to explain the workings to someone who cares and can be trusted. The task of the analyst is to discover them and to make the researcher's ambiguous social role more clear, so that the informants' rights, interests, and sensitivities are protected. Even informants who may appear so sophisticated as

[1] See J. P. Spradley, *The Ethnographic Interview* (New York: Holt, Rinehart & Winston, 1979), and *Participant Observation* (New York: Holt, Rinehart & Winston, 1980).

not to require such protection need a clear understanding of the analyst's role.

Once the ethnographer finds the informants, they must be interviewed as well as observed. The interview should simply be a friendly, comfortable conversation. Within these social boundaries, whatever the interviewer is able to remember (through tape recordings, written notes, informal questions, etc.) will determine the quality of the analysis. The congregation analyst will discover that careful observation of details and extensive participation in membership activities will help to formulate questions for the interviews and conclusions for the final report. The analyst should expect false starts and blind alleys. But in most cases an ethnographer who is also an accepted member of the church fellowship will have the distinct advantage of being involved in the field setting, and of sharing its faith and knowing most of the religious rules, symbols, and rituals of the congregation. Participation, however, does have its dangers: overcommitment to the setting, loss of objectivity, and multiple role expectations. However, the analyst can become a fully participating member in the congregation notwithstanding the possible hindrances of such immersion. Such membership allows for early identification of key events, important factions, leadership hostilities, powerful and influential members, and irreconcilable differences. Jules-Rosette has called such a member observer an "observing participant." Using his or her knowledge, the analyst selects key informants who will be both knowledgeable and communicative.

The ethnographer must constantly guard the data, as Jules-Rosette explains:

> In his study of the Kachin of Highland Burma, Edmund Leach noted that many informants' categories are often ambiguous and highly variable. This ambiguity permits a wide range of social and linguistic distinctions which the researcher may find expedient to prune or eliminate from his study. In spite of the researcher's goal of critical detachment, he actually selects and remolds the informants' commentaries into a consistent account of cultural facts.[2]

---

[2] Bennetta Jules-Rosette, "Rethinking Field Research: The Role of the Observing Participant," presented at the 79th annual meeting (1980) of the American Anthropological Association.

Accuracy requires the analyst to keep a detailed diary of experiences during the analysis. Such a diary allows the analyst and other readers to check the researcher's decisions and conclusions in interpreting the congregation. The researcher may reject the explanations of the informants about the problems and crises in the church because of the scope and goals of the chosen interpretation. But ethnography is always a study from one perspective or another. No one must forget that the interpretive process permeates the entire study.

Translation competence is what Spradley[3] calls the tendency of the informant to translate his own language into that of the researcher. To the extent that the researcher exhibits a lack of cognition about the subculture or world of the informant, the informant will attempt to translate it. The analyst must work to avoid such translations in order to obtain unscreened information. A full member in the congregation should require no translation from the informant. Furthermore, every ethnographer's description is a translation itself. So the analyst must strive to use as much of the native or church language as possible in notes and the final report.

Just as a new pastor seeks to understand and interpret the traditions, social networks, precious objects, daily routines, and common commitments of a congregation, so the ethnographer seeks to lift up the belief system of the community as explained in the language and in the behavior of its members. What the new pastor must learn (and the older pastor assumes), the ethnographer tries to make explicit. Ethnography provides an interpretation that may be useful to others for motivation and leadership in the church.

Basic Assumptions

The analyst will comb through the data to discover patterns of social behavior, looking for meanings that reside in that behavior for the members of the congregation. Soon he or she will discover that social behavior is replete with a complexity of meanings. Thus the analyst may decide upon an ethnographic focus. In my Pittsburgh study, I decided to focus upon the meanings in the

[3] Spradley, *The Ethnographic Interview,* p. 21.

congregation that contributed to community in that church.[4] In a Lafayette study, I focused upon the meanings in the congregation that contributed to social involvement in the community at large.

Of course, the analyst may decide not to have a particular ethnographic focus but to do a "surface investigation" of several areas of congregational interaction. Once these decisions are made, the researcher is prepared to return to the congregation for focused observations—those observations that will help discover particular patterns of behavior that relate to the area of concentration. Over and over, the analyst will ask those questions that will provide the essential information.

The analyst searches for patterns in the interviews and observations that will yield a list of themes that dominate the congregation's behavioral activities. These themes will provide an interpretation of what is distinctive in the subculture of that congregation.

An adequate ethnography also introduces the pastor or the consultant to various members of the congregation and prepares the pastor for the known relationships that exist among them. This congregational analysis is designed to facilitate the pastor in serving the people of the church. It is what Spradley calls "strategic research."[5]

Such an endeavor is designed to be useful to members in resolving their own congregational predicaments. Because of this I do not want the material I present to offend its intended audience. The presentation must be understandable in their idiom. This chapter is designed to assist pastors and congregational consultants as well as researchers. Thus it is different from the research I have written in the past.[6] Here, the exposition of deep bonding is secondary to my efforts to assist those who would understand and minister to their congregations.

Wiltshire Church

The case study of Wiltshire Church was largely based upon ethnographic data collected by a husband-and-wife team of par-

---

[4] M. D. Williams, *Community in a Black Pentecostal Church: An Anthropological Study* (Pittsburgh: University of Pittsburgh Press, 1974).

[5] Spradley, *The Ethnographic Interview.*

[6] See Williams, *Community in a Black Pentecostal Church,* and *On the Street Where I Lived* (New York: Holt, Rinehart & Winston, 1981).

ticipant observers. Neither had prior training in ethnography, but as participants in the congregation, they were accepted as part of the people they studied. Participant observation is the distinctive methodology for ethnography.

We will discover that there are certain themes that are the basis for a significant cleavage in the Wiltshire Church. Those themes and that cleavage help us to explain the actions, customs, social networks, feelings, and issues of the congregation.

The framework for this analysis is borrowed from the work of Victor Turner, who described the distinction between "structure" and "communitas."[7] Structural groups are pragmatic, goal oriented, and intentionally organizational. Communitas, by contrast, signifies spontaneous relationships of intimate bonds without regard to status, wealth, or property. A similar and more familiar distinction was developed by Ernst Troeltsch in the concepts of "church" and "sect."[8] Troeltsch notes that churches tend to be large and mutually dependent upon the culture, while sects are comparatively smaller and seek their identity apart from or against the culture.

From the reports of the tensions in the Wiltshire Church, the basic cleavage in the congregation appears between the majority who are satisfied with the structural "corporate" church and a minority who seek a more demanding "spiritual" communitas. These differences can be seen (1) in their attitudes toward the larger society, (2) in their orientation toward congregational organization, and (3) in their expectations of pastoral leadership.

First, the structural approach of managers and executives dominates and supports both the town and the church. Throughout its history the Wiltshire Church has been a reflection of the wealthy members, especially the officers of the Adams Company. It is located in the center of town, symbolic of its position in the culture. Although not all members have been wealthy, the church has projected the style and image of an establishment agency for affluent upper-management people, the corporation mentality. For most members, it is the anchor and extension of the most signifi-

[7] V. W. Turner, *The Ritual Process, Structure and Anti-Structure* (Chicago: Aldine, 1969; Ithaca, N.Y.: Cornell Paperbacks, 1977).

[8] E. Troeltsch, *The Social Teaching of the Christian Churches,* trans. Olive Wyon (New York: Macmillan, 1931).

cant values that hold the town together. The church fits the neighborhood.

By contrast, some members want to participate in spiritual communities that are less structured and more intimate. They reject the dominant image of affluence. They want more involvement with people in the larger community who are economically deprived, whose poverty demands concerted Christian social action. Their professed identity is not in upward mobility, but in the recognition of human need, spiritual need for themselves and economic need for others. They seek not a larger congregation but a smaller group of other Christians who share their spiritual commitments.

Secondly, the organization of the case material, and apparently the church, reflects the values placed on proper organization and due process. The members recognize the need to constantly recruit new members, to keep present members, to maintain their financial base, and to retain their prestigious reputation. They would not settle for less than the "best show in town." Success has reinforced the growth and stability of the church. Most members are concerned about "what works." Although the church frequently celebrates the Eucharist, the theology of the members remains undeveloped. The present pastor accepts his "agnostic" members where he finds them and leads them in areas of proven effectiveness: personal counseling and expanding programs for children and youth. It is the "in" church in Wiltshire.

By contrast, those who seek mutual fellowship through more demanding commitments seem to feel that the pastor is lacking in spirituality. Some have separated the organizational activities of the pastor from the more "spiritual" groups of the music program, the church school, and study groups. Others have challenged the organization to clarify its goals in reflection and planning. They feel that the corporate commitments of the church have impeded the spiritual growth of the congregation.

Thirdly, the pastor experiences the tension between the advocates of the corporate church and the seekers for spiritual commitment. He has developed into a good team player in the "corporate realm." He is aware of the corporate pressures on the lives of his members, and does not make time demands that conflict with their busy schedules. In recognizing the Shangri-la image of the town, he avoids continual invasion of their belief systems. He admires their way of life, and has become a corporate manager in his leadership style.

Significantly, the pastor's sermons provide a kind of mass counseling program designed to assist corporate managers to endure and to feel understood. Things are kept peaceful, and the world is held together, by the pastor's counseling from the pulpit and with individuals.

But still, some members hunger for a more spiritual relationship with the pastor. One member confronts him almost every week about his sermons. She is trying to feed her spiritual needs by her own individual efforts. The pastor enjoys the challenge of an individual encounter. He is able to grapple with spirituality on an individual basis and to minister to each member in her or his time of crisis. But he is not able to bridge the "corporate-spiritual" chasm in the aggregate. Taken as a whole, the congregation asks too much of him. They want him to provide a successful establishment church and an intimate spiritual communitas at the same time.

The Pastoral Dilemma

Some members would like to push the pastor and test his elasticity. I think he cannot endure these tests much longer. He has tried to communicate his limitations. He told his congregation that he was under psychiatric care, that he failed his doctoral examinations. He told other members that he is considering leaving the ministry to be a consultant in corporate counseling. Many refuse to hear.

The pastor has much experience with this kind of population. He does his corporate job well. But the church is not a corporation. He is denied the perks and rewards of a job well done in the corporation. He is over 50 and is showing signs of job burnout. He is tired of preaching "thou shall not be a failure" (materially), when he suspects that he may be one himself. He is tired of ministering to the crisis needs of people whose net worth far exceeds his own and who would deny him any substantial increases. He is tired of being concerned about the well-being of people who would deny him a four-bedroom house. He wearies of counseling people who "don't care about me." He despairs at the disloyalty of those who joined.

The members sense the pastor's "spiritual" weakness, and some of them are attempting to exploit it. They object to the pastor's building expansion program because he appears to be trying to reassert control and influence over the church school. Historically, this is the style the pastor has used to assert himself, building structures and changing personnel.

In this analysis of this congregation, my focus has been upon the congregation as an interactional group. From this distance much individual variation has necessarily been neglected. Suffice it to state that omission. When I state that the church represents corporation-like commitments, I am aware that many individual members hold deeply spiritual commitments. Although Wiltshire Church is not the kind of community I have observed in Zion,[9] but rather an expressive aggregation, there are some members who perceive and respond to it as their spiritual community of primary involvement.

A Comparison

The previous analysis might be helpful to lay leaders, pastors, executives, and others working with the Wiltshire Church or with another, perhaps their own, congregation. But there are many ways to assemble ethnographic data once it has been collected. The following categories are suggested as areas that might interest pastors, consultants, and denominational committees as they seek to better understand and motivate local congregations. These categories are adapted from my book *Community in a Black Pentecostal Church:* (1) history, (2) formal and informal organization, (3) behavioral dynamics, (4) church activities, (5) symbolic expressions, (6) physical setting, and (7) quality of community. These categories suggest how ethnographic data from two churches (Wiltshire and Zion) demonstrate the distinctive character of each congregation.

The Zion Holiness Church (Pittsburgh, Penn.) has a *history* of

[9] Williams, *Community in a Black Pentecostal Church.*

migrants from the rural South to the urban North, where they feel ostracized and excluded. This exclusion occurred, in part, because of local perceptions that: (1) they were creating ghettos and slums; (2) they were causing a race problem where none had previously existed; and (3) they had habits of speech, dress, and behavior that were inferior.

Wiltshire Church has a history as a company church in a company town for company people. The company was paternalistic. It built houses, a town, and a church for its people, and it provided the resources to sustain that church. Though the company is no longer dominant, the attitude remains.

Both histories have a continuing effect upon the life and style of their respective churches. In Zion, the members depend completely upon one another. In Wiltshire they are struggling with new forms of paternalism.

Zion and Wiltshire have a formal *organization* that is determined by their respective denominational affiliations. Yet both have informal organizations determined by their respective histories and circumstances. In Zion, those who collect the most money from nonmembers and give it to the church become very powerful. In Wiltshire, a few who have the pastor's ear and "blessing" are very influential.

Power is fluid in Zion, depending upon how many of the members one can influence. Such influence depends upon exposure in the congregation, fellowship with members, and collection of donations to support the church. Power in Wiltshire is circumscribed by the will and influence of the pastor, who makes the agenda, controls the communication, and sustains the necessary votes to provide leadership.

Behavioral dynamics in Zion are dominated by mobility within the church and by the church-community character of the congregation. One finds intensive interaction in a church that dominates the lives and interests of its members. Dress, especially women's hats, provides conversational interest, invidious comparison, and exposure. Seating arrangements reflect the social rank of individual members. Membership relationships, and rumors of relationship, encourage gossip and controversy. Fund raising accrues power and its abuse. Love and fellowship provide influence and a sense of security within the community. All of these create vitality and meaning for Zion Holiness congregation.

In the Wiltshire Church, most of the reported behavioral dynamics of the congregation are confined to the administrative tasks of managing the church, especially the administrative board meetings and retreats. Other dynamics are reported in relation to the crises generated by these meetings. The choir, youth programs, church school, study groups, and regular worship include innumerable unrecorded important relationships. The emphasis on structure is typical of the orientation of this congregation.

Activities of Zion's members are all centered in and determined by the church, except for the time spent in outside employment. The members of Zion interact together at church dinners and food sales, church plays and rehearsals, music rehearsals, church trips, picnics, membership household movings, membership legal actions, funerals, and worship. The church is the center of their socioreligious activity.

The members of Wiltshire exert most of their efforts in the children's school and the music program. Involved members are eager to participate in these few activities. Other members attempt to be a part of decision-making processes by belonging to strategic committees, keeping the "ear" of the pastor, or campaigning against the "pet" projects of the pastor. Most members are satisfied to participate peripherally by attending worship services and routine activities.

Symbolic expressions in Zion are from the rural South and its hills and valleys. The members' language is full of references to farm animals, food, and water ("cool well water," not refrigerated). The members emphasize the enthusiasm of their fellowship in order to attract new members. They are a community of people who attempt to "love everybody," especially their fellow members.

In Wiltshire we discover a competitive church, not just with the outside world but within the congregation. Two themes are in tension. The structural approach is dominant, with its emphasis on good management and success through concentration on children, youth, music, and counseling (including preaching). The subordinate theme is a hunger for commitment to spiritual relationships and to people in physical need. Tension exists between those who see the church as an extension of upper-middle-class values, and those who see Christianity as a spiritual commitment to people in need.

Physical setting in the sanctuary of Zion Holiness Church provides a critical index to the power and importance of particular persons. Although all of the sanctuary is sacred, some places have accumulated more status than others. Not only do the chorus and choir have their designated places, but the missionaries, church officers, and pastor's wife, as well as the pastor, have their places within the inner sacred space of the liturgical event every Sunday. Within this inner space, the offering is received, preaching is lifted up, Communion passed out. The closer to the inner space, the more powerful a person is perceived to be. One's seat in Zion is more than a place to sit; it is an expression of one's status.

Members of the Wiltshire Church are uncomfortable with the concept of sacred space. Since their Communion table is surrounded by a low railing, in the act of Communion they come forward in small groups to share the sacrament. No place in the sanctuary is set completely apart. But conflict revolves around the allocation of space resources. In Wiltshire, importance is attached not to where the space is located, but to how much is allocated. The pastor, the church school, and others are constantly vying for more space.

The *quality of community* in Zion is intense, abiding, and continual—in gossip and on the phones—the very stuff of its members' lives. News about the church or its members can be a source of great anxiety until it is shared with someone who is similarly concerned. Informal subgroups have developed in the congregation, so that the same people often come and leave together; they often testify on the same nights and "feel the spirit" at the same time. They respond to and support each other in loving and courageous ways.

The lack of community in the Wiltshire Church appears to short-circuit the development of similar social networks and feelings of intimacy. The church seems to have little impact upon values and actions of most members. On the contrary, their wider neighborhood, family relations, and employment obligations seem to dominate their lives. Only to the extent that the church is an extension of these concerns does it impinge upon most congregants' major interests. The sociological approach in this volume (Chapter 6) will expand on the impact of social context.

As I have stressed before, the pastor has utilized this focus to create a successful church. The issues that abound within this congregation involve the separation between "corporate church" and "spiritual community" and the personality conflicts that are based upon that cleavage. The pastor is a strong-willed, management-oriented person. He tends to control his domain. Those persons who would influence the direction of the church must engage that personality. They often fail. Most members have been largely content to allow the pastor to control a successful church. But with the pastor showing signs of burnout, some officers and those who espouse various spiritual communities are becoming increasingly aggressive in the affairs of the church. The future of this congregation cannot be determined in isolation but must be assessed in the context of the community where it is located. The question here is whether a different kind of pastor and a different kind of church would be as successful as this one has been. Is the nature of the neighborhood changing? Do they need a different kind of church to meet changing conditions? Or are we seeing some superficial rumblings that always occur when an aggregate of human beings interacts, desiring, but unable to become, a spiritual community?

SUGGESTIONS FOR RELATED READING

Heilman, S. C. *Synagogue Life: A Study in Symbolic Interaction.* Chicago: University of Chicago Press, 1976.
An excellent example of ethnography applied in a Jewish congregation by a sociologist.

Jules-Rosette, Bennetta. *African Apostles: Ritual and Conversion in the Church of John Maranke.* Ithaca, N.Y.: Cornell University Press, 1975.
A recent study that is particularly helpful in identifying the problems of intimacy in collection of data.

Spradley, J. P. *The Ethnographic Interview.* New York: Holt, Rinehart & Winston, 1979.

A useful introduction to ethnography and to interviewing in the field situation. It is written in a style and format for beginners in the discipline.

———. *Participant Observation.* New York: Holt, Rinehart & Winston. This is a companion volume to his *Ethnographic Interview.* Together they are a useful introduction to the entire area of ethnography.

Troeltsch, E. *The Social Teaching of the Christian Churches.* Translated by Olive Wyon. New York: Macmillan, 1931.
Specific discussion of "church" and "sect" may be found in volume 1, p. 331 f., but concepts used frequently throughout.

Turner, V. W. *The Ritual Process, Structure and Anti-Structure.* Chicago: Aldine, 1969. Ithaca, N.Y.: Cornell Paperbacks, 1977.
The study of community ritual and its oscillation between structure and spontaneity.

Williams, M. D. *Community in a Black Pentecostal Church: An Anthropological Study.* Pittsburgh: University of Pittsburgh Press, 1974.
One of the first ethnographies written about an American congregation by an anthropologist.

———. *On the Street Where I Lived.* New York: Holt, Rinehart & Winston, 1981.
An example of the ethnographic approach applied to understanding a neighborhood.

5. The Jovial Church: Narrative in Local Church Life

Literary Symbolism

JAMES F. HOPEWELL

A story, of all things, mobilizes the disciplines and techniques featured in this book. It is a narrative account, the Wiltshire case study, that here gives anthropologists, sociologists, theologians, and management consultants both reason and instance to use their skills. Story, that most ancient of human reports, has here drawn together those modern methods of inquiry normally parted by their task and jargon. Surely part of seeing how we understand the local church involves our looking at not just our scientific conclusions but also the narrative matrix of that understanding.

Consider how story (that is, the representation of a succession of happenings) permeates the corporate life of a parish and its interpretation. It is the primary medium by which the systemic imperatives of that institution—identity, values, goals, perceptions, and strategies—are communicated among its members, especially when these need emphasis or justification. Just ask of a systemic signal "how come?" and its human transmitter *accounts* for it. It is often these accounts that a social scientist reduces to rules and findings; yet story re-appears when that analyst tries to explain these facts to those who were investigated. Such a basic way of accounting for and to corporate life—the Wiltshire Church story—is examined in this chapter.

Every congregation has a story. Although this narrative aspect of parish life is seldom explored, it can be helpfully probed by ethnography and literary symbolism. The disciplines complement each other. Ethnography explores the pattern of symbols by which a particular congregation gives meaning to its life and language. Literary symbolism works with these same symbolic components—pattern, meaning, and language—to see how human imagination gives narrative structure to corporate life. Together these disciplines help us consider the full imagery of a local church.

For the observer such study may disclose unexpected dimensions of the symbolic interaction among members and groups within a church, or it may lead to refined comparisons among the lives of different churches. It may enhance an appreciation of the rich cultural complexity of even the average congregation. For the local church itself the full recounting of its story has benefits similar to those found in families who carefully recall and play with their own stories. Narrative can reinforce (as argued above) identities, values, outlooks, and goals. It seems to facilitate corporate discussion of church life: its peculiar, often painful, problems, its needs, its mission.

The Wiltshire story can be analyzed according to its plot, setting, and characterization.

PLOT

The plot of a congregation's story is its history: its consciousness of its struggle as an organization through time and circumstance. A good example of the unfolding plot is seen in the Wiltshire Church case study. In that study a causally connected series of events is related, its progression noted in the study's section headings (Company Church, Sid Carlson Appointed, Growth, Recent Changes, Board Retreat, Housing Proposal, Tensions Increase . . .). As in other plots these events form only a small fraction of the total number of happenings in Wiltshire Church; their recounting as plot is a selective but not arbitrary action. Finding the plot of a church is an imaginative undertaking for the historian but also for the community that lives it out. Both the community and its historian (or case study writer) give significance to only certain events. Both treat certain instances as critical to the struggle for corporate life: certain scenes of strategy and decision, certain times of conflict and response, only some programs and only some results. In that the thickening of these into plot is so evident in the case study, however, we can move on to those less obvious aspects of the Wiltshire story: its setting and characterization.

SETTING

Wiltshire Church not only has a plot; it also has a world view. Its life is narrated not only by events but also by what it suspects to be really going on in that life. This is the setting of the Wiltshire story: the world and its process as viewed by the participants in the plot.

Full ethnographic inquiry into world view at Wiltshire Church would require months of observation and interview. Since that was not possible, a summary way of analyzing Wiltshire's world view was employed. Members completed a test instrument based in part upon Northrop Frye's typology of literary archetypes. Distinguishing four basic interpretations of the world, this typology has been helpful in development of a questionnaire to differentiate the world views of various congregations. In brief the four world view types (here given their narrative designations) are:

Comedy, in which complications of life are found to be illusory when participants find the right knowledge (or gnosis). Harmony is gained in the end.

Romance, in which life as adventure leads to conflict between hero and antagonist. Struggle, however, results in a sacred union or charism.

Tragedy, in which a flawed hero suffers the consequences of breaking the canon. Resolution comes in a final submission to that law.

Irony, in which heroes and heroic situations are found by empirical evidence to be all too human. Life is lived without illusion or recourse to the sacred.

Different local churches live out their plots in the light of these different settings. Each setting, of course, has its peculiar religious dimension. Implied in the comic world view is a *gnostic* framework in which life is dislocated until the truth is realized and union with the ultimate achieved. The romantic world view is as well that of the *charismatic,* involving the lover's search for the beloved, the excitement and anxiety of the quest, and the mystic sweet communion between God and the person. Within the tragic world view is the *canonic* interpretation of life in terms of its obedience or disobedience to God's ordinances. And the ironic world view reflects the *empiric* understanding of life that rejects any gnosis, quest, or pattern not verifiable through one's own senses, but affirms the integrity of human experience. This fourfold differentiation of world view has proven more useful than the usual liberal-conservative polarity used to categorize the belief of a congregation.

Of the thirty or so churches in the eastern United States tested so far, Wiltshire had the highest ironic and lowest romantic scores yet found. Wiltshire interprets its world as playing out an empiric, not a charismatic, story. Wiltshire's script is ironic. The case study ends not with a gnostic solution, nor in romantic ecstasy or tragic judgment. As does Alan Hyatt in its first sentence, the study instead smiles and shakes its head at its supposed heroes and unfulfilled promises.

CHARACTERIZATION

The third narrative dimension of corporate life at Wiltshire is its characterization. Although closely related to the other dimensions, the character of a congregation is neither the life plot that church follows nor the world it views. It is instead its ethos, its pattern of values. Pastors who have encountered the character of several churches and who, perhaps ruefully, recall their decided differences, term this narrative mode the church's personality.

The narrative form of that personality is imaged in myth. Myths are the primal, yet still powerful, tools by which a people accounts for its value, its character. There is a surprisingly close correlation between a specific myth and the character of a particular congregation, and Wiltshire is a case in point. In this instance the myth is that of Zeus, the father of gods and men.

In her anthology Edith Hamilton relates that myth in the following way:

> The Titans, often called the Elder Gods, were for untold ages supreme in the universe. They were of enormous size and of incredible strength. . . . The most important was Chronus, in Latin, Saturn. He

> ruled over the other Titans until his son Zeus dethroned him and seized the power for himself. . . .
>
> The twelve great Olympians were supreme among the gods who succeeded the Titans. They were called the Olympians because Olympus was their home. . . . The entrance to it was a great gate of clouds kept by the Seasons. Within were the gods' dwellings, where they lived and slept and feasted on ambrosia and nectar and listened to Apollo's lyre. It was an abode of perfect blessedness. . . .
>
> Zeus became the supreme ruler. He was Lord of the Sky, the rain god and the cloud-gatherer who wielded the awful thunderbolt. His power was greater than all the other divinities together. . . . Nevertheless he was not omnipotent or omniscient, either. He could be opposed and deceived. . . .[1]

Both the narrative of Wiltshire Church and that of Zeus are characterized by the following themes:

1. The defeat of the chronic
2. Moral rule
3. Joviality
4. Ultimacy

At Wiltshire these themes appear to develop with the advent of Sid Carlson in 1970. Their interweaving throughout the next decade creates, as in the Zeus myth, a plausible and powerful identification between local life and a sacred cosmos. In the "distress" and "turmoil" reported by church members in recent months, however, we see the ironic unraveling of these themes and their point-by-point repudiation. We shall look first at the symbolic pattern that seems to characterize Wiltshire Church throughout most of the seventies. In the latter part of the chapter we look at what may be its recent deterioration.

Parish Character in the 1970s

The Defeat of the Chronic

Chronus was the tyrant father of the gods, who swallowed his offspring at their birth. As his Latin name suggests, Chronus

[1] Edith Hamilton, *Mythology* (New York: New American Library, 1940), pp. 24–27.

was saturnine, heavy, and dull. Although in some accounts the time of Chronus was remembered as a golden age, it was more generally depicted as a time of lengthy and saturnine imprisonment of spirit.

For over a century Wiltshire Church lived in the belly of the Adams Company. "A company church in a company town," the congregation was a virtual subsidiary of the Adams Company; its sandstone skin was that of the company buildings and its physical structure was conceived and maintained by the company head. It was dulled by chronic leadership: "tired old men, ready for retirement" and weighted by a chronic "congregation of elderly people." The later Greeks considered Chronus to be Chronos, Father Time, the old man with the scythe who rounded out the year.

Zeus is the lastborn son of Chronus, who by deception escaped being swallowed by his father (Sid Carlson masquerading as Mr. Mueller?). When strong enough he administers a strong emetic to Chronus ("Sid was probably just the right prescription for this church"), who vomits up his children to begin the Olympian age.

A titanic battle, however, was required before the rule of Zeus was secure. Chronus throws his fellow Titans against the gods. The Titans are followed by the giants and, finally, by the terrifying Typhon. Although shaken and sometimes despairing, Zeus and the gods finally win out. Typhon is buried by Zeus under Aetna, Europe's largest volcano. With Typhon trapped by Aetna, the earth is no longer victimized by chance disaster.

A titanic overthrow occurs with Sid's leadership. Four trustees die in late 1969. "Sid challenged the entire administrative board literally to vote itself out of existence." The church secretary and the choir director leave. He confronts the opposition in their lair and dares them to call the bishop. He purges the church rolls, collapses the double service routine, and restricts administrative board membership. Sid, with support from his bishop and a good number of laypeople, decisively defeats the chronic.

Moral Rule

In addition to the political power his bishop and lay supporters provided, Sid uses extraordinary moral force in "straightening this place out." "I was going to push for what I thought was correct." Early on Zeus gains a moral personality and is seen as the protector of laws and morals.

Sid presses early against the ethically indefensible postures of Wiltshire Church. From the pulpit he says that they sing as if God is dead, that they are in the pocket of the Adams Company, that membership is trivialized by inclusion of 220 lost members, that the building that houses their children has seventeen fire code violations. He finds fault in both the secretary and the choir director, and they leave. Accusing the average member of giving only twenty-five cents each week to God, he transforms their $400,000-portfolio complacency into the guilt of indebtedness.

Zeus not only punishes the wrongdoer, he also advises the suppliant. At the topmost peak in Olympus he gathers the other gods for counsel. Mortals gain his advice through divination, the word spoken at his shrines. He is known as an undeviating protector who punishes only those mortals who seek divine prerogatives. In the pulpit, Sid preaches authoritatively to a congregation needing guidance toward "success and survival in the context of the values of the present culture." Sid is not saturnine in his preaching; he is "provocative," speaking directly to the middle-management families of Wiltshire, advising them how to live decent, honorable lives in uncertain times. The business managers of Wiltshire recognize in Sid a person of great management gifts capable of high secular office had he not chosen rather the role of community divine. Sid could make it big, but his obvious sacrifice of material goods gives him instead a pre-eminent moral power.

Like Zeus, Sid exercises this power with pivotal authority. As the maypole, Sid represents the center of human life. Before his tenure the church building did not have a pastor's office, but Sid appropriates the room with the hearth, the central room heretofore tended by the old women. As maypole, Sid marks the *axis mundi*—the world center—in a church building situated at the power center of a town whose citizens manage one of the nation's most potent industries.

As "a man who could take charge of a situation in the best corporate sense," Sid has both the "charm" and moral strength to provide "very direct leadership . . . very emphatic . . . very strong leadership." He is "a one-man show," clearly in charge of a small board and a part-time, inadequate staff. Only a "small cluster of laypersons in this eleven-hundred-member church make decisions for it," and these under Sid's guidance. "Ye God," Sid says in late 1979, "I was trying to run this place alone—there was no help at all."

Zeus controls his family and mortals with thunderbolts, inflicting severe penalties on those that displease him. A method of control Sid uses increasingly as years pass is "a pattern of getting people," exposing them to embarrassment and ridicule if they cross him. "Let no god, let no goddess attempt to curb my will," Homer quotes Zeus, "or I shall seize him and cast him into darkest Tartarus."

Joviality

The Olympus of Zeus is, however, a basically happy place. Throughout its days the gods live serenely in merriment and laughter. Listening to the sweet music of Apollo's lyre and the Muses, they dine on celestial nectar and ambrosia. At night they retire to marvelous dwellings fashioned for each by the cunning Hephaestus. Life under Jove is jovial; Olympus is the land of the blessed.

"If you can't join Wiltshire Country Club, join Wiltshire Church." The joviality of this congregation, so attractive to so many in Wiltshire, has two related aspects. In the first place, the church is entertaining: "the best show in town." Its pastor is described as lighthearted and is pictured in tennis togs. Even in his sermons some see him "playing with ideas." The music of the church is considered excellent; its pews are comfortable and its welcome, warm.

The blessing of Jove, however, also brings kindness and compassion. A second aspect of the joviality of Wiltshire is its ministry of "love" and "acceptance." Father, Son, and Holy Ghost are manifested in their jovial natures. More than any other minister in town, Sid reaches out to the single people, the widowed and divorced. The church over which he presides is not just the best show in town, it is also an Olympian "sanctuary" that "provides nurture and caring for those who must go out of the sanctuary and do battle" in a tough outside world. Many echo the blessing that one parishioner finds in Sid's preaching: "through Sid's sermons I am aware that I am not alone, that I am strong enough to take care of my problems, that there is hope, that there is a God and my many friends in that church who care."

Loving many gods and mortals, Zeus peoples the world with his offspring. Wiltshire Church membership doubles during Sid's tenure.

Ultimacy

The Greek gods are like humans in most ways, except that the deities enjoy superior stature, strength, and beauty and through their veins flows the ichor that makes them immortal. Though subject to the contingency of fate, gods live and do as they please, beholden neither to mortal need nor to some more final deity. The gods of Olympus are not themselves spiritual, that is, inspired by or aspiring to some nature beyond their own.

The stature, strength, and, indeed, beauty of Wiltshire Church are superior to those of others. Its members are the "people with the financial power and clout." The district superintendent sees it as the "strongest church in the district"; it pays its pastor more than does any other Methodist church in the conference. Its "highly select group of people" inhabit a building remarkably more attractive than "the struggling wooden church on the edge of town" that is the usual lot of Methodists in this region.

There is also in Wiltshire Church the inference of immortality. The membership tends to be young, "with relatively few older people." Although over 50, Sid looks perhaps fifteen years younger and, according to his district superintendent, is immune to the ritual death of the denomination's appointment system. The church, moreover, is "child-oriented," the perpetuation of its being, its moral rule, and joviality assured in its very strong church school.

And, like inaccessible Olympus, Wiltshire is a place apart from human society, a Shangri-la, a town with a drawbridge mentality nestled between the ridges.

These intimations of its own ultimacy reinforce the general disregard that Wiltshire Church shows toward any system of church, society, or doctrine beyond its own. There is a lack of concern for the world beyond Wiltshire Church. Neither Sid nor the church takes responsibility for working with the denomination's district and conference. Sid, in fact, is "really turned off by Methodism." Nor does the church find that it has "a primary responsibility to be present in, active in, or related to the world outside the community of the church." With candor, Sid reports that he has "minimal interest in impacting major social and economic problems in the community."

A similar independence is expressed by the congregation toward orthodox Christian doctrine. Sid says that he addresses "a secular, agnostic congregation of people" who are biblically illiterate and theologically unread: "people who wish they could believe the message of the Christian church but really find it difficult to do." New members at Wiltshire face little indoctrination; they are oriented in a single session. In a congregation that seems to celebrate its present ultimacy there is little emphasis on adult education.

The world view test instrument completed in spring 1981 by Wiltshire Church members confirms their basically empirical understanding of a here-and-now world. No congregation that has used this instrument gave as few charismatic interpretations to its questions as did Wiltshire Church. In the narrative of this congregation, God does not break into life from some more ultimate source. Spirituality, insofar as it represents a personal relationship with a more ultimate being, is not widely practiced in Wiltshire Church.

The Challenge to Character

An absence of overt spirituality does not, however, imply that Wiltshire Church is irreligious. If the above retelling of the congregation's story according to the myth of Zeus is anything more than my fantasy, it would suggest that Wiltshire Church, secular as it might seem, is in fact expressing through its word and deed a fundamental form of human piety. In playing out the social drama that is at least similar to that which the Greeks told as the story of Zeus, this congregation makes its particular sense of existence, its corporate commitment to a cosmos whose verities its behavior reflects. Rather than stay at home, the people of Wiltshire Church gather, worship, plan, gossip, play, and fight in a complex, engrossing narrative whose pattern has a recognizable mythic counterpart.

Recently, however, "some have commented on the lack of clarity about the goals and direction of the church." The pattern that characterized the parish in the 1970s appears to be breaking down, its basic structure challenged with such pointedness that the congregation may be approaching a crisis in meaning. In part this crisis may reflect the ironic disenchantment that time and contradictory experience bring to any sacred pattern; in part the crisis may be the result of the subversion of religion worked by the kerygma in Wiltshire's own Word and Sacrament. While its causes are unclear, the point-by-point relation between the crisis as reported and the previous pattern seems significant.

The Return of the Chronic

Time catches up with Sid. He passes fifty and is "more anxious about retirement." The "exciting upward movement" of the church, its membership spurt, and its economic potency seem to slacken. The time of Chronos, the old man with the scythe, has not yet returned, but there are signs of its coming.

The Collapse of Moral Rule

Earlier the moral arbiter, Sid is now the accused in moral judgments. In his letter of resignation from the administrative board, its chairman cites two basic causes of disturbance, the more intractable being "the seemingly un-Christian behavior of our minister." Whatever the nature of that behavior—it is elsewhere identified both as leading to "personal charges" and as "a recurring pattern of attacks by the pastor" on congregational "victims"—it undermines the theme of moral rule.

In 1980 Sid, moreover, "pushes for something for myself for the first time in ten years." He wants a private home somewhere other than at the *axis mundi.* He seeks to get away from the singular, central role he plays as maypole: "the senior pastor has by his own decision withdrawn from his usual directive leadership style."

The Decline of Joviality

"Earlier sermons used to be upbeat, uplifting, warm—something to stand by you all week. Now—no more humor, joy. There used to be a lot of laughter." Division regarding the appropriateness of enlarging the church building and the "emotion-laden issue" of alternate housing make this a time of "distress" or "turmoil" rather than joviality.

Earlier emphasis was placed upon the accepting, commiserative ethos of Wiltshire Church. Now, an aspect of the congregation's distress is its unfulfilled need for a nurturing community. Opposition now is met with "contempt, not dialogue." "We are far from being a redemptive fellowship in part because we are full of fear."

The Repudiation of Ultimacy

Tempers flare. Someone formerly considered superior in stature and beauty is profaned. Sid witnesses his own demystification: "They don't give a goddamn about me."

Less *ad hominem* is the apparently growing concern that the church is "not spiritual enough," that there is a reality beyond that expressed in the church that is not sufficiently acknowledged. A similar argument against the prevailing sense of local ultimacy focuses on increased involvement of the church in social issues.

NARRATIVE IN UNDERSTANDING THE LOCAL CHURCH

Congregations are imprisoned in prosaic self-description. Pick up virtually any parish report or church announcement, listen to almost any sermon or church board meeting, and note how statistics and program titles bind the language by which the local body is described. Public talk about a congregation is caught in a convention of numbers and tags. Although this body is called to the eloquence of theology and urgency of human need, its formal words about itself are usually a drone of data concerning money and membership and meetings.

This mumble is not merely dull, it is also evasive. By picturing itself in mechanistic terms (numbers and programs also describe washing machines) the congregation avoids semantic inference of either God or people. This prison of self-description is thus a fortress. Its fix on meetings, money, and membership walls out the implication of the group in human suffering and hope. Talking about one's church in terms that picture neither the pain nor the promise of the world is not only dull, it is also immoral.

Now narrative is a tool that springs the church from such bonds. It undermines cliché by relating what people see and do in their complex shaping of life. It literally tells the rest of the story, which is that part forgotten in the rush to reduce corporate experience to controlled data. Narrative recovers the metaphors that connect local to larger events; it represents the recurrent drama of humanity; it evokes the microcosm. It shows that structure of human imagination. For a surprising number of people, involvement in a local church embodies their week's most sustained imaginative activity. For these the congregation is a stage upon which the world story is played out live. For them, church life is not just a program but also a history whose plot members both relate and inhabit. What is worth telling about a church is first its story.

Using narrative does not, however, necessarily build up one's expertise about congregations. In reaching behind and beyond controlled data, narrative loses the latter's certainty. Because, as Northrop Frye reports, story tells the "and then" rather than the "hence" in life description, its form is never final. As the story unfolds, its telling is an account to be retold, not a conclusion to be pronounced. In finding and telling the story one does not inevitably become an authority regarding congregations in general, any more than an ethnographer of a particular people is thereby qualified to assess all others.

Neither ethnography nor literary criticism is therefore the most helpful to congregational understanding when it comes to *(a)* explaining, as do psychology and sociology, why a particular pattern of behavior occurs in a local church, or *(b)* judging, as would theology and ethics, how acceptable that pattern is, or *(c)* changing the pattern, as might organization development. The strength of both ethnography and literary criticism lies rather in their capacity to explore this pattern; to understand its meaning among those people who undertake it. In describing anthropology, Clifford Geertz talks of its uncovering what Max Weber termed a society's "webs of significance." In combining ethnography and literary criticism we are most concerned with finding the webs of meaning that shape the culture of a particular people. The culture of, for instance, Wiltshire Church may require the sort of explanation, judgment, and modification that other disciplines provide more abundantly. But if any information from other disciplines is to be conveyed to the church itself, it must be through the symbols and signals that ethnography and literary criticism explore.

Church leaders interested in these explorations find them useful in addressing such perplexities in ministry as *(a) communication,* as between the language of the pulpit and that of the pew; *(b) concepts,* the force and form of ideas, fears, and dreams shared by churchgoers; *(c) conflicts,* the messages conveyed in particular tensions and fights; *(d) initiation,* patterns of socialization by which new and young members gain entry; and *(e) commitment,* what it means to be marginal or involved in local church life.

What then presents these issues powerfully to the congregation itself is more likely story than theory. Although ethnographers may by observation and interview gather in their minds what they find to be the more abstract themes of a church, their subsequent talk within that culture about these themes tends to assume narrative form. Narrative historical accounts were often the source of these cultural themes, and story is often the framework that carries their import on-site. Story is not then just the play of children nor the protoscience of primitives. It is the mastery of metaphor by which a group interprets its common life. Any ongoing ministry in a church relies upon story in its attempt to interpret its life. It is not just sermons that need illustration; all of corporate life needs imaging for its communication.

Once one begins to sense the power of narrative in congregational life one finds it everywhere. It constitutes the news that members share about their common life. A large part of that news is gossip. In one of the best of ethnographies of a congregation Samuel Heilman shows how gossip—that is, stories about other members—is essential for corporate existence. Heilman even demonstrates the presence of four layers of gossip, increasingly private and potent, that enrich activities and relationships in a congregation. Stories of origin and narrative explanations of behavior also define life together, as do schemes for the future and reports of the past. Introductions, confessions, testimonies, and other accounts further tie individual lives to the group story. Even jokes serve the common narrative pattern, their telling deemed tasteful if they somehow advance the common story. Longer sequences of group behavior such as fights and social events have a dramatic framework that holds actors, plot, props, and setting. Added to all of the above is the more consciously storied nature of divine worship: its liturgical drama, its Scripture, hymns, sermons, and symbols. From its conception to its death the local church exists by the persistent imaginative construction of its members.

Some hints about finding and telling a congregation's story:

a. Begin with ethnographic practices such as those featured in Melvin Williams's chapter. By participant observation and interview seek information about how this congregation makes sense of life and death and makes use of space and time. Learn how the group orders itself through patterns of submission and dominance. Consider the categories that underlie its systems of belief and value.

b. Although events in this local church have their parallels elsewhere, resist the satisfaction of pointing out these similarities as one's most significant "finding." That is the habit of outside observers, and it does little to deepen an apprehension of a group's unique idiom.

c. As that local idiom becomes more clearly defined, note how it is expressed in modalities of imperative, indicative, and subjunctive speech. These have narrative counterparts in the three aspects of story described earlier in this article: plot (the imperative behavior of a church that effects its history), setting (its indicative actions that constitute its world view), characterization (its subjunctive stance that forms its ethos).

d. Discover the narrative that gives life to these aspects. In the history of human imagination the range of narrative options was determined fairly early and is preserved in the world's mythology. The local story and its primal counterpart touch each other in four basic ways. Both concern a form of murder or other extinction that results in an integration of participants. Both display a style of behavior deemed essential for survival as a group, and both promote a dominant mood for that life. And both seek a similar outcome.

The congregation's story is the access of that local church to human history. It is here and nowhere else that corporate life is related as event and inference. Either God's call and the world's cry sound in what this church tells as its own story, or it as a body does not hear them.

SUGGESTIONS FOR RELATED READING

Frye, Northrop. *Anatomy of Criticism: Four Essays.* Princeton, N.J.: Princeton University Press, 1957.
The range and interrelationships of Western literature described in ways that suggest symbolic options in the social construction of reality.

Geertz, Clifford. *The Interpretation of Cultures.* New York: Basic Books, 1973.
Ethnography as entry into the conceptual and conversational worlds of a people. "Doing ethnography is like trying to read a manuscript" (p. 10).

Hamilton, Edith. *Mythology.* New York: New American Library, 1940.
The major Greek, Roman, and Norse myths told clearly.

Heilman, Samuel C. *Synagogue Life: A Study in Symbolic Interaction.* Chicago: University of Chicago Press, 1973, 1976.
Heilman uses a "dramaturgical framework" in this ethnographic approach to a congregation.

Turner, Victor. *Dramas, Fields and Metaphors: Symbolic Action in Human Society.* Ithaca, N.Y.: Cornell University Press, 1974.
A study of social dramas in the life of a community.

6. From the Outside In and the Inside Out

A Sociological Approach

JACKSON W. CARROLL, WILLIAM McKINNEY,
and WADE CLARK ROOF

Introduction

Local churches are community institutions. Historically in America most churches have defined their community geographically, although other definitions (ethnic, racial, ideological) are possible. As community churches have complex and changing relationships to their environment, they depend on the community for resources that are essential for their continued existence, such as members, finances, and services. They also contribute to their community in both direct and indirect ways. Among the obvious contributions are services offered by a church to its neighbors, ranging from education for the young to food for the poor. They contribute in indirect, subtle ways as well by fostering a sense of well-being among their members, advocating and enforcing standards of individual and social behavior, and providing visions of community life that transcend short-term self-interest.

A congregation's relationship to its community is a product of several factors, among them the history and character of the community itself, the church's denominational heritage and local history, the religious environment of the community, and choices made by the congregation and its leaders. The case of Wiltshire Church illustrates the complexity of the church-community relationship and the impact of choices made by the church within its immediate environment.

As sociologists, we share the conviction that in recent years congregational analysis has overemphasized the internal dynamics of congregational life and has failed to take sufficient account of the influence of the social and ecological context on the church's inner life. We argue, in other words, that congregational analysis should work from the "outside in." While we do not subscribe to a deterministic view, we believe that the environment both sets limits on, and provides opportunities for, a congregation. Therefore we begin with an examination of the Wiltshire Church's community and regional context, looking at population characteristics, physical setting, community institutions, and relationships between the town and the region. Secondly, we turn to the "social worlds" of Wiltshire residents, the perceptions of reality that guide their daily lives, lifestyles, values, interests, and needs. Finally, we view the church from "inside out" to see how the internal life of the church relates to its community setting.

Throughout this chapter we use an analytical framework suggested by Rachelle and Donald Warren.[1] That framework organizes various data under three broad rubrics, or "orienting questions": (1) *Identity:* What is this community's (congregation's) understanding of itself? How do members define its boundaries, both geographically and socially? What are the chief characteristics or qualities of the community (congregation) and the dominant myths and symbols that shape community life and give it meaning and flesh? (2) *Interaction:* In what ways and places do people interact with one another? Who talks with whom and about what? What are the boundaries between formal and informal communication and behavior? How do groups define their special space? What institutions and practices symbolize change over time? (3) *Linkages:* How do persons and groups relate to the world around them? In what ways are external forces transmitted and resisted by residents (members)? Where do points of tension between individual and outside interests find expression?

FROM THE OUTSIDE IN

Demographic Setting

Although the town of Wiltshire traces its history to its founding by Yankee settlers some three hundred years ago, it is in many

[1] In *The Neighborhood Organizer's Manual* (South Bend, Ind.: University of Notre Dame Press, 1977).

respects a new community. In this section we look at some of the characteristics of the "new" and the "old" Wiltshire that provide the social and ecological context for Wiltshire Church. Our focus is on demographic and other statistical data that illuminate the community's identity and patterns of interaction and the linkages between Wiltshire and other communities in the region.

Identity. Interspersed throughout the data collected for this project are suggestions of Wiltshire's self-understanding. From interviews with community residents and from data from the U.S. Census and local sources, we see three components of Wiltshire's identity: its rapid population growth, youthfulness, and affluence.

Perhaps the central dynamic in Wiltshire community life is its rapid growth since 1940. Once a sleepy New England town, the community has now become one of the larger suburbs in its metropolitan area. With a 1980 population of over 21,000, the town has grown more than fourfold in forty years. Having undergone one transition from an agricultural village to a "company town" in the nineteenth century, Wiltshire has undergone another transition in the twentieth to become a suburb.

Wiltshire's growth pattern, as shown in Table 6.1, is that of a "second-ring" suburb. During the forties the community grew, but only slightly; its rate of growth was considerably lower than that of other suburban communities in its Standard Metropolitan Statistical Area. Its population more than doubled in the fifties as the metropolitan area expanded to the west; the town experienced a gain of over five thousand people in this decade. Growth continued in the sixties as the population increased by over 70 percent and more than seven thousand people. Wiltshire's growth slowed in the seventies to 21 percent with a gain of over three thousand residents.

Table 6.1 Population Growth of Wiltshire and Its Region

	Percent Population Change			
	1940–1950	*1950–1960*	*1960–1970*	*1970–1980*
Entire Metropolitan Area	14	35	21	1
Central City	7	−9	−3	−14
All Suburbs	97	169	31	5
Wiltshire	22	210	72	21

The table also shows the growth rate of the region as a whole and its central city and suburban components. The city areas have been losing population since 1950 and declined fully 14 percent in the past decade. The suburban communities of the region, however, have grown quite rapidly. Wiltshire's growth in the 1940s lagged behind other suburbs, but since 1950 it has grown more rapidly than other towns. Its rate of growth in the past decade is more than four times that of other suburbs in the region.

Although 1980 census data on housing construction are not yet available, the 1970 census showed that only 19 percent of the owner-occupied housing predated 1950. Thirty-two percent of these units were built in the 1950s, 20 percent between 1960 and 1964, and 29 percent in the late sixties. Other data from 1970 also suggest the high mobility of Wiltshire. During the single year 1969–70, 5.5 percent of the owner-occupied housing (excluding new units) changed hands (compared to 4 percent in the rest of the region). Less than half (47.4 percent) of the 1970 residents over age 5 resided in the same household in 1965; this compared with 56.4 percent in the total region.

A real estate agency's brochure gives a sense of the community's self-understanding and its appeal. "Recreation opportunities are so extensive," the brochure states, "that it would be impossible to describe them on this page. The 'showplace' of Wiltshire is the town-owned Wiltshire Farms Recreation Center, which opened in 1972. It houses a championship 18-hole golf course, four swimming pools, tennis courts, paddle tennis courts, skating rink, cross country ski trails and unusual play areas for children." Residents, the brochure continues, "are education-oriented and, as a result, the school and other facilities for children are excellent. Seventy-six percent of the graduating seniors from Wiltshire High School continue their education. . . . Within the Town of Wiltshire there are five private schools with outstanding educational programs and facilities."

A second important feature of Wiltshire is its youthfulness. The 1970 census showed that 42 percent of the community's residents were under age 18 and 28 percent were in the prime childbearing ages of 25 to 44. Its median age was only 26.1 years. In the region as a whole, 34 percent were under 18, and 25 percent were 25 to 34; the median age was 28.6 years, or fully 2.7 years older.

Wiltshire's youthfulness is reflected in the community's public school enrollments. Between 1963 and 1970 the enrollment increased 61 percent. Enrollment grew another 3 percent from 1970 to 1975 but began to decline in the late seventies; there are 14 percent fewer students in 1981 than there were in 1975. Though enrollments are down in Wiltshire, the declines are far less severe than in neighboring communities closer to the region's central city.

Local YMCA officials estimate a decline in Wiltshire's youth population of about 8 percent in the past ten years and an increase from 25 to 33 percent in the over-45 population. Increasing property values, a recent slowdown in housing construction, and community resistance to low-income housing make it likely that the median age of Wiltshire residents will continue to rise. At the same time the town remains young relative to the rest of the region.

A third major feature of Wiltshire life is the community's affluence. Wiltshire is one of the wealthiest communities in the region. Commercial demographic analysts estimate that 20 percent of the community's families have incomes of $50,000 a year or more; another 29 percent have incomes of $35,000 to $49,000; and 30 percent earn between $25,000 and $34,999. In 1981 the town is home for four families with incomes over $50,000 for every family earning less than $10,000.

Wiltshire's median family income of $34,445 is 30 percent higher than the regional median of $26,597. The increase in the relative affluence of Wiltshire families is suggested in the fact that in 1950 the community's median income was only 13 percent higher than that of the region.

In 1970, the latest year for which complete census data are available, 45 percent of Wiltshire's employed residents were in professional or managerial positions. Adding clerical and sales workers to this total puts fully 76 percent in white-collar jobs. In the region, 28 percent of the workers are professionals and managers and 58 percent are white-collar employees. Adults (over 25) in Wiltshire averaged 13.7 years of formal education in 1970, with 54 percent having completed at least some college. The regional median education was 12.3 years with only 26 percent reporting any college training. Eighty-eight percent of all families in Wiltshire were living in single-family homes; the comparable figure for the region was 58 percent. Seventy percent of Wiltshire households owned two or more automobiles compared to 43 percent in the region as a whole.

Interactions. Wiltshire's recent transition from a small agriculturally based town with a single major manufacturing employer to a growing suburban community that is dependent on the rest of the region for its economic vitality has left its mark on patterns of interaction within the community. Religious life in Wiltshire provides a "window" on the old-timer/newcomer relationships of the past three decades. In Figure 6.1 we have plotted the membership trends of seven of Wiltshire's major congregations. The data were supplied by the congregations themselves, and as usual among denominational statistics, there are varying definitions of membership. They nonetheless suggest changes in Wiltshire's religious population.

The oldest church in town is Old First Church, which traces its history to the founding of the town itself. For some two hundred years it was recognized as "the church in town," the religious home of the community's leading citizens. Even today it contributes a disproportionate share of Wiltshire's civic and political leadership. Old First Church grew very rapidly in the early stages of Wiltshire's suburbanization; its membership grew from under 800 in 1950 to nearly 1,400 in 1970 as its strong Sunday school program attracted large numbers of young families. During the 1970s, Old First Church began to show slight signs of decline. Membership decreased by some 300 people despite the community's continued growth. A study of the congregation showed the membership to be considerably older than the community at large. Average Sunday church attendance declined from 376 in 1970 to 290 in 1980, and the church school enrollment fell from 850 to 180 students. Old First Church is viewed by many in the community (and many of its members) as the church of the "old guard," of those who have controlled Wiltshire in the past.

The Methodist church was founded in the 1800s with leadership from one of the founders of the local textile plant. The church building resembles the plant in construction materials and is based on plans chosen by the wife of the plant's owner.

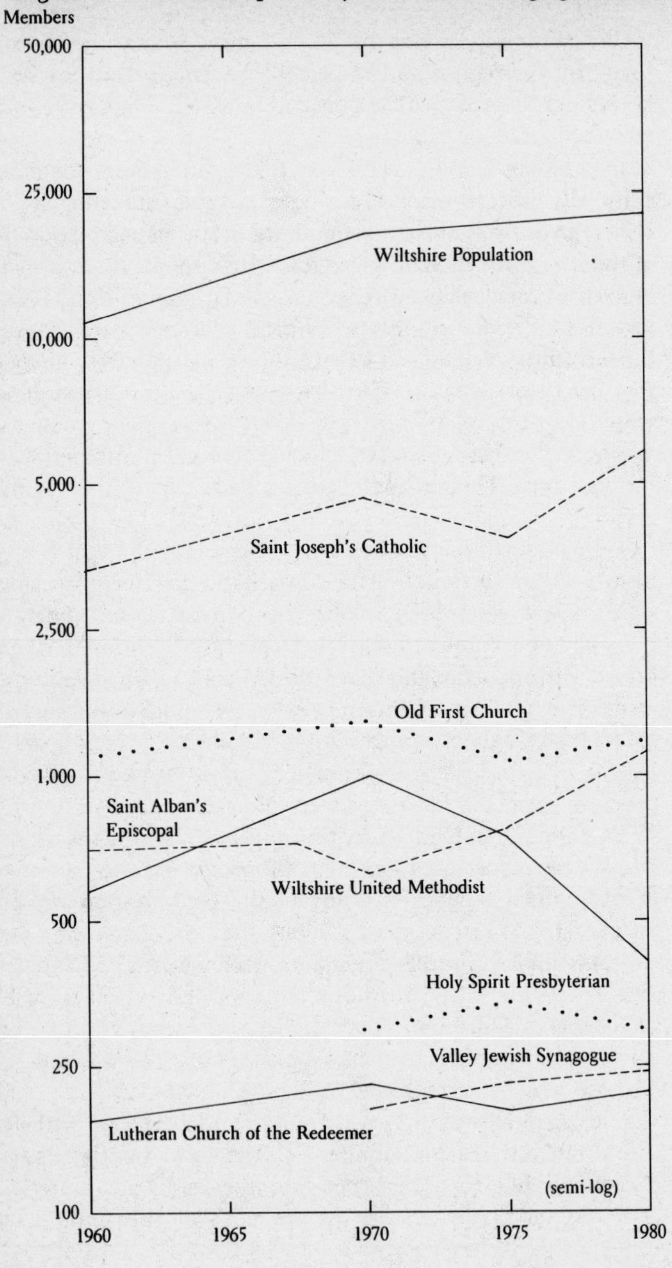
Figure 6.1 Membership of Major Wiltshire Congregations
Members
50,000
25,000
10,000
5,000
2,500
1,000
500
250
100
1960
1965
1970
1975
1980
Wiltshire Population
Saint Joseph's Catholic
Old First Church
Saint Alban's
Episcopal
Wiltshire United Methodist
Holy Spirit Presbyterian
Valley Jewish Synagogue
Lutheran Church of the Redeemer
(semi-log)

Through most of its life the church was known in the community as a "company church." Many of its members and most of its leaders were factory employees; the annual deficit was covered each year by the company's chief executive. During the early years of Wiltshire's recent growth, the Methodist church was largely unaffected, its membership remaining fairly stable through the fifties and sixties. In the early seventies, new leadership effected a psychological and economic break with the church's historical identity as a "company church," a break that was facilitated by changes in ownership of the plant. The church has grown and changed considerably since 1970. Its membership has risen from 689 to 1,101 in the decade; church school enrollment has increased from 309 to 503; average Sunday worship attendance is up from 163 to 305. It has earned the reputation as "the best show in town."

Saint Alban's Episcopal Church, the third of the older Protestant churches in Wiltshire, also benefited from the community's growth in the postwar period. Between 1960 and 1970, Saint Alban's membership increased from 773 to 1,020. By contrast with Old First's growth in this period, however, Saint Alban's new members were older. Church school enrollment remained stable through the 1960s and average church attendance actually declined. Around 1970 the church began to suffer rather dramatic membership declines as inactive persons were removed from the rolls.

The most dramatic change in Wiltshire's religious life is the growth of the Catholic population. Saint Joseph's Catholic Church, which serves the township, has shown enormous membership gains. Enrollment in the parish rose from 3,230 to 4,644 in the sixties, prompting the diocese to split the parish and form a second congregation in the western part of town. Despite the loss of a thousand members to the new parish, Saint Joseph's still reported a net increase of more than a thousand members in the seventies. The new parish has itself grown to over three thousand members.

In addition to the second Catholic parish, other congregations have been formed in the past two decades in response to population growth and changes. Among these new congregations are a

Lutheran parish, at least two conservative evangelical churches, and a synagogue that serves the area's growing Jewish population.

To get a sense of the change in Wiltshire's religious population we totaled the membership of the larger congregations in the community and compared the result with the Wiltshire population. In 1960, 71 percent of the population were on the rolls of these congregations; 32 percent were members of Saint Joseph's Church and 39 percent were members of the five largest Protestant congregations. In 1980, 61 percent of the town population were on the rolls of the major religious groups in the community; 42 percent were members of the two Catholic parishes and 19 percent were members of the five Protestant churches.

Although church membership statistics are notoriously imprecise and we lack data on some of the smaller congregations in the community, it appears that in the past two decades there have been two important developments in religious group interaction. The first is a decline (from 71 to 61 percent) in the percentage who are are members of any major religious body. The second is a decline in the proportion of the population who are members of Wiltshire's historically dominant Protestant congregations; the decline is from 39 percent in 1960 to 19 percent in 1980.

The head of Wiltshire's clergy association, a pastor who has been in the community for two decades, reflects on the changing role of religious organizations in Wiltshire: "You know, years ago the church was really the center of the community and people pretty much rallied around the church that was there as a way of finding expression for their social needs as well as spiritual needs. There was great respect for the influence of the church in the community which I think has been lost now. . . .When you see churches pretty much struggling for survival and competing with so many outside interests, they have lost a great deal of their effectiveness and especially their influence."

The shift from a sleepy community dominated culturally and religiously by a tight-knit elite of old families and executives of the Adams Company has created an increasingly heterogeneous town whose political and social life are far more fluid than in the past.

Linkages. Excerpts from a session with black students living in Wiltshire as part of an educational enhancement program provide a unique perspective on the community's relationship to the outside world. "It reminds me of *The Brady Bunch* on TV," said one student. "It's the typical American town that people in other countries hear about. You don't see the real America. It's an ideal."

Another spoke of his high school classmates: "Kids here don't have a very realistic understanding of what it's like to live in a city. All they ever see is the theaters and hotels. It's a stereotyped view of how a city is. They just know what they see on television." Another feels the same is true of his teachers. "I remember seeing a film at school on bullfighting, with lots of blood and everything. The teacher was surprised that I was shocked by it. She said, 'Well, you come from the city. You must be used to seeing things like that all the time.'" In the words of still another student, "Their parents work in the city. They only see the downtown area. They have a view of the city as a place where minorities live, as run down, as ghettos and slums. They grow up in this type of area. They're born here, they go to school here, then they go to work in this type of area. . . . It's two different worlds, really."

In actuality, the community of Wiltshire has an integral relationship with the city and the region. Although the Adams Company and the town of Wiltshire employ a sizable proportion of the town's residents, more than one-quarter of the residents commute to the city to work; even higher proportions of the newer residents depend on city employment for their livelihood. Wiltshire participates in the regional council of governments and relies on social service agencies located in the city. Residents depend on regional newspapers and radio and television stations for information about community activities and developments throughout the nation. Many serve on regional boards of voluntary agencies such as the United Way.

Wiltshire's central function on behalf of the whole region is to provide residential housing for upper-middle-class people. Its residents' occupations and income and education levels, as we have noted, place Wiltshire as one of the most affluent towns in the region. This affluence makes relationships to the rest of the region somewhat ambiguous, as is illustrated in two recent controversies.

The first involved an attempt by the Adams Company to develop a parcel of property for multifamily dwellings. Community opposition (based largely on conservationist grounds) was fierce, and the proposal seeking a zoning variance was denied. Within a matter of months, on the other hand, an area corporation was given permission to build a major computer facility in Wiltshire that promised new jobs and the prospect of lower property taxes for residents. The proposal found virtually unanimous public support.

The New England tradition of local autonomy is valued by old and new residents alike and provides an important lens through which its regional relationships must be viewed. The tradition places major emphasis on local community loyalty and responsibility but contributes to the problematic relationship between Wiltshire and its surrounding region. As pressures rise from demographic changes and increasing economic disparities between the central cities and communities like Wiltshire, one can expect further strain on historic forms of government.

The Social Worlds of Wiltshire

Turning from social and demographic characteristics, next we look at the social worlds in which Wilshire's residents live. By "social worlds" we mean the perceptions of the world that inform their daily lives, values, lifestyles, interests, and needs. Wiltshire is more than just a place to live, a commuter suburb of nearby Springfield. It is a community experience providing residents a sense of meaning and belonging. Indeed, the community lends itself especially to psychological "world building," for a variety of reasons. Its three-hundred-year-old heritage of New England individualism and independence, its geography ("in between the ridges"), and its comfortable, suburban affluence all help to create a distinctive self-awareness as well as a sense of isolation and of values to be protected. Thus, to understand the dynamics of congregational life in Wiltshire, it is essential to understand Wiltshire as a social reality and to recognize the values and outlook people in the community bring to church experience.

In analyzing the social worlds of Wiltshire, again we draw upon the three categories of identity, interaction, and linkages.

Identity. Of all the clues to understanding Wiltshire, none is more potent or revealing than the "Shangri-la" image used by a leading town official. People move to the town, according to the official, to have their own piece of suburbia in a retreatlike setting: "to get between the birches and the elms," "get between the ridges every night," in search of their "own little island."

The retreatist atmosphere of Wiltshire is sustained, in no small part, by its high degree of homogeneity. Few residents are poor. Virtually all are white. Many are upwardly mobile, professionals and corporate executives who have "made it" in the system. Most have moved to the community and do not have deep roots within it. The traditional nuclear family with the husband employed full-time and the wife devoting her energies to raising a family (at least while the children are young) remains the norm. Residents share an awareness of job-related stress, knowing that corporate transfers are frequent and that daily commuting to the city takes a toll. Divorce and family tension are real.

In Shangri-la, however, there is escape. For people in Wiltshire there are two worlds—the public and the private. Wiltshire offers an environment in which everyone has ample opportunity to retreat from day-to-day stresses from the job and the city—alone or with one's family—through recreational activities and community-based interest groups. Here there is opportunity to explore and to develop the private life, a chance to expand a realm quite different from the public, job-related realm. Unlike the corporate workplace, which is cool, rational, and ordered, the private world of Wiltshire is warm, expressive, and unstructured. Activity in the workplace is regularized and calculative; activity in Wiltshire is more voluntary, open to personal preferences and choices.

Wiltshire's residents recognize these two worlds are different and to some extent experience a tension between the public and the private. But the two realms are not in opposition to one another; instead, they should be regarded as complementary, the fusion of instrumental and expressive aspects of everyday life. The pressures of corporate life, long hours, and heavy travel schedules take on meaning to the extent they make life in Wiltshire possible. Commuters return to Wiltshire to shift gears, to return to time for oneself, one's spouse and family, for tennis, friends, and church.

Because of its upper-middle-class character, the town is dominated by values of individualism, hard work, ambition, success, and achievement. Having made it to Wiltshire, residents attach great significance to their own social standings, achieved by the investment of effort and sacrifice. To live in Wiltshire is to recognize this achievement, to celebrate a way of life called the American Dream. Furthermore, it promises to offer their children what they need in order to follow them in the company of the affluent—the best education possible, a safe neighborhood in which to grow up, and an environment supportive of individual growth and well-roundedness. Not surprisingly, Wiltshire residents often joke about "buying a school, not a house." Investment in the children represents an extension of their own lives, as well as affirmation of a lifestyle they claim as their own.

Wiltshire symbolizes the success that residents feel they deserve, yet it also presents some tensions for them. They know that life at the other end of the thruway is different, that not all share in the prosperity to which they have become accustomed. The community's homogeneity both reinforces the tension and provides a form of legitimation for the residents' good fortune. Proximity to others who have "made it" (or who are making it) is its own form of reminder that one can fall behind, that one can fail. Residents see that some of their neighbors fail in their attempts to climb the corporate ladder, that others face marital and family problems, and are reminded that life is not always easy, that life *is* a challenge. To be able to feel that one is meeting life's challenges helps to legitimate the rewards that have been obtained. By meeting the challenges one earns the right to the rewards.

Interaction. To grasp the social worlds of Wiltshire, we must also look at the social networks, or patterns of interaction, within the community. People's values, interests, lifestyles, and outlook are typically anchored in some social base, wherein they are affirmed and mutually reinforced. In a small-town, suburban setting like Wiltshire particularly, the social networks and cleavages between them are readily identifiable; despite the apparent homogenity of the community, social group differences are real. Moreover, the social networks and divisions become part of the fabric of congregational life—both shaping, and being shaped by, what takes place within the religious institution.

Wiltshire's transition to a growing suburban community has led to tensions between those who built and led the community through the Second World War and those who have made it their home in the past three decades. Not that they don't have some things in common. To an extent there is an affinity between the newcomers' values and the old town spirit of individualism and independence; both also place high value on traditional family life and morality. Yet there are differences. Newcomers over the years, and in the high suburban growth period of the fifties and sixties especially, accentuated the upper-middle-class character of the town and made more visible its affluent, consumption-oriented styles. The character of the town changed, becoming more transient, more a commuter community. In more recent years, the distinction between old-timers and newcomers appears to have become less important. Increasingly, one senses that Wiltshire has different meanings for the various cohorts of in-migrants, ranging from those who came in the fifties and sixties to those who arrived quite recently.

Wiltshire is a community turned inward upon itself. Boundaries are drawn, particularly by those who have moved in over the past couple of decades, on the basis of having earned the right to belong. The mayor, speaking of the "drawbridge mentality" of the town, puts it this way: "There is an attitude in some quarters that we worked to get here and anyone else who wants to be here can also work to get here. On the other side of the issue are the descendants of the original residents of three hundred years ago, who are saying to the new people, 'We made room for you and we think you should take an example from us and make room for others.' "

Boundaries have also been drawn between those who have earned the right to belong. These boundaries find symbolic expression in local housing patterns. In many neighborhoods, one sees only the driveways; the houses themselves are invisible, nestled among the birches. Consequently, when interaction occurs within Wiltshire, it is mainly among upper-middle-class persons who share common private—individual or family—interests and needs. Social activities are frequently organized along lines of hobbies or sports (e.g., tennis), and children and youth (e.g., PTA), religious activities, and personal needs (e.g., AA, singles' clubs). Bonding takes shape to a considerable extent around personal concerns and interests, as opposed to a shared community, ethnic, or religious heritage. This makes for a situation in which social ties are often tenuous and short-lived. In many ways it seems to be a community in search of greater sharing and belonging. This search is an issue both in the Wiltshire Church, as we shall see, and in other religious groups in the town.

Linkages. As already noted, life in Wiltshire must be understood in terms of the bifurcation between the public and private, between life in the workplace and life at home in suburbia. Aside from a somewhat divided existence, this also makes for carefully defined boundaries between the two worlds. The private life is valued and protected, not to be confused with the public realm. By keeping the two separate, Wiltshire maintains its meaning and identity.

Despite its introverted, localistic character, Wiltshire is not an isolated place. The residents are sophisticated, cosmopolitan people. They are aware of what goes on in the larger world; their lifestyles and values reflect the positions they hold in the nation's corporate economy. Indeed, as a result of their position in the larger system, they bring to Wiltshire all sorts of external realities—the corporate culture, stresses and anxieties, dreams and failures. By their very presence, the external realities create the need for a place of retreat and re-creation, for a meaningful private life, for Wiltshire itself.

Because of the carefully circumscribed character of the private world, not surprisingly in Wiltshire there is no great outpouring of concern for broad social problems. It's not the place for contending with poverty and social injustice or for working out solutions to difficult social issues. The latter are part of public, not private, life. Local community life is geared to protecting residents from the intrusion of the outside world on the inside world of home and family. Cognitive boundaries are reinforced by the town's strong sense of political autonomy and self-control. If there are problems, they are local and personal: drugs in the schools, tension and divorce in families, alcoholism for particular persons. Over these, Wiltshire expresses concern. But beyond these locally defined problems, there is little attempt to deal constructively with vexing social issues.

Wiltshire is a place of professionals where competence is known and appreciated. If there are problems, residents here seek help from professional experts. The stance is one of hiring others to check the problems out, to get someone to take care of these needs for them. Their affluence, combined with a privatized outlook, fosters a reserved, somewhat hands-off approach to social and personal needs.

FROM THE INSIDE OUT

We began this analysis by considering the "outside" of the congregation—aspects of local and regional context and the social worlds of its members. Now we turn to the "inside" of the congregation to examine both internal characteristics and their functional relationships to the congregation's "outside." The analysis continues to be organized around identity, interaction, and linkages.

Identity

A number of dimensions of the congregation's identity may be noted. We have organized them under the headings of heritage, member characteristics, beliefs, and norms of membership.

Heritage. It is obvious, but nonetheless important, to note that Wiltshire Church stands within the Christian tradition, and this fact is not insignificant for understanding its current identity, interaction patterns, and linkages. From the Christian heritage leaders and members selectively appropriate core beliefs, symbols, and rituals. Even when only parts of that heritage receive emphasis by the congregation, that which is emphasized gives character to the identity or ethos of the church, and that which is neglected is nevertheless "available" and may be a resource for critiquing or challenging the congregation's current focus. For example, the groups within the church currently calling for more emphasis on spiritual growth and greater concern for social justice do so by drawing on neglected aspects of the church's heritage.

That the church stands within the Methodist tradition also contributes to its identity, although its Methodist heritage seems to be of importance in relatively limited ways. Indeed, its building and its current style make it different from the typical Methodist churches of the region, as the district superintendent acknowledged. Its building, he noted, gives it the appearance of an Episcopal church, rather than a more typical white-frame Methodist church on the edge of town. Differences from traditional New England Methodism are also reflected in pastoral style and tenure, membership growth, age of membership, and relative affluence.

The local history of the congregation is a further contributor to its current identity. That it was once a "company church in a company town" is not of great, continuing significance save as a point of comparison to what it was before the coming of the present pastor in 1970. Even from this comparative perspective, the post-1970 transformation and growth has been rather remarkable, as was noted earlier. It is, therefore, not surprising (and probably accurate) that the pastor's telling of the history of the church to new members emphasizes that most that is of importance has happened since (and largely because of) his arrival.

Member Characteristics. The kinds of people joining the church since Sid arrived (as well as the few remaining who preceded him—approximately 15 percent) contribute importantly to shaping the congregation's identity. The distribution of particular attributes or characteristics of members—for example, age, social class, values, or beliefs—gives a congregation a particular identity or ethos. These attributes or characteristics may be homogeneous or heterogeneous. The more homogeneous they are, the more clear or distinctive the congregation's identity will be.

Concerning the age structure of the church membership, from what information we have available, Wiltshire Church can be described as middle-aged, with the majority of adult members falling between 30 and 50. This is a relatively homogeneous age structure. Since this age range is also the primary period for families with children present in the home, the experience of child rearing is also an important shared characteristic of a majority of the members and a concern that they bring with them to the church.

A common socio-economic status contributes to congregational identity. Although specific occupations of members differ, a majority of breadwinners are in middle- and upper-management positions, earning substantial salaries, many in excess of $50,000 per year. In addition to providing homogeneity of outlook, the fact that so many members share a corporate management background leads to what one member called a "middle-management style of leadership." Such a style places heavy emphasis on professionalism. Said one leader, "We don't know what we want and expect from the church and staff, so we hire talent to give it." If there is a problem, hire a consultant; if good music attracts people to the church, then hire professional musicians. This style seems to be a part of the congregation's identity.

Racially, the church is predominantly white, although several black families are members. The latter are mostly longtime United Methodists who have moved to Wiltshire and affiliated with the congregation. They are essentially similar to white members in age and socio-economic status.

Members also share another trait. Approximately 50 percent are relative newcomers to the congregation, having joined within the past five years. Less than 10 percent of the current members have been associated with the church since childhood. This led one leader to observe that it was necessary to regroup and reorganize every five years.

Considerable homogeneity in such characteristics as age, child rearing, socio-economic status, race, and even mobility creates commonality of outlook, style, needs, and expectations for the church. In response, congregational leaders have developed a church program—especially attractive worship services and a strong church school program—that "speaks to" the members' needs and expectations. In all of this there seems to be little contradiction between the status of being a Wiltshire resident and the status of being a member of Wiltshire Church. A young family, newly arrived in town, would find a congregation of peers whose hopes and fears are similar to their own, and whose members are not too far above or below on the corporate ladder.

There is a remarkable fit between the current pastor and the constituency the church is attracting. The pastor makes no secret of the fact he is ambitious, has been open about his concern for the economic security of his family, and is comfortable with traditional middle-class social and political values. He identifies with and has affection for his members. His appeal, however, seems to go beyond a willingness to be "one of the boys." He is willing to act out what remain fantasies for many of the members: expressing public disdain for ecclesiastical superiors, confessing personal failures and self-doubts, and discussing topics seldom allowed "out of the closet" in community life. He is willing to stretch the congregation's intellect and emotions, but only within a framework of basic acceptance of the rules that govern Wiltshire public and private life.

Beliefs. Beliefs and values are another important attribute constituting a congregation's identity. In Wiltshire Church, diversity is the rule in religious convictions and beliefs. There is no formal statement of faith to which assent is required or encouraged. To be sure, the use of creedal affirmations, hymns, prayers, and other elements of worship, including the sacraments, function to articulate the basic identity of the church as standing within the Christian heritage. However, it appears that these more formal beliefs are not especially salient for a majority of the members in the sense of informing attitudes and behaviors. The minister perhaps overstates the case when he refers to members as "secular agnostics," but others confirm that commitment to core Christian beliefs is "limited" and "nominal."

Although we never have complete data, we can hazard an inference, based on interviews, questionnaires, and sermons, about the "operational" beliefs of the congregation. These are centered in belief in a God who loves individuals, calls them to fulfill their potential as individuals, forgives and supports them when they fall short and are hurt, and blesses them with the good life. There is an especially strong belief that individuals are called to fulfill their potential and must refuse to give up or to sell themselves short.

This operational belief system also seems to carry over into the belief that the congregation itself must refuse to sell itself short or to be less than "the best show in town." It is highly important that things be done well. Indeed, the dissatisfaction with the current church school facilities seems to reflect the belief that such inadequate facilities are a "selling short" of the congregation. Additionally, the theme, repeated several times by leaders, that the congregation must be a "hospital" to bind up those hurt by the stresses and strains of life seems also to be a part of the operational belief structure and parallels the individual's belief in a loving, forgiving, supporting God. These operational beliefs support a generally privatistic orientation and lifestyle.

Some members who are concerned about spiritual shallowness and superficiality complain about the belief structures described above. These essentially privatistic and nonthreatening beliefs also frustrate members who want the church to become more involved in issues of mission and social justice. Likewise, the belief structure reinforces and legitimates the isolation of the town from significant issues in the region. Beliefs are also dysfunctional, as we shall note below, in their failure to foster among members a strong bond of religious commitment, personal as well as institutional. There is a lack of any compelling and unifying set of doctrinal affirmations.

Norms of Membership. One further aspect of congregation identity may be seen in the norms of church membership. New members are desired; congregational growth is viewed positively; and the minister and others work hard to seek out and bring in new members. At the same time, joining the church is easy. There are few, if any, expectations for new members, with the possible exception of giving to the church and participating. Discussing criteria for membership, leaders used the following expressions: "We're not an evangelical church"; "we don't actively go out to work on 'true belief'"; "we don't open ourselves up to nonbelievers"; "we don't exclude anyone." These norms regarding membership open the congregation to the community and make it easy for new residents to join. At the same time, the absence of clear-cut expectations makes the congregation vulnerable to whatever values or interests new members may bring with them, adding to the heterogeneity of congregational beliefs and increasing the likelihood of conflict.

Further, norms regarding membership limit the church's claim on members. It becomes an organization of limited liability. Thus, when members perceive that their needs and expectations are not being satisfactorily met, they may be little inclined to honor their membership covenant. Church records provide indications of the casualness of church life. While membership in the church increased 66 percent between 1972 and 1980, average attendance at Sunday worship increased only 50 percent. The ratio of those in attendance to total members declined from 34.8 to 31.6 in this period. Sunday school enrollment increased from 309 in 1970 to 543 in 1980, but average Sunday school attendance actually declined from 247 to 215. The church's 1981 budget of $155,500 represents an average member contribution of $141.24; assuming the congregation's per capita income to be approximately equal to Wiltshire's estimated per capita income for 1981, the average contribution is only 1.2 percent of income.

Interaction

We turn now to patterns of interaction in the church, focusing on both formal and informal patterns. Under formal patterns, we consider both governance and programs. Under informal patterns, we consider the bonding (or lack thereof) between congregation members.

In its governance, the congregation loosely follows Methodist polity. The administrative board plays the key role along with the pastor-parish relations committee. Other committees are primarily organized around program functions. When Sid arrived, he deliberately reduced the size of the church's leadership. Now there seems to be a small group of laity, probably fewer than the administrative board or PPRC, who, with the pastor, make most of the major decisions. The pastor, in particular, has considerable authority and has an unusually broad role in shaping policy and determining the direction of the church. Although Methodist polity is partly responsible for the way his role is defined, Sid's power seems especially to derive from four sources. One is what he describes as his "mandate" from the bishop at the time of his appointment "to straighten out the mess." Second is his demonstrated competence, which contributes to his authority. Third, there is what we have called the "managerial style" of the church, the willingness of the members to "leave it to the professional." Finally, there is his relatively long tenure as pastor.

It is not particularly surprising that power should be concentrated in the pastor and a relatively small number of laity in

Wiltshire Church. For reasons just mentioned with reference to Sid, coupled with the relatively large size of the church, the voluntary nature of membership in which members are not materially rewarded for involvement, and a high rate of member turnover, we might expect a concentration of power. It follows what Roberto Michels called the "iron law of oligarchy."[2] Although such a concentration of power might be suspected of leading to member apathy and indifference, this need not be so. As long as member expectations of the church are being met, the church is functioning effectively, and there is no serious conflict, most members are likely to be willing to allow the pastor and a small group to make major decisions. But when groups find expectations or needs unfulfilled (e.g., those in Wiltshire Church asking for spiritual renewal and the others concerned with social justice), or when a conflict develops (e.g., over the pastor's housing), there is likely to be a challenge to oligarchical rule. Furthermore, the slowing of mobility in Wiltshire and among church members seems to be increasing the interest of a broader spectrum of church members in having a "say" in the direction of the church.

In addition to governance, another aspect of the more formal interaction patterns in the church centers in its programs of ministry and mission. The programs that exist in the church are generally well done, as might be expected in a congregation that emphasizes professionalism. This is especially true of those program aspects directed toward current members, which constitute the large majority of what is undertaken. The church's worship services, particularly the preaching and music, are exceptionally well presented. Likewise, particularly the church school and youth program receive considerable attention and positive evaluation, affirming the child- and youth-centered values of the town. Although adult education has received attention in past years, the current disposition of the staff has left a void in this area. Another positively appreciated ministry of the church is pastoral care, in which the minister, through his counseling and preaching, is viewed as effective in relating to the myriad of issues facing members—painful interpersonal experiences, hard decisions, illness and suffering, divorce, and family difficulties.

---

[2] In *Political Parties* (Glencoe, Ill.: Free Press, 1949).

What seems generally underemphasized in the program is outreach beyond the congregation. Only 18 percent of the total budget of $155,500 is directed toward programs beyond the congregation, and two-thirds of that amount goes to Methodist apportionments, much of which is used for maintaining the denomination. The lack of budgetary outreach is matched programmatically by the apparently limited programs that serve or engage people and issues beyond the congregation. There are a few such programs, directed at the problems of the aging, participation in clothing drives, participation in a local ecumenical refugee resettlement program, and beginning exploration of a relationship with a coalition of urban churches in the nearby city. These latter programs, however, seem to involve only a limited number of members. The pastor does become involved in some social ministries and community concerns, but sees his ministry as primarily within the congregation and to its members.

In general, this review of programs within the church suggests that ministry is seen in individualistic terms, focusing on congregational members in their private rather than public lives. Generally, the members see themselves as ministered to, rather than as ministers, as receiving ministry rather than giving it; hence, they are concerned that "employed leadership should serve our needs."

Given the focus on individual needs and on ministry *within* the congregation, considerable effort goes to building up the community from within, creating fellowship among members. It is surprising, therefore, at first glance, to hear members complain of lack of fellowship (over half the congregation surveyed would like the next pastor to be gifted especially in "deepening our fellowship with each other"), of superficial relationships with other members, of a failure to experience much community within the church. Both the efforts directed at building fellowship and the considerable homogeneity of members on a variety of personal and social attributes would suggest the contrary to be true.

On further reflection, however, the lack of deep bonding among church members could be anticipated. One reason is the absence of any deeply shared theological commitment or strong commitment to a denominational heritage, which makes it difficult to build community within the congregation (and even more difficult to reach out to the broader world in the name of the church). Second, the church's membership size makes it difficult to develop strong primary group ties, especially when the programs of the church involving adult members seem primarily geared to atomistic individuals participating as spectators. A principal exception to this lack of bonding among members appears in the choir, where primary, nonsuperficial relationships have developed. We can understand, therefore, why the choir is a locus for some of the present conflict in the congregation. It is one of the few places in the church where individuals have developed sufficient social solidarity to respond to a threat to one of their own or to care deeply about the direction of the organization.

In general, then, the privatization that exists within the lifestyle of the community residents as a whole is reflected in the church, and efforts at community building have not succeeded in overcoming it.

Linkages

Given the previous discussion of the inward and individualistic focus of the congregation, it follows that linkages of the congregation with much outside of itself are few. Yet there are linkages to be noted.

Wiltshire Church identifies with its local community. It is proud of its history in the community but makes little effort to dwell on history. Its focus is on its youthfulness and the freshness and relevance of its program for the Wiltshire of today.

We previously noted that the Methodist heritage contributes little to the congregation's current identity. Members are aware of their Methodist connections, but function as Congregationalists. Yet, there are continuing linkages with the Methodist heritage. First, the church is dependent on the Methodist system for its ministerial leadership. Sid Carlson serves under the appointment of the bishop, and should he or the congregation seek to sever that relationship, the bishop must give approval. Second, the denomination's polity provides a formal organizational structure for the congregation, and although this does not seem to be followed rigidly, it gives the pastor and administrative board considerably more authority than would be the case if the church actually was

Congregationalist. Third, its Methodist identity accounts for at least some of the church's membership growth in recent years, as Methodists have moved to the area and looked for a compatible Methodist congregation. (This does not, however, seem to have been a major factor in the church's appeal to many new members.) Fourth, the church, as noted, contributes to the denomination financially, and Sid Carlson participates in some conference activities. Finally, the Methodist connection provides a context in which some leaders evaluate the congregation. Considerable pleasure is taken in being the largest, most active, most vital church in the district, and near the top in the annual conference.

The church recognizes it is in a competitive relationship with other churches in town, and though relations are cordial, there are few efforts to deepen interfaith ties or engage in cooperative efforts in Wiltshire or beyond. Linkages with other congregations are perfunctory, formal relationships, as expected in a suburban community; however, Sid Carlson and the congregation's commitment to these linkages is relatively minimal. The church's major efforts go into maintaining a program that responds to the needs of its own members. The pastor avoids pressing members to involve the church in activities that bring contact with issues and concerns that cloud the boundary between private and public life. The church does not actively discourage those who seek close ties with the denomination or who would involve members in regional issues but makes it clear that these are not its major priorities.

Wiltshire Church, for most of its life a "company church" in a small town, has emerged as a community church in suburbia. It is aware of the boundaries between local and regional life but shows little motivation to transcend them.

The congregation is broadly accepting of the way things are in community and national life. Members recognize problems in the world but see traditional means of resolving these problems as adequate.

Contemporary social problems do not receive a great deal of attention from the pulpit or, as we have noted, in church programming. Where attention is given, it tends to be in terms of the impact of social problems on the lives of members and is aimed at helping individuals to cope with this impact. There is little recognition that the church's members are well off relative to others in the region, that church members have disproportionate financial resources and power, or that Christian stewardship implies any special responsibility for community, regional, or national life.

We conclude with two propositions basic to our sociological approach: First, a congregation—its theology and ethics; its worship, program, and style of operation; what it does or does not do in ministry and mission—is profoundly shaped by its social context, especially the local community and the social class of its members. Second, a congregation, by virtue of its relationship to a religious or faith tradition, has the capacity, in a limited but crucial way, to transcend the determinative power of the social context, so that it influences the values and interests of its members as well as being influenced by them. A congregation that participates in a faith tradition contains within it the ideas and inspiration, beliefs and experience, on the basis of which the status quo may be challenged and at least partially transcended. The more church leaders and members are helped to see and understand the impact of their context upon their congregation's life, the more likely they will be to discover ways of influencing this context rather than simply being influenced by it. This is characteristic of what sociologists call "open systems." They have the capacity for self-renewal based on feedback and insight.

The Wiltshire Church can never escape the influence of social context. Recognition of this fact offers a limited but crucial freedom *from* its power and freedom *for* becoming an influential and shaping force within it. Sociological analysis will not prescribe to the church what it should be or do. But it can provide the congregation with comprehensive information and fresh insight about itself and its setting that create new possibilities for a people with the resources of faith.

SUGGESTIONS FOR RELATED READING

Berger, Peter L. *The Sacred Canopy.* Garden City, N.Y.: Doubleday, 1969.

A theoretical approach to the sociology of religion that has informed this chapter's discussion of social worlds.

Carroll, Jackson W.; McKinney, William; and Rozen, David A. *The*

Varieties of Religious Presence. New York: Pilgrim Press, forthcoming 1983.
This book grows out of an extensive sociological study of diverse ways local churches and synagogues interact with their communities in a single metropolitan area.

Douglass, H. Paul, and Brunner, Edmund deS. *The Protestant Church as a Social Institution.* New York: Russell & Russell, 1935.
The summary of hundreds of studies of churches and communities conducted in the 1920s and 1930s by two pioneer religious researchers.

Earle, John R.; Knudsen, Dean D.; and Shriver, Donald W., Jr. *Spindles and Spines.* Atlanta: John Knox Press, 1976.
A study of Gastonia, North Carolina, that re-examines this community two generations after Liston Pope's classic community study, *Millhands and Preachers.*

Gustafson, James M. *Treasure in Earthen Vessels: The Church as a Human Community.* New York: Harper & Row, 1961.
One of America's leading Christian ethicists takes a multidimensional look at local churches.

Hoge, Dean R., and Roozen, David A. *Understanding Church Growth and Decline, 1950–1978.* New York: Pilgrim Press, 1979.
A number of social scientists and other scholars look for the reasons for the membership declines in "mainline Protestantism" since the mid-1960s.

McKinney, William; Roozen, David A.; and Carroll, Jackson W. *Religion's Public Presence.* Washington, D.C.: Alban Institute, 1982.
An examination of community leaders' expectations and evaluation of the religious community's role in public life in a metropolitan area (Hartford, Connecticut).

Roof, Wade Clark. *Community and Commitment: Religious Plausibility in a Liberal Protestant Church.* New York: Elsevier, 1978.
A sociologist looks at church participation patterns among North Carolina Episcopalians and stresses the importance of social worlds on member views and behavior.

Vidich, Arthur J., and Bensman, Joseph. *Small Town in Mass Society.* Princeton, N.J.: Princeton University Press, 1968.
One of the most important community studies published in recent decades that gives considerable attention to the community role of religion.

Warren, Donald, and Warren, Rachelle. *The Neighborhood Organizer's Manual.* South Bend, Ind.: University of Notre Dame Press, 1977.

An extremely useful volume for those persons seeking to understand the dynamics of community life.

Wood, James R. *Leadership in Voluntary Organizations: The Controversy over Social Action in Protestant Churches.* New Brunswick, N.J.: Rutgers University Press, 1981.
A short, lucid analysis of factors affecting organized religious responses to community issues.

7. Theologian at Work

Theological Ethics

JOSEPH C. HOUGH, Jr.

A theological analysis of a particular congregation must proceed in two directions. In the first place, the "documents" of the congregation, living and written, available to the theologian must be examined in order to determine the present, concrete working understanding that the congregation has of itself. This analysis should make transparent the purpose of the congregation as it is articulated and understood by the members. This should be followed by an analysis of the institutional practices of the congregation in order to determine whether, in fact, the lived reality of the community conforms to the expressed understanding of itself. In this way the congregation determines whether or not its intentions as a community are adequately expressed in the organization of the congregation and the functions of its ministry.

Second, the theological analyst must examine the self-understanding of the congregation together with its practice in light of broader convictions about the nature and purpose of the church. Utilizing an explicit understanding of the nature of the congregation based on interaction with the biblical and theological sources, the analyst becomes an external critic, raising questions about the adequacy of the congregation's self-understanding in light of the universal theological dialogue in the church about the mission and ministry of the church as the body of Christ in the world. Theological analysis has this normative function: It calls the church into account to be faithful to its convenant with God and to respond creatively to the promises of God for the church and the world.

THE THEOLOGICAL SELF-UNDERSTANDING OF WILTSHIRE CHURCH

At the very beginning of the analysis of the theological perspective of the Wiltshire congregation, it is interesting to note that the pastor of the church does not think there is any theological understanding among the members at all. They are "biblically illiterate" for the most part and agnostic about many matters of faith. They are "wistful hearts" who wish they could believe. They come to church largely for the purpose of gaining insight and inspiration to enable them better to cope with the pressures of family and corporate life. A leading layman summarizing a board discussion adds the observation that the congregation is a group of people who profess belief in Christ but really have only a nominal or limited belief in his teachings. He noted that there are few demands placed on persons who wish to become part of the congregation and that the primary focus of the life of the church is on the needs of those who are part of that church.

The material available to me and the conversations I have had with observers of the congregation indicate that this is a fairly accurate picture of the theological state of affairs at Wiltshire. Considerably more specificity can be given to the congregation's self-understanding from various interviews and questionnaires provided by church members. Taken together, a profile of faith emerges.

God

The idea of God characteristic of the congregation is very vague, but a relatively large number do believe in a God related to them personally. For example, almost half the respondents to a questionnaire indicated that they had experienced God "speaking to them" and their situation. However, half of the members did not experience God speaking to them in this way, and only a third of the respondents even asked for God's guidance in a time of crisis. There is little evidence that those who experienced God speaking to them really expect intervention in any noticeable way into their lives. God is mostly a source of comfort and a source of inspiration, a sort of coping hypothesis. "There must be something higher than ourselves." God is the name of courage, perseverance, and strength—all resources found within the self. This is perhaps the so-called spark of the divine within each human being mentioned often by the respondents. The divine person is not experienced as the holy, one who governs, judges, and redeems, though there are some who are seeking more clarity about the "holy." The notion of God at Wiltshire is far from the God of the Reformed tradition who inspires awe and wonder. God is rather the "urge to go on," "the inspiration to do right," and a kind of "presence" that one feels within oneself. This idea of God is not tied in any special way to a clear biblical understanding of God, although there is a curious anomaly here. Although a third of the people say God "speaks" most clearly in the words of the Bible, they have very little enthusiasm for biblical study. In fact, there is not even much interest in having the minister know more about the Bible.

Jesus

Jesus is not perceived to be the revelation of God except in the sense that Jesus reveals the "spark of the divine" more fully than other men. Jesus has much in common with other great leaders. He functions primarily as a moral example for uplifting the sight of human beings and inspiring them to take new courage and new hope. Even the most significant parts of the Easter message become transformed into inspiration for human trust and love and the possibility for overcoming loneliness.

Jesus is seen as a particular kind of moral example. He does not challenge the present order in the name of a coming kingdom. Rather, the Jesus of Wiltshire Church is the one who reflects those survival virtues necessary for the people of Wiltshire themselves. He is the one who loves children, who fearlessly does what he thinks is right, who exhibits courage and honor and good sportsmanship. He is not a model of personal piety. He is the one who forgives mistakes and then denounces those who condemn persons who exhibit minor moral improprieties. Though there is strong agreement that Jesus "saves from sins," that salvation results in no change of world view. It is simply the result of following Jesus' example and forgiving ourselves and then forgiving each other.

In other words, the story of Jesus is the prime example of a person who cared about other people and who stuck to his principles through everything. He did not challenge Caesar. Caesar killed him. Yet Jesus was decisive, intentional, and held his honor. At the end, he could be at peace with himself.

The Nature of the Church's Ministry

The Wiltshire congregation gives a very high priority to ministry to the suffering. Most respondents to the questionnaire felt that it was terribly important for the pastor to visit the sick and counsel the troubled. They are persons with problems of their own, according to one respondent. These personal and family problems are magnified by the pressures of corporate life and the pressures of upward mobility. The church for them becomes a kind of "sanctuary," a place of refuge from the pressures on their lives, a place for inspiration and solace, assurance and support. A highly transient people caught up in a highly competitive environment, they seek a place to identify with others of like mind. They also seek a source of reassurance and a sense of acceptance in the midst of their doubts about themselves and life in general.

This characterization of the ministry of the church is to be understood as ministry to *this* community, to the suffering and the troubled of *this* church. The respondents reflect little interest in having the church as such involved in ministry beyond the membership of the congregation. This is evident in the overwhelming agreement (with some dissent, of course) that the church should not concern itself with the major social issues of the day. The social ministry of the church should be carried on by inspiring moral concern and courage in individuals who then go out into the world as positive influences for good. This moral inspiration is focused on personal honor and character, not social criticism. Little attention is given to questions of social ethics, such as poverty or militarism.

This understanding of ministry is a reflection of the needs that attracted most people to the town of Wiltshire. The city is referred to as a "Shangri-la," a retreat from the pressures and stresses of the corporate life. One primary factor in choosing Wiltshire has been its reputation for excellent schools and family living. Wiltshire families want a safe place for their children where they will get the best education possible and where the "atmosphere" of the community inspires them to take advantage of their opportunities. Wiltshire is a haven, a place to escape with one's family from the stresses and dangers of nearby Springfield. One observer noted the "drawbridge mentality," a desire to separate their world from the world they have just left beyond the turnpikes. Yet, Shangri-la is not merely an escape, it is a community filled with like-minded people who are upwardly mobile, ambitious, and decisive. Almost all the newer residents of Wiltshire are in similar income brackets and have growing families for whom community activities are terribly important. As corporate middle-executives, they are also transient and mobile. They do not have time to search out community. It must be there when they arrive. It must be obvious and immediately available. A sense of belonging must come with the territory.

It is therefore not surprising that their sense of ministry is community building for *their* community in *their* church. They want the best music program and the best church school and the best speaker in town. Only the "best show in town" is capable of adequately meeting all their needs, including community, status, and upward mobility.

With so little time to give to any activities other than their own careers and precious moments of recreation and family activities, the people of Wiltshire do not look for a church that makes heavy demands, nor are they, for the most part, eager to probe the depths of personal meaning and faith. Their search for meaning is defined by their vocational choices. It is closely related to the possibility of advancement in a particular corporate setting where they find themselves. This is not to say that there is an absence of interest in the deeper questions of meaning, but they much prefer to have simple, anecdotal, and clear answers to the questions that they face on the practical plane of life. In the words of one respondent, "something we can take home and use during the week." They feel little need for involved and probing discussions of issues about the ministry of the church or the challenge of the Christian life. They come to church to be served, not to be disciplined. They come to church to receive ministry, not to be ministers.

THE PRACTICE OF MINISTRY

My brief and admittedly inadequate observation of the practice of the church would indicate that this conception of ministry coheres with the actual life of the congregation. There are study groups for interested adults. Though these rise and fall and usually are not well attended, they are available for those who wish them. For the most part, however, the ministry of the church focuses on three activities—the Sunday school, the regular morning worship service, and the program of enlistment and visitation.

The church school is largely run by laypersons. Most of them are women. They are dedicated teachers and seem to do an exceptional job. The church school has defied recent demographic trends and continues to grow while other church schools decline. This is a tribute to the effort that is invested by leadership and the tremendous support that it receives from the church constituency. If there is an educational program at Wiltshire Church for their children, it will be "the best." Many people in the Wiltshire congregation firmly believe it to be the best anywhere in the area.

The worship service focuses on the sermon, but almost equally important is the music program. The music program is primarily composed of volunteers with part-time paid singers and a choir director. It is widely conceded in the community that Wiltshire Church has the best music program available, and the congregation is extremely proud of it. The pastor is known as one of the outstanding public speakers in the area. His delivery is flawless and his sermons are filled with practical hints at wisdom. Often there is little in the sermon that is specifically Christian, but the overwhelming majority of the people find the sermons helpful, clear, and on most occasions, inspiring.

The visitation program of the church is largely the program of the pastor. There is little evidence that the congregation engages in enlistment or visitation of the sick on any organized basis. However, the pastor is constantly on call. Many members commended him for his promptness in calling on them when they came to the community as well as his responsiveness in times of trouble and crisis. Most people felt that the pastor really cared for them.

However, not all is well in Wiltshire. There seems to be growing dissatisfaction, although those who are involved are not clear about the causes of their dissatisfaction. At the present time, most of the discontent has focused on particular actions or recommendations by the minister. There have been charges of lack of confidentiality and of excessive demands on the congregation for his own benefit. Seen from the standpoint of the minister, these charges are preposterous. He believes that the persons responsible for the charges are primarily irritated because they have been removed from the positions of leadership or because he has been hard-nosed about business decisions concerning his future and the future of the church.

This mention of conflict in Wiltshire Church as part of the theological analysis is here simply to indicate that although my basic judgment is that the ministry of Wiltshire Church very clearly coheres with the expectations and theological self-understanding of the congregation and the minister himself, this does not mean that harmony reigns supreme. The conflicts at the present time appear personal and do not reflect widespread theological disagreement about what the church ought to be doing or about the nature of the church and its ministry. On these matters, the pastor and the overwhelming majority of the members seem to agree. The ministry of the church, as carried on by the pastor and under the direction of laity in the church school and music programs, very adequately implements and coincides with the congregation's self-understanding its own nature and task.

A THEOLOGICAL CRITIQUE OF WILTSHIRE CHURCH

Much of what I have described as the self-understanding of Wiltshire Church is in an abiding tension with the notion of the congregation that arises from an encounter with biblical and theological sources. This tension is analogous to the tension in the life of the individual Christian. The Christian is called by God into fellowship with God and with other Christians, and at the same time is alienated from God and separated from other persons. In the same way, the congregation is at once the people of God called together to be the body of Christ, a community of reconciliation and redemption for all the world, and at the same time it is a self-centered, exclusive, compromising religious institution that has struggled to accommodate itself to the needs of its culture and to ensure its survival. In other words, this congregation at Wiltshire is no more and no less than human.

Therefore, I avoid any flight of rhetoric toward a "mystical church," "church within the church," or "church incognito," because that would seem to me to be a stubborn manifestation of the refusal to acknowledge that this church, like myself, is what it is only in the mystery of grace alone. It is true that this congregation falls far short of the biblical promises of what the congregation can be, but for all of that, we must remember that it is a community of the people of God. That is the audacious claim they can make and that claim is an expression of hope in God. I therefore begin my theological critique with the statement that this church is the body of Christ. That statement is one of belief in God's promise to be with Wiltshire Church and to be for Wiltshire Church. It is an expression of my expectation that community is, has been, and will be justified by God in her gracious and steadfast love.

Yet, hope in God is not simple flight of fancy, and this church, like others, is called in its confession of hope to be what it has been promised. It is called to struggle to achieve integrity and authenticity as the body of Christ in the world.

The call to integrity and authenticity raises the question of how one proceeds to discover and justify normative criteria for the life of the congregation that do not arise in the self-understanding of the congregation itself. In what sense can a theologian presume to know what this particular congregation ought to be? This important question deserves more attention, but I am limited to suggesting certain directions.

In the first place, if the congregation is the body of Christ in the world, one must have some understanding of the world in which this particular congregation lives. What is the global context of the life of this congregation? What are the issues and problems for this congregation as a community dedicated to Jesus Christ?

There are, of course, a number of ways in which one can describe the contemporary world. I have chosen three significant components of the global situation that form the content of my perception of the world of Wiltshire Church. In the first place, this is a world of relative isolation of persons from one another. It is, therefore, a world of selfishness and loneliness. Secondly, the global world of Wiltshire Church is a world of extreme poverty. More than 60 percent of the world's peoples live at subsistence level or lower. This is a world of injustice and inequity that confronts Wiltshire Church with these problems. Thirdly, the world in which Wiltshire Church lives is a world living on the edge of time. Its very existence and survival is threatened by environmental destruction. The paradigmatic form of that destruction is the possibility of nuclear warfare, but there are other less obvious trends that point us inexorably in the direction of self-destruction.

If this is a limited but fairly accurate description of the world in which Wiltshire congregation lives, then what are the biblical and theological sources that illuminate the appropriate pattern of life for a community that understands itself to be a church? I propose three affirmatives about the congregation as the body of Christ that shed light on the past problems of Wiltshire Church and offer inspirational promises for the future of this congregation.

1. The Body of Christ Is a Human Community

God became human in Jesus Christ. God became flesh of our flesh. This means that the church as the body of Christ is a human community. It is not just any human community, however. It is a people who are to be with each other in a particular concrete way. Because it knows its Lord is the one to whom and by whom all things are made, it knows itself to be the community that bears the marks of its origin in God's creative act.

What are the marks of the community that is created by God? Karl Barth's discussion of the basic form of humanity is helpful in describing the marks of truly human community. Barth begins with the assumption that there is no question as to whether we shall live in community—that has been decided by creation. We are created irrevocably social. Barth outlines four "levels of humanity" which move progressively closer to the norm of a fully human community that manifests the marks of divine creation.

The first level is what Barth calls eye-to-eye relationships. By this he means the capacity to see each other. Almost paradoxically, he insists that if we are to be with each other in community, we must see and recognize the uniqueness of each one. Only as each one becomes this one or that one does he or she come to be really with us. Otherwise, he or she may be "around" but not with us. To be able to say "I know you by name, I know you by sight" is the first level of humanization in community. However, this must also be a willingness to be seen and to not hide myself from the other. Visibility to each other and seeing each other then constitute the first level. Secondly, there is a necessity for mutual speech and hearing. The obvious need for communication is at the heart of the truly human community. But perhaps it is less obvious that communication as such is constitutive of community, our being together. I literally cannot know who I am unless I hear from you about who I am. And you cannot know who I am unless I will tell you who I am. The same is true for you with respect to my speech and hearing and your own self-understanding. The development of the self is a social phenomenon that involves your speaking to me about my origins and my place in society and my integrating those words in my own way and projecting myself out beyond the previous boundaries set for me by the social world. Thus, my becoming who I am is contingent upon your willingness to speak to me and hear me speak to you. If we are to be "in communion" at any level deeper than the mutual dependence of individual selfhood, then speech and hearing take on further importance. Not only does the community protect my right to speak, but the community has a right to hear what I have to say. As a member of the community, I have the obligation to address the community with genuine and significant speech and thus to participate actively in the growth of community by augmenting authentic communication.

The third level to which Barth refers is mutual assistance. This is a broad-ranging claim upon us. In Christian terms the need of the neighbor becomes the form of God's command for us to act. This is not a program of reform. But armed with sensitivity to human need, we live ready to assist when a need is discovered. Equally important, we are ready to receive graciously when we are in need. The key again is mutuality. It requires willingness to receive from others and readiness to respond in obedience to assist others in need.

The fourth level of humanity has to do with our attitudinal stance toward community life. Sensitive to the human tendency to become moralistic and deadly serious about doing what must be done, Barth insists that such attitudes deny the humanity we seek. Being together easily becomes a burden that we must bear, a complex network of duties that we fulfill grudgingly and purely for the sake of meeting our own survival needs. The human community created by God, however, is not characterized by drudgery, but by joy and gladness. We are together because in being together we are being who we are and what we are. We come to each other for each other's sake as well as our own, and in that coming together, we recognize that we are becoming ourselves and what we hope to be. In genuine giving and receiving, that which we hope for—human fulfillment in community—becomes a reality for us. The joy of knowing that we are received by others and that they receive us gladly enables us to give, knowing that our gifts will be received in the same joyful mood. We trust the other one, knowing that that other one is trustworthy, and at the same time is trusting us. We are not alone, and we shall not be left alone. We care and we are cared for. Such a life together creates a community of perpetual celebration in which we abandon our inhibitions and exhult in the promise and possibility made known by our being with each other.

At this point, it is worth noting that creation, for Barth, is a postcovenantal doctrine. Because the covenant community understands all community to be created by God, and the possibility of community to be a gift of God, it will expect to find many communities that more or less manifest the marks of the divine creative act. Furthermore, the covenant community will make a serious mistake if it sees itself to be somehow "better" than other communities, as if it, too, were not human and did not partake in all of the ambiguity that that implies. The uniqueness of the community of the people of God does not rest in its moral achievement. It resides rather in the fact that it knows a secret—that God's creative act is the basis for all genuinely human community. The people of God rejoice in community wherever it is found because they know they have discovered more than a human achievement. They have discovered a gift of God.

Knowing that all community is a gift of God means that the community of the people of God will be an open community. Because the community itself owes its existence to a gracious gift, it will be open to new gifts of persons from God into its community. The One whose gift has made their being together possible is the One whose love is fully given to all. Therefore, whosoever desires may come and share the mutual joy, hope, and fulfillment of the congregation. There can be no exclusiveness about the body of Christ. The body of Christ can never become a clique or a closed circle. They will be attentive to the center of their life and not to its boundaries. God is that center and God alone sets the boundaries of the covenant community by her own free choice.

2. The Body of Christ Is a Community for the Poor

God's choice of Israel and of Jesus Christ is a choice of a particular people. In Jesus Christ we know that God has chosen a people for the world, but there is a particular people who were objects of Jesus' special attention and to whom his ministry and his call were especially directed. Jesus Christ became human for the poor.

The church has long understood that Jesus Christ was for the poor, reflected in the historic preoccupation of the church with service to the poor. But, as Gustavo Gutierrez has said, "The poor today, rather than being regarded as merely a 'problem for the church,' raise the question of what 'being the church' really means."[1]

Jesus' own understanding of his ministry was characterized by a primary concern for the poor. To illustrate, it is useful to point to a series of significant events reported by Luke. The first was a baptism at which time the title "Son of God" is given to Jesus, and the descent of the spirit upon Jesus is described.

The second event is the temptation in the wilderness. Here

---

[1] Gustavo Gutierrez, "The Poor in the Church," in Julio De Santa Ana, *Toward a Church of the Poor* (New York: Maryknoll, 1981), p. 122.

more New Testament commentators have agreed that from the mouth of Satan came popular notions of messiahship that were in vogue at the time. In each case, a proposal is suggested by Satan. Jesus spurns the proposal with an aphorism from the Scriptures. The fact that the subject matter between Jesus and Satan is really the nature of messiahship is a strong indication that the wilderness period was thought by Luke not only to be a time of temptation but of growing clarity for Jesus about the direction of his ministry. It is not surprising to discover that Luke places Jesus in an active teaching role when he returns from the wilderness.

The third event in the sequence takes on special importance because it is the first return to Nazareth by Jesus after the wilderness experience, which Luke saw as crucial in setting the tone for the ministry of Jesus. When Jesus appeared in a synagogue, he was handed a scroll to read. He chose a familiar passage from Isaiah: "The spirit of the Lord is on me because he has anointed me to preach good news to the poor and the recovery of sight to the blind, release to the captives and freedom to the oppressed, to proclaim the acceptable year of the Lord." Luke then reports that as the eyes of all were fixed on him, Jesus announced that what they heard was fulfilled before them.

This passage clearly has the force of a revolutionary concept of messiahship. It picks up aspects of the most important revolutionary social innovation in Jewish history, the Year of Jubilee, the acceptable Year of the Lord. The legislation establishing the celebration every fifty years included a provision for the canceling of debts, the re-assignment of land to the dispossessed, the freeing of slaves and servants, and the freeing of the land for itself and for nonhuman creatures.

In this cultural context, we can understand why a group of the good citizens of Nazareth tried to push Jesus off the cliff. Jesus had asserted the primacy of concern for the poor in God's creative and messianic relationship to the world. This was said in a cultural milieu that was based on the theological understanding that rich people were the objects of God's special favor. In spite of their position as a colonized people, the Jews within their own ranks associated riches and religiousness, so that to be poor was almost by definition to be a sinner—at least the poor were not among the truly religious. This convenient theological perspective also undergirded the political alliance of the Sadducees and the Pharisees that finally formed the spearhead of Jewish opposition to Jesus on religious grounds.

What Jesus said at Nazareth turned established theology on its head. Not only were the poor to be included in the covenant people, they were the object of God's special concern. God is God for the poor, and the people of God are the people for the poor—living, working, and moving on their behalf.

Recent New Testament scholarship suggests, however, that this analysis does not go far enough. Not only was Jesus *for* the poor in his ministry, but he called together a community that *was* poor. The community of the people of God is revealed in Jesus Christ as a community of the poor. The community that gathered around Jesus may have been part of the general movement referred to in historical literature as "the piety of the poor." It was a grass-roots protest against the alliance between riches and religiousness that characterized official religion.[2]

In light of this, wealth became the problem for the followers of Christ. The poor needed no justification, only the rich. This means that the community that is the body of Christ must be becoming a community that is *for* the poor in a peculiar way. Too long the poor have suffered the indignities of paternalism and condescension from the religious rich. The act of giving, even generous giving, has often been a taking-away. What is more, giving has often been a way of keeping a safe, discreet distance. Being *for* the poor means far more.

For one thing, it means being with the poor. The body of Christ will include the poor within it. Where it exists apart from the poor, this fact alone will be a matter of great concern. Within the community of people of God, those who are rich will be profoundly disturbed at their separation from the poor. This concern will manifest itself in a persistent and genuine reaching out for community with the community of the poor.

Secondly, if the congregation is for the poor, it will be for the

---

[2]See Luise Schottroff and Wolfgang Stegemann, *Jesus von Nazareth: Hoffnung der Armen* (Stuttgart: Kolhammer, 1978).

poor even at the risk of itself. The body of Jesus Christ will be and is sacrificed for the poor of the world. The community of that body will be willing to assume whatever risk is necessary and to do those things required to be sure that the poor have good news preached to them—genuine good news that there is new life, new hope, and a new order coming for them.

The poor will know that the community of God's people see them, the poor, as the vanguard of the Year of Jubilee. The signs of the Year of the Lord will be *their* freedom, *their* hopes, and *their* new life. In short, for the body of Christ, progress of the poor out of oppression and captivity is the sign of the Jubilee, the New Kingdom. All other progress is, as Bloch has put it, darkly progressive.[3] The good news will be heard only when the body of Christ understands the heart of its community to be the poor.

This kind of understanding will not be possible from afar. Only the poor can speak fully for the poor. A community that claims to be for the poor and remains *far from* the poor is not what it claims. To be the body of Christ in the world, the community will be the community for the poor when it becomes a community *with* the poor. In this way not only is the body of Christ the hope for the poor, but the poor are the givers of hope for the body of Christ. As Dumas has put it, the two faces of Christ, the poor and the church, cannot remain alienated and expect to be whole.[4] When they are together fully with each other and for each other, the faces of Christ are united and the body of Christ becomes one.

3. The Body of Christ Is a Community for the World

The fact that the community of the body of Christ is seen to be the community for the poor should not blind us to another important aspect of the ministry of Jesus. Jesus Christ came not only for the sake of human beings, the poor or otherwise. *Jesus Christ became human in and for the world.* As a body of Christ, then, the congregation is the human community in and for the world.

---

[3] Ernst Bloch, *A Philosophy of the Future,* trans. John Cumming (New York: Herder & Herder, 1970), p. 113.

[4] Benoit Dumas, *The Two Alienated Faces of the One Church,* referred to in Julio De Santa Ana, *Toward a Church of the Poor* (New York: Maryknoll, 1981), p. 99.

It is not as if God created a community and suspended it, as it were, in thin air. The community created by God is created in a place, a world. The body of Christ is not estranged from the world. They feel at home here, knowing that they have been given their place by the grace of the One who gives them everything. Without this place there is no possibility for the beginning of community or its growth and sustenance. Our place, then, is our place only in the sense that we are part of it. The world, living and nonliving, is woven together in a mutually sustaining web of interdependence. We are, as Aldo Leopold put it, a part of the life pyramid, the complex, dynamic, and vital ongoing system in which each part is integral to the world and in which the good of each part derives from and participates in the good of the whole.[5] The boundaries of community are larger than a simple reference to human community implies.

Here the relationship between the creation and covenant is important, but in a different way. Though the faith of the covenant community is a presupposition of any notion of creation at all, it is clear in the biblical accounts that covenant is for the sake of the whole creation. Thus the scope of the covenant is defined by the accounts of creation, and the wider meaning of God's covenant with Abraham is clear only when it is referred to the covenant with Noah. The children of Abraham become Abraham's children precisely because they are to be the people of the rainbow, those who are party to God's covenant with all the earth.

It is not as if the rest of the world is at the disposal of humanity to be simply *our* place. On the contrary, one might say that we are at the disposal of God for the world. Those who are in the image of God through Christ are in the image of a God who loves the world because she has made it. Therefore, our dominion over the earth, which itself is a gift, must be a dominion that is in every way analogous to the dominion of God over the earth. God's rule is loving, caring, and creative—one that bestows upon the world a gift of life with the hope of fulfillment.

There can, therefore, be no radical distinction between human and nonhuman life with respect to their value. Although it is true

---

[5]Aldo Leopold, *A Sand County Almanac* (San Francisco: Sierra Club, 1971).

that because God became a human being human life is more important than nonhuman life, we can in no way assume that only human life is important. The world is good because it is good for God. We live in a place with other creatures, all of whom have value for God by virtue of God's own pronouncement of their goodness for her. We also know that the goodness of creation for God lies precisely in the beauty of its interrelationships, whereby the being of each one is constituted by its being with all the rest.

This is the vision for which the prophets were groping as they spoke of wolves lying down with lambs and the pounding of swords into ploughshares and spears into pruning hooks. The peaceable kingdom is a vision of God's relationship to the whole world, and that relationship is a redemptive ecological connection. This is why the writer of Colossians can speak of Christ as all in all, everything for everything; and this is that to which Paul pointed when he told the Romans of the eager longing and straining of the whole cosmos toward the coming of Christ and Christ's people. They are the community of the body of Christ, the one in whom all things were made and in whom all things now find their hope. Jesus Christ is the harbinger of God's ecological community. The bridgehead, the locus of the redemptive secret that is at the same time the meaning of creation, is the congregation.

THE BODY OF CHRIST IN WILTSHIRE CHURCH

The theological self-understanding of Wiltshire Church is a far cry from these promises to the body of Christ. The ministry that it offers is so narrowly focused on itself that it relates only marginally to the universal promises and claims of redemption manifested so clearly in the faith of Israel and in the church's understanding of the reality of Jesus Christ. Wiltshire Church is not really concerned about the world beyond itself and its own inner community. This is not to say, of course, that there are no persons of compassion who contribute to such causes as Bread for the World, nor is it to suggest that there are no conservationists and ecologists in the membership of the congregation. Indeed, there probably are! What I am suggesting is that there is nothing in their understanding of themselves as a congregation that would indicate that their being gathered as a Christian community entails these sorts of commitments to the poor in the world. The reigning theological understanding of Wiltshire Church as well as the programs of the congregation give no clues as to how much it is identified with the body of Christ for the poor and for the world.

To be sure, the Wiltshire Church does understand itself to be a fully human community, but it is a community closed in on itself. It is almost a classic case of the American culture Protestantism that identifies salvation and success with each other. If this church is a community of the faithful, the faithful are also upwardly mobile. Yet, as Bellah has said of nineteenth-century American religion, there is an ambivalence here.[6] There is a hint of the knowledge that "something more" is required than the trappings of "Shangri-la." Thus, though many may be in this community precisely because it is the "best show in town," there are others who are there because all of the "best show" trappings in the world do not quite satisfy them. Many are there because they are hurt, and they do not receive ministry. Many are there because they are confused, and they do not receive guidance and counsel. Others are there because they hope for a renewal of faith for their children. Wiltshire Church as a community does meet many of these needs. People have felt the healing of being present together there.

Even though there is healing in the community of Wiltshire Church, there is also conflict. Although it does not appear to be theological in substance, it does have important ramifications for our theological analysis. The tone and the issues of the conflict at Wiltshire have become serious causes of interpersonal alienation. Distrust has surfaced to the point where the humanity of the community is at stake. There is very little "presence" of the one to the other in many cases, and mutuality in speech and hearing apparently has disappeared in the face of a cacophony of mutual recrimination. This sort of response is a violation of the bond of community and is proving to be personally destructive to a number of persons. Thus, in spite of the healing that has gone on for many, and in spite of the common focus that binds Wiltshire

---

[6] Robert Bellah, *The Broken Covenant: American Civil Religion in Time of Trial* (New York: Seabury Press, 1975), chap. 3, pp. 61 ff.

people together, the fabric of the congregation is in danger of being shattered by anticommunal, authoritarian, and heedlessly vindictive styles of interpersonal communication. Human community at best is fragile, even when everyone works at it. At present, the parties to the conflict seem to be little inclined to make much effort toward mutual ministry.

In the midst of the problems in the life of Wiltshire Church, there is a sign of hope. Church members place heavy emphasis on the importance of worship, particularly on the importance of Communion. This priority was reflected in the responses of members to the questionnaire on beliefs. The majority view the giving of Communion as one of the most important tasks of the minister. Although I do not want to make too much of this, they do seem to be groping for a community identification with the body of Christ that has universal dimensions. There is a hint that the community of Wiltshire Church is not simply a community for itself, but that in some way it is a community of persons identified with and implicated with the redemptive suffering of Jesus Christ for the world and for each other. That may be all that can be said at this point. If it is a hint of deeper awareness, it is only a hint.

In short, Wiltshire Church partakes very much in the paradox of the people of God. It is at once a self-centered, fractured, and culture-bound community of like-minded persons, and at the same time, by the miracle of grace, it is the body of Christ symbolized in the bread and wine, called to be for each other and for the poor and for the world. The fact that the church is not completely for the world and for the poor—or even, for that matter, fully for each other—in no way negates the fact that it is called by God to be those things. The theological challenge for this church is to involve itself intimately with discerning external critics of their religiosity by hearing from those whose needs are not being met in Wiltshire, Springfield, and elsewhere. They also need to expose themselves to those who are actually poor, and to Christians with global perspectives on the church and ministry. That kind of communication will reveal to Wiltshire the promise of God that it can claim for itself and by which it can be claimed. If this happens, its vision of its ministry will change, its suffering will become redemptive, and its presence will provide new hope for those who are now in the community of Wiltshire Church; and an increasing number of those now on the periphery of concern might join the center.

SUGGESTIONS FOR RELATED READING

Barth, Karl. *Church Dogmatics*. Vol. 3, part 2. Edinburgh: T & T Clark, 1960.

In this section of the *Dogmatics,* Barth discusses the doctrine of creation. Here the marks of human community are presented under the rubric "the basic form of humanity." As is the case in all of Barth's *Dogmatics,* all humanity is humanity understood in light of Jesus Christ's humanity, but the humanity of which Barth speaks is not identical to that of Jesus. In other words, the humanity described at this point is humanity as such, creative humanity, and not the promised humanity with God that is revealed fully in Jesus Christ. It is humanity "with each other" by virtue of its origin in the creative act of God, but it can exist yet ignorant of its origin.

Bonhoeffer, Dietrich. *Sanctorum Communio*. New York: Harper & Row, 1963.

This is Bonhoeffer's basic book on the nature of the church and society. It is here that Bonhoeffer develops a notion of the self as social as opposed to the individualism of his forebearers in idealism. He also argues that all being is relational whether that being is a single human being or a community of human beings in relation to other communities. Since it is not possible to be human except in relation, Bonhoeffer grounds the humanity of all humankind in relation to God. As the community before God, humankind is a real community. Without this relation, there is no ground for any conception of the reality of humankind as a total community.

Metz, J. B. *Theology of World*. New York: Herder & Herder, 1969.

This is a series of essays by Metz in which he develops a sociocritical approach for the church. Though Metz moves toward a "political theology," he is not clear just how this relates either to congregations or to the church as a whole. What he argues essentially is for a change in the historical perspective of the theology of the church from the past to the future. This eschatological perspective then places the church in a critical posture toward all past and present sociopolitical realities, including the theology of the church itself. The theology of the church becomes creative in the sense that the church knows that the world is called to hope for peace, justice, and reconciliation in the future. It is militant in the sense that it calls into question at all times past and present contradictions of its hope for the future.

Niebuhr, H. R. *Radical Monotheism and Western Culture.* New York: Harper & Brothers, 1943.
I refer to this book primarily because of the essay on "the center of value," where Niebuhr argues that in the final analysis all value is relational and that all valuing is therefore relative to the valuing center. The unity of value is constituted by God as a valuing center. For God, what is has value. Any less universal perspective on value that makes value instrumental to centers of value other than God is not a genuine monotheistic faith.

Schottroff, Luise, and Stegemann, Wolfgang. *Jesus von Nazareth: Hoffnung der Armen.* Stuttgart: Kolhammer, 1978.
This is a New Testament study, primarily in the gospel of Luke. The basic thesis is that Jesus' ministry was focused on liberation for the poor. They argue that not only was Jesus' ministry for the poor, but the community Jesus gathered was a church of the poor.

Steck, Odell Hannes. *World and Environment.* Nashville: Abingdon Press, 1980.
This is a study of the biblical understanding of world as it relates to the whole natural milieu. The focus is upon the accounts of creation in Genesis and the creation psalms. Though Steck admits that there is little direct application that can be made of biblical understanding of creation to the present environmental crisis, he does argue that the biblical writers understand clearly the interdependence of creation in a way that contradicts a strict subject/object distinction between humanity and world characteristic of post-Cartesian philosophy and modern science.

8. Professionalism, Breakdown, and Revelation

Philosophical Theology

DAVID S. PACINI

When the Reverend Sidney Carlson came to Wiltshire Methodist Church, it was in the midst of collapse. Its principal benefactors had recently died, and the principles by which the church had been run were breaking down. Sid established new procedures for its management and new programs for its membership, effectively revitalizing the church. To all appearances, Sid was, at first, eminently successful in rebuilding the church. But quite suddenly the new principles and programs he introduced seemed to be falling apart. Again, the church was tottering on the brink of collapse. How are we to understand this?

Owing to our predisposition to conceive of ourselves as citizens of a secular world, we are inclined to use secular categories to interpret our experience. Secular categories appear different from religious categories. Indeed, it is for us a commonplace assumption that methods of secular inquiry are distinct from the methods of religious inquiry, the one the negation of the other. For example, secular inquiry, such as that of the social sciences, begins with social experience and the conditions of that experience. Religious inquiries, on the contrary, seem to be anchored in a dimension that is beyond human experience, to which humans respond. When cast this way, our current understanding of "church" appears to reflect a theological posture that emerged at the beginning of the century, that the Word of God is wholly distinct from social experience. Accordingly, reflections issuing from social experience do not lead to God. Instead, they culminate in the deification of social experience, and so in the worship of false gods.

Theological investigations, in sum, cannot arise from the analysis of social conditions.

This way of putting the issue is both right and wrong. What is right about it is the notion that there are distinctions between the analogies of social science and theology. What is wrong is the presumption that sociological analyses do not already contain an implicit theological viewpoint, or that theological analyses are not contingent upon an implicit sociological setting.[1]

In this chapter, I want to bring out the force of this observation by bringing into view the underlying metaphors that are at play in the life of Wiltshire Church and that insinuate themselves into our thinking about its social collapse or breakdown. I have chosen metaphor as a focal point for my analysis owing to the ways in which it reflects the capacity of minds to make connections, transferring modes of regarding, of loving, and of acting from one context to another in order to grasp a sense of the whole.[2] Understood in this way, metaphor is more than a colorful addition to our spoken and written expression. Rather, metaphor is fundamental to the way in which we think and act, introducing coherence to the manifold diversities of experience. Whenever we use a word or phrase to bring different things together in interactions, we engage metaphor.

I am also interested in the relation between a knowing, acting subject and metaphor. Coherent patterns of meaning are ex-

---

[1] Within the limits of this essay, it is not possible to expand upon this particular claim or to elucidate its implications. But this much should be said: we have come to think of the character of our time as essentially secular. And though there is a sense in which this is so, there is equally a sense in which it is not. On the surface of our languages, we do indeed appear to be secular. But at a deeper level, the structures within which our languages cohere are fundamentally theological. Thus the sense that our age is marked by secularity is, at best, superficial; the character of our time is marked more by the religious than we have heretofore recognized. For a more detailed treatment of this issue, the interested reader may wish to see my forthcoming essay, "The Character of Modern Religious Thought."

[2] For a more extensive treatment of metaphor, see I. A. Richards, *The Philosophy of Rhetoric* (New York: Oxford University Press, 1965), and Stephen Pepper, *World Hypotheses: A Study of Evidence* (Berkeley: University of California Press, 1970).

pressed by or for subjects. Thus, identifying the ways in which we understand the relation between subjects and their sense of the whole as it comes into expression in the Wiltshire Church community is essential to our task of interpretation.

To draw these themes together, I shall begin with an assessment of the collapse of Wiltshire Church from the perspective of the underlying metaphor of democratic consensus. This metaphor informs our sense of organizational process, and it was doubtlessly a part of Alan Hyatt's thinking about how the polity of Wiltshire Church had broken down. I shall look, too, at the way in which Sid Carlson's notion of being "professional" defines his relation to this metaphor. Next, I will take up a theological metaphor, "the sovereignty of God" that runs through Sid's preaching. I will attempt to show that this metaphor stands implicitly behind what Sid called "the veneer" of democratic consensus. And I shall point up the way in which the God of Sid's preaching is related deus ex machina to Sid's metaphor. But after observing the points at which these metaphors obscure the interplay between theological and sociological factors, I will push us further still. I will argue that the logic of the relation between the knowing, acting subject and the metaphors I have lifted up recapitulates the logic of, and constitutes a factor in, social breakdown or collapse in the larger culture. Grasping this phenomenon in its own right, and the extent to which our ways of relating to metaphor contribute to it, may help us to understand breakdown in the church. It may as well, I conclude, enable us to engage in new ways of theological thinking that grow out of such experience in our congregational lives.

DEMOCRATIC CONSENSUS

Wiltshire Church had been dominated by the Adams Company, with its principles of paternalism and primogeniture. Before 1970, church officers had enjoyed uninterrupted tenure. Changes in the practices of the church that accompanied the ministry of the Reverend Sidney Carlson included abolishing the tradition of two Sunday morning services in favor of one, the removal of inactive members from the rolls of the church, and the establishment of the principle that no individual would hold office for more than three years. In order to broaden involvement in church stewardship, the church entered into a program of debt.

Sid's personal style complemented the organizational transition to broader congregational involvement. On his first Sunday in Wiltshire, Sid admonished his congregation for their ineptitude in hymn singing, requiring them to re-sing the opening hymn. The secretary and organist/choirmaster whom Sid had inherited left their posts and he involved the congregation in the search for their replacements. Perceiving his parishioners as "secular agnostics" with "wistful hearts," as "biblically illiterate," and as disillusioned by the failures of the "American dream," Sid honored their desire to expose their children to basic religious values. Church programs focusing upon church school, music, and preaching all grew out of Sid's sensitivity toward the experiences of his congregation. Gradually, the constituency of the church changed from persons who were primarily workers in the Adams Company to persons who were upwardly mobile middle-class executives. Throughout the transition, Sid worked adroitly to retain the backing of the majority of the congregation and its votes. In this way, at least, one could say that Sid succeeded in altering the experience of Wiltshire Church from dependency upon the Adams Company to self-sufficiency. Indeed, one might argue that the focus upon democratic consensus had an emancipatory effect upon the life of the church.

From such a reading, it would appear that the Wiltshire Church program collapsed when the process of democratic consensus broke down. One event that highlights this is the church retreat. Essential to the process of democratic consensus is the free and equal participation of all parties in communication. Impediments to such freedom can only be tolerated within a range that still satisfies the generalizable interests of the participants.[3] When,

[3] For extended commentary upon this point, see: Jürgen Habermas, "A Social-Scientific Concept of Crisis," in *Legitimation Crises,* trans. Thomas McCarthy (Boston: Beacon Press, 1973), pp. 1–31; "On Systematically Distorted Communication," *Inquiry,* 13 (1970), pp. 205–218; "Towards a Theory of Communicative Competence," *Inquiry,* 13, pp. 360–75; *Knowledge and Human Interests,* trans. Jeremy J. Shapiro (Boston: Beacon Press, 1971).

at the retreat, the concerns of a growing number of parishioners about the nature of the church were cut off in favor of discussion about staffing concerns, the process of democratic consensus broke down: staffing concerns did not reflect the generalizable interests of those who were actively pursuing questions about the nature and identity of the church.

Sid's intervention at the retreat brings into focus his relation to the metaphor of democratic consensus. Sid understood himself to be a "professional," meaning by this one who is able to manage successfully the process of democratic consensus. He came to Wiltshire Church with the charge from his bishop to "shape it up." He expected that his congregation would "push back or shut up." He was not afraid to confront the initially disaffected parishioners who were seeking his removal. Nor was he reticent about altering the discussion at the retreat from general questions about the nature of the church to specific questions about staffing and other professional matters. Indeed, his sense of professionalism was for him a strong suit, but it was as well the cause of his downfall. By putting the emphasis upon his professional capacity to manage the process of democratic consensus, rather than upon his ordination to be sensitive to the context of the process, Sid lost touch. Subsequently, speculation centered upon the person of Sid Carlson. Was Sid's aberrant behavior a reflection of his mid-life crisis, of his anxiety over economic instability, or of his desire for private housing? Why did Sid feel that his parishioners didn't give a damn about him? And what was actually at stake in his personal conflicts with various members of the church? Insofar as the church community sensed Sid's loss of control, suspicion about the nature of his "professionalism" emerged. To some, Sid appeared to be disillusioned with the tradition and practice of his denomination, insufficiently "spiritual" and "theological," uninterested in "fellowship and support," and even devoid of interest in social outreach.

Now the difficulty that accrues to the use of the metaphor of democratic consensus is that it promotes an interpretive view whose focus is process rather than content. To put that differently, the metaphor of democratic consensus unites a formal principle—majority rule—with legitimate social conduct. Because the principle of majority rule is self-referential, no appeals to external authorities are required to adjudicate social conduct: the principle of democratic consensus and its practice are co-incident.[4] From a historical perspective, it is easy to see that the institutionalization of this principle at the outset of modernity had an emancipatory and secularizing effect. Human conduct now would be judged from the perspective of self-legislated principles rather than from the hierarchical principles of feudal society and its church.[5] One could say that this historic transition from feudalism to self-sufficiency was effectively re-enacted in Wiltshire Church. But the inward turn toward self-sufficiency is simultaneously a turn away from the social world.[6] Consequently, the ideal of self-legislation assumes greater reality than the specific social context to which the ideal is addressed.

Although the formal approach to human conduct is one way of understanding social practice, it is not the only one. Other approaches attribute greater weight to the issue of the content of the procedure, but these do not come into focus with the metaphor of democratic consensus. When viewed historically, this apparent lacuna in the metaphor of democratic consensus assumes special significance in our reflections about Wiltshire Church.

The development of the principle of democratic consensus, owing to its independence from external religious authorities, precipitated the emergence of what we call secular culture. That culture, of which we are a part, is preoccupied with organization. But it is ill equipped to deal with matters of content—especially religious content.

The dimension of religious content cannot be divorced from the interpretation of church life, however. For this reason, the meta-

[4] Jürgen Habermas, "Legitimation Problems in the Modern State," in *Communication and the Evolution of Society*, trans. Thomas McCarthy (Boston: Beacon Press, 1979), pp. 183–88. The reader is referred as well to Jürgen Habermas, "On the Logic of Legitimation Problems," in *Legitimation Crisis*, trans. Thomas McCarthy, pp. 95–143.

[5] This is the view especially of Max Weber, of Niklas Luhmann, and of Jürgen Habermas, although there are numerous others who have embraced it.

[6] This insight has its origins in Fichte and in G. W. F. Hegel; a more recent expression of this insight may be found in Clifford Geertz, *The Interpretation of Cultures* (New York: Basic Books, 1973), esp. chaps. 4 and 5.

phor of democratic consensus takes us part of the way, but not far enough, in the interpretation of Wiltshire Church. It does not, for example, tell us what were the genuine differences of religious viewpoint among the various groups who were unsettled about the direction in which the church was going. Nor does it help us to see the extent to which Sid is becoming, like his predecessors, a tired old man. It is interesting that Sid himself confessed that the decorum of the church and the process of democratic consensus was itself a veneer, behind which stood something else that was really operative. The theological metaphor, to which we now turn, brings this other dimension into view.

THE SOVEREIGNTY OF GOD

The theological metaphor of the "sovereignty of God" is operative in a subtle but continuous way in Sid's preaching, in his hymnody, and in the psalters that he uses.

On his first day at Wiltshire, Sid declared "God is in his heaven and all is well with the world." Over the years, Sid amplified this view in his sermons:

> God made the heavens and the earth and his sovereignty is never usurped. It is God's will so to turn history as to "put down the mighty from their seats" and to exalt "them of low degree."
>
> The love of God reaches out to each of us locked in our loneliness and separation. That love comes with power capable of redeeming the times of stress and peril through which we from time to time must move . . . in fact, the Lord God omnipotent reigneth. Hallelujah!
>
> The fulfillment of God's power needs us. . . . Every one of us here is the end product of history. We are the focal point at this time of the creative forces of God.
>
> Blessed are those with a living faith in the reality of the divine world and such interior fellowship with it that amid the alien pressures of the world they can live for the approbation of the highest.
>
> It is only through the grace of God and the redemptive power of the Holy Spirit that any of us can hope for the grace of salvation.
>
> Turn to me, O God, prayed the Psalmist. But God turned to him even in the man's seeking. We need to root ourselves in something that is greater than we ourselves.

> God, so the record runs, said to him [Ezekiel]: "Get up upon thy feet, O son of man, and I will speak to thee." God cannot do business with people in a supine condition. Paul, in his second letter to Timothy, uttered these encouraging words: "God has not given us the spirit of timidity, but of power and of love and of self-control." . . . The groundwork of our grit and determination is lodged in our understanding of ourselves as creatures of God.

Reinforced by his hymnody (e.g., "O Worship the King, All Glorious Above," "Rise Up O Men of God," "March On O Soul, with Strength," "Spirit of Life in This New Dawn," "Give Us the Faith That Follows On," "Come Down O Love Divine") and his selection of psalters (e.g., "Rejoice in the Lord, O ye Righteous! Praise befits the upright," "Preserve me O God, for in thee I take refuge," "Give the king thy justice, O God, and thy righteousness to the Royal Son!"), Sid's theological metaphor of the sovereignty of God consists, in rough outline, in the conviction that God is at the helm, controlling the outcome of history. Through God's grace humans may exert self-control, rise up upon their feet, and do business with God. Only in this way can God's creative forces redeem the times of stress and peril; only in this way will God's plan be fulfilled in the course of history.

This metaphor of the sovereignty of God affords us a view of the content of the process at Wiltshire Church. In broad strokes, it fills in the backdrop of what Sid thought ought to happen. Through programs of self-help, humans do get to their feet, do conduct business with God, and do retain some sense of control in a world in which they are uncertain about the extent to which they have control. This view was borne out as well in Sid's programs for individuals, even though he was suspicious of their motives for involvement. Nonetheless, Sid had seen such outreach as part of his larger professional ambition of getting people back on their feet who were having trouble. Similarly, his program for the elderly, even though basically programs to feed senior citizens of Wiltshire Church, embodied the intent of keeping them on their feet so that they could do business with God. So, too, trying to provide a better Christian education program for the young people who were the future of the church reflected Sid's aim of enabling people to do business with God.

Sid frequently states the relation of God to his theological metaphor. The economy of history, for Sid, is not divine. God is clearly Other, one who can turn toward us, one who can intervene—"putting down the mighty" and "exalting those of low degree." Those are times of stress and peril, which God, through intervention, can redeem. The objectivity of God, understood as the sovereignty of God, is the fulfillment of history. But the subjectivity of God, the God who elects to intervene, is not God immanent or God with us. The subjectivity of God is tacitly understood to be deus ex machina, the manager who intervenes to reinforce our "self-control," our "grit and determination," and who intercedes when we are "locked in our loneliness and separation."

By virtue of the metaphor of the sovereignty of God and of the concomitant assumption about the relation of God to the divine economy, it becomes possible for us to achieve a clearer sense of what Sid thought the content of the church program should be. Moreover, the peculiar character of the metaphor and its assumption of God's relation to the divine economy to which Sid alludes is wholly co-incident with Sid's understanding of the metaphor of democratic consensus and his relation to it. Both Sid and God are managers. For Sid, the emphasis falls upon the success of managing the process of democratic consensus. For God, the emphasis falls upon managing the divine economy. Both Sid and God are to direct the process toward goals they think appropriate. For Sid, the goals are masked by the church's metaphor of democratic consensus; for God, the goals are masked by the church's metaphor of the sovereignty of God.

Once the links between the metaphors of democratic consensus and the sovereignty of God and the roles of professional and deus ex machina come into view, it is not difficult to see how the connections in Sid's mind, and in the minds of many at Wiltshire Church, committed Sid to the stance of an outsider, like God, whose task is to raise up other people and to align them with the will of God. For Sid, the stance of the outsider manifested itself in numerous ways. His surreptitious entry into Wiltshire under a pseudonym, his scolding of the congregation, his unilateral termination of staff, his contempt for the choir, his manipulation of denominational church polity, and his dissolution of existing church practices are all reflections of this stance.

Grasping the extent to which Sid stood outside the church adds another dimension to our understanding of Sid and of what was going on in the church. Such understanding also affords us a glimpse into why the programs broke down. For this notion of the sovereignty of God is not something that was rooted in Wiltshire, or that grew out of the experience of Wiltshire. The members of Wiltshire Church were "wistful hearts," secular agnostics, and "biblical illiterates." Sid brought this metaphor from the outside to Wiltshire. A more formal way of putting this point is that Sid's theological metaphor is not rooted in the sociohistorical conditions of the church. For this reason, the metaphor appears to stand over against the social world of Wiltshire. Again, the parallels between the secular metaphor of democratic consensus and the theological metaphor of the sovereignty of God are striking. The secular metaphor assumes that the religious is something wholly distinct. This religious view assumes the same posture, that the religious is something distinct, not from culture as we know it. Consequently, we are now more aware of the content that informs the program of the church, but this is not the content that grows out of the actual life of the church. Insofar as the church is implicitly guided by this outside metaphor, it is unable to sustain its program, because it reflects neither the church's own identity and direction nor the church's own growth and awareness of the tensions that occupy our culture.

We may summarize all this by saying that the theological metaphors that our generation avoids steer our thought and conduct as much as the secular metaphors that we accept.

BREAKDOWN

At this point, it is worth recalling the central thread of my argument. Discussing the underlying metaphors of clergy and laypersons helps us to interpret the life experiences of Wiltshire Church. Moreover, inasmuch as patterns of meaning are expressions for and by subjects, it is essential to determine what relation obtains implicitly between subjects and metaphor. Then it is possible to discern the extent to which theological hypotheses are distinguished in practice from sociological factors. In Wiltshire

Church, the secular metaphor of democratic consensus, with its accompanying relation of deus ex machina that incorporates the subjectivity of God, broadens its focus to include ideological content. But both metaphors fail to link social context and theoretical views in a convincing interpretation of practice.

It is not sufficient to stop here. We have not yet come to an adequate understanding of why Wiltshire Church is again tottering on the brink of collapse. We are not yet able to account for the belief that the church was a one-man show. Nor can we account for the paradox that Sid, like his predecessors, is now getting older and contemplating retirement, practicing the arts of preaching, visiting the sick, and burying the dead. Finally, we have not yet found a sufficient interpretation for the differing visions of the nature of the church and the growing sense that the congregation needs to retain the services of a consultant. To understand all of this, we need to think in a more theoretical vein than we have until now.

Few social phenomena are as difficult to assess as breakdown. Breakdown, as we have seen, is a collapse of social relations. But it is, as well, the collapse of patterns of coherence; the inadequacy of basic metaphors that we use to understand social relations surely contributes to our quandary. What may have been suspected but needs to be said clearly is that the phenomenon of breakdown surfacing in Wiltshire Church is manifest as well in the larger society—in families, in communities, in states, and in nations. All of us have to contend with breakdown in one way or another, although none of us is suitably prepared for the task. As we have noted, metaphors can establish connections, or deepen our experience by envisioning more encompassing unities. We now must explore the significant power of those metaphors in our lives, especially in our attempt to contend with the dissolution of familiar patterns of relationship.

Metaphors function for us as a way to orient us to our experience. This orientation has to do with what is occurring at present. It has to do also with our ways of relating to our past. Our metaphors reflect our deepest beliefs, aspirations, and accomplishments in Western society. We hold dear such metaphors as the kingdom of God, which is a religious metaphor, or the land of the free, which is a sociopolitical metaphor, or the age of anxiety, which is a psychological metaphor, as ways of understanding the temper of our times.

We are so accustomed to using metaphor that we don't realize how often we use it, the extent to which we use it, or its importance for our daily conduct. Rather, we take metaphors for granted. When we try to talk about metaphors, some people become confused, claiming that they don't know what metaphors are all about. Experience, however, belies this claim. That metaphor is an omnipresent principle of our thinking can be shown by looking at our situation.

In recent decades we have begun to face troubling questions with the metaphors that we use. The war in Vietnam brought us the metaphors of the light at the end of the tunnel and peace with honor. How many of us lived our lives in the belief that it was just a little bit longer before that horror would come to an end, transformed, finally, into a just cause? Similarly, the events in the Falkland Islands, South Africa, Ireland, and the Middle East have made us wonder about the metaphor of political sovereignty. Our belief in the metaphor of a democratic free society contributed to our outrage when United States diplomats were held captive in Iran. We were ill disposed to ask what the infusion of Western metaphors, practices, and gadgetry meant for a non-Western country. When members of the civil rights movement began to insist upon black power and pointed out the complicity of white liberals in the continuing practices of racism, we began to wonder about our metaphor of "freedom and justice for all." When the women's movement pointed out that we had fashioned God in the image of the white male patriarch, we began to wonder whether we could ever again easily hold the metaphor of God the Father. In short, many events of our lives in recent years have called into question numerous metaphors that we have taken for granted as ways of understanding the course of our lives. Some, in response to these questions, have attempted to reinstate so-called traditional values. Others have tried to find new, more encompassing metaphors. But all of us have to acknowledge the metaphors we employ, and all of us have come to feel the malaise caused by challenge to the metaphors we have used to orient ourselves.

We begin to comprehend more fully, perhaps, the import of

metaphor for our lives when we recognize that certain among our metaphors assume for us a central position, around which other metaphors coalesce. We refer to such a configuration as a world view, meaning by this a pattern of ordering that characterizes our sense of objective totality. Thus, the world view of democratic consensus shapes what we mean by the metaphor of freedom and justice for all, just as the metaphor of the sovereignty of God shapes what we mean by the metaphor of redemptive grace. Moreover, the distinctive ordering of a world view functions as a principle to which we appeal in order to justify our actions. Metaphors that function as world views, then, not only orient our conduct, but also incorporate principles of legitimation to which we appeal as warrants for our conduct.

Throughout history, of course, metaphorical world views have changed. The transitions accompanying the breakdown we experience today have prompted some to suggest that nothing more is required of us than has been required of generations in other historical periods: we need to adopt more realistic metaphors that reflect the temper of our time. Some would even say that, if we were to develop more realistic metaphors, we would be able to stabilize our present situation. We would not feel shaken by threats to our world views and so to fundamental ways of orienting and legitimating our lives. These observations seem sound, but there is a sense in which they are not sound at all.

Though it is true that world views undergo change, it is not true that we really know how metaphors change or why some assume the role of world view. Thus, to suggest that what we need is more realistic metaphors is to engage in sleight of hand. We don't make metaphors by introducing a rule regarding the manner in which they are to function. Nor can we make metaphors more inclusive by appealing to some unstated principle of inclusion. For example, the metaphors of the social sciences begin with a keen sensitivity toward culture-specific expressions. They then move beyond those expressions to lawlike generalizations and probability formulations with strong predictive powers. In this way, the metaphors of the social sciences achieve, ostensibly, greater inclusivity. But what kind of inclusivity? What does it mean to say that we can develop metaphors that are governed by laws? For a law to be law it must be always and everywhere efficacious; otherwise it is not a law. If a law is always the case, it is so on its own merits alone, and not with reference to human beliefs, intentions, reasons, fears, and the like.[7] But is this not a very odd way for us to conceive of human behavior? Does not the view that there are fundamental laws, which operate independent of human beliefs, reasons, intentions, fears, pains, and the like, but which are the key to interpreting human life, seem impoverished?

Odd or impoverished as it may be, there are those who hold such "inclusive" metaphors to be useful devices. To what does holding such a metaphor implicitly commit us? Implicitly we are bound to the notion that human life is essentially mechanistic, that is, that life processes take place according to mechanical sequences that admit of predictability. Worse, if we think that this is true of life, then we are committing ourselves to a preoccupation with social mechanisms and the way in which they function, while averting our gaze from questions about values, beliefs, intentions, and the like. So if we think that metaphors can be made more inclusive by virtue of some covert appeal to the formulation of lawlike generalizations, we are aligning ourselves with a very narrow view of life indeed.

This narrowness is one of the key factors that comes into play in breakdown. If we become preoccupied with a world view that we think is inclusive and all-embracing, without recognizing the extent to which it is simply a reflection of our own notion of inclusivity, then we are implicitly excluding all whose world views differ from our own. Moreover, in the case of the so-called secular society in which we find ourselves, the use of such metaphors that claim this form of universality reflects nothing other than the world view of the middle class, ordered by its penchant for management and its conviction that life processes are to be

[7] For systematic exploration of this point, see: W. V. O. Quine, *Word and Object* (Cambridge: MIT Press, 1960), esp. chap. 6. The reader is referred, as well, to the views of Alasdair MacIntyre, *After Virtue* (Notre Dame Ind.: University of Notre Dame Press, 1981), chaps. 7 and 8; Charles Taylor, "Hermeneutics and Politics," in *Critical Sociology,* ed. Paul Connerton (Middlesex: Penguin Books, 1976); and Steven M. Tipton, *Getting Saved from the Sixties* (Berkeley: University of California Press, 1982), esp. chaps. 1 and 5.

managed according to standards of predictability and lawlike generalization. Although this world view has its origins in the Enlightenment and historically is the basis for the rise of the middle class, it is nonetheless a world view whose legitimation principles of management have been employed by the middle class to safeguard its interests. Oftentimes this has meant exploitation of working class people, through subtle reinforcement of their bondage to their station in life. By imputing status to ourselves and thereby giving ourselves a form of leverage over the lives of others, the phenomenon of social breakdown is, in part, set into motion.

A corollary of this is that institutions and lifestyles that appeal to the world view of the middle class are committing the same kinds of errors as individuals who subscribe to this world view. Insofar as institutions reinforce anonymity, the responsibility for their role in breakdown is more difficult to identify. But the corporate force of metaphor is certainly pervasive.

No single one of these factors, but their interplay, constitutes the social phenomenon of breakdown. The inadequacy of world views and related metaphors to orient us in the face of complex experiences generates questions about the ways in which we orient ourselves. These questions, in turn, precipitate the search for more inclusive metaphors. And our search for more inclusive metaphors brings us face to face with the ways in which our conception of inclusivity commits us repeatedly to narrow views of life. Confusion is rampant in the collapse of institutional forms of twentieth-century social life. Family, community, church, and nation exhibit the phenomenon of breakdown. The extent of the collapse is underscored by the shrill claims of conservative religious and political groups that are attempting to reimpose that posture as traditional values. In fact, what they advocate are simply old world views that purport to give us security. What these world views negate, however, is the multiplicity of lifestyles to which we are heir and of which we have become unavoidably aware.

In what ways do these theoretical remarks bear upon our capacity to understand breakdown in Wiltshire Church and to discern new avenues for theological thinking? This question hinges, in key part, upon our readiness to concede that our metaphors fail to bring about the greater portion of their declared ends.

At one level, the metaphors of democratic consensus and the sovereignty of God fail because they are inadequately conceived. The metaphor of democratic consensus, for example, lifts up its pattern of ordering as a principle of legitimation, while simultaneously suppressing its function as world view. Specifically, its preoccupation with form that is self-sufficient overrides its recognition of its determinative role for other metaphors. The sovereignty of God is thus tacitly determined by the metaphor of democratic consensus. What this points up is that the attempt to separate a principle of legitimation from world view falters; although we have taken over this assumption, which has been shown to be characteristic of modernity, in the belief that it is justified, it is wrongheaded.[8] Metaphors and principles of legitimation or obligation are co-eval. In the absence of this recognition, patterns of social relations are bound to embody the same mistaken assumption. The sense that Wiltshire Church is a "one-man show," that there is no room for differing world views, and that Sid has become a "tired old man" reflects this assumption, as does the growing sense that a consultant is needed. Neither the metaphor of democratic consensus nor the metaphor of the sovereignty of God can bring about or sustain a comprehensive interpretation of the life of Wiltshire Church.

At a deeper level, the recurring problem in Wiltshire Church's use of metaphors is the way in which they tacitly understand their relation to metaphors. They, like us, suppose that metaphors are made according to some preconceived notion of inclusivity. Indeed, we frequently act as if metaphors lead us to some hidden central principle, to some basic underlying order of life. To be sure, the metaphors we use embody patterns of coherence that inform the course of human events. Yet when we think of metaphors as a means of access to independent underlying principles, we are also inclined to suppose that our relation to metaphor is simultaneously a relation to the principle that orders the course of human

---

[8] The distinction I am challenging here has been drawn by Habermas, if I understand him correctly, in "Legitimation Problems in the Modern State," pp. 179–83.

events. In this way, we imagine ourselves as getting to the center of things. This understanding of our knowledge of principles we express by means of another metaphor: the center of meaning.

However innocent that metaphor may appear to be, it is, in fact, anything but innocent. We assume that our metaphors are heuristic devices, enabling us to identify fundamental life-ordering principles that are actually at work. In order to identify such a principle, such a center, we tacitly think of ourselves as standing over against that center, looking at it objectively, naming it amongst other principles as "the" principle that is governing life. When we adopt the standpoint of the outside observer who is picking which of these principles is the actual principle that is ordering life, we are implicitly positioning ourselves outside of life.

This is a very curious place in which to stand. We are claiming that somehow we are independent from life structures. We are also claiming, implicitly, that the life principle is independent of life structures. For example, when we survey a situation such as Wiltshire and claim to identify the life principle that was operative, even as we survey the collapse of Wiltshire Church, we are suggesting that, somehow, that life principle continues to operate even independent of the life structure in which it was supposed to be functioning. Simultaneously, we are standing independent of that life situation, looking at it. So both we and the life principle now turn out to be independent!

Now this way of presenting the problem of our relation to metaphors is nothing other than a more general expression of the forms of relatedness to metaphors that we encountered earlier, namely,"professionalism" and "deus ex machina." Insofar as it depicts accurately a more diffuse assumption about our relation to metaphors in which we all participate, it helps us to see the extent to which the members of Wiltshire Church, and in a larger sense, all of us, play into the phenomenon of breakdown. This way of relating to metaphors is, at bottom, self-serving.

Let me elucidate one way in which this is so. The problem with the claim that both we and the life principle are independent, aside from the difficulty of how we would ever make good such a claim, is that we are presuming a kind of absolute sovereignty for both ourselves and the life principle. We are suggesting that the life principle is sovereign because it does not collapse when structures collapse. We confer sovereignty upon ourselves, because somehow we are on the outside of the structure that collapsed. We and the life principle turn out to be one and the same. This is nothing other than a way of imposing our view upon the structure from the safety of an outside standpoint.

To me, this suggests that the notion that we can have an objective report of breakdown is a distortion. In breakdown, which is the loss of a center, any interpretation imposes a new center. It is the center of the person who is looking at the structure. In a very subtle way, our imposition of centers upon structures undergirds our aspirations to universal empire over the affairs of life, reflecting our bourgeois orientation. It is, therefore, inherently opposed to the sensitive interpretation of persons whose culture, position, and life experiences differ radically from our own. Again, our metaphors fail to achieve their avowed intent.

Breakdown, then, is a sign of our times, of our imperiousness, and of our pretentiousness. What we are called to is a way of being faithful that encourages us to step outside the confines into which our world views deliver us. But this step, as I hope this account has made clear, is more difficult than is generally imagined.

Doubtless, it will be said that I, to maintain this theses, am also standing outside, as an objective observer witnessing breakdown. But that would be said wrongly. I am as much a victim of the patterns of our language, our institutional practices, and our patterns of conduct as is Sid or anybody else in our culture. Even so, we still turn to the church in an attempt to bring faithful witness to the gospel. From this an important theological insight emerges. It is not finally our way of understanding the kingdom to which the gospel points. Rather, the gospel points repeatedly to the inbreaking of the kingdom that overturns our ways of understanding. In stating that we are all caught then in the phenomenon of breakdown, I am urging the view that it may be possible for us to catch some glimpse of the inbreaking of the kingdom in our own time. I say a glimpse because I think that our predilection to hold fast to metaphors that are self-serving is greater than our faithfulness to the God who would be God in spite of us and because of us.

This breakdown may be disquieting but it is also a sign of hope. We may perhaps begin to reconceive of our ministry not primarily in terms of professionalism and of the various resources of the professional, be they ethnography, sociology, organization development, psychology, or, indeed, theology. In the proper light—which, as yet, has not been determined—each of these may be instructive. But of greater importance, our responsibility is to a calling that cannot be neatly packaged in the metaphors of our time. This is the distinctiveness of theological thinking that needs to be understood and reclaimed. To respond faithfully to revelation as a calling, and to think deeply about its meaning, may well mean that we are for our own generation sentinels, standing guard, watching over a church that has grown weary with the insipid metaphor of our age. To abandon the bourgeois dimensions of professionalism may enable us to peer out into the darkness of the night and to make bold our attempt to discern the as yet unnameable, proclaiming itself both in our midst and beyond.

SUGGESTIONS FOR RELATED READING

Connerton, Paul. *Critical Sociology: Selected Readings.* Middlesex: Penguin, 1976.

A superb anthology of readings that traces themes of critical thought from Hegel and Marx through such contemporary figures as Habermas and Marcuse.

Habermas, Jürgen. *Legitimation Crisis.* Translated by Thomas McCarthy. Boston: Beacon Press, 1973.

———. *Communication and the Evolution of Society.* Translated by Thomas McCarthy. Boston: Beacon Press, 1979.

Both volumes by Habermas are difficult going, because they present working papers that Habermas has shared with colleagues at the Max Planck Institute and presuppose a working knowledge of numerous theories that are not widely known in United States circles. Nonetheless, with the aid of the introductory material in both volumes, Habermas's views reward the patient reader.

MacIntyre, Alasdair. *After Virtue*. Notre Dame, Ind.: University of Notre Dame Press, 1981.
A provocative assessment of the reasons behind contemporary moral disagreements, with far-reaching theological insights.

Tipton, Steven M. *Getting Saved from the Sixties*. Berkeley: University of California Press, 1982.
A model of sociological inquiry, guided by philosophical and theological reflection.

III

FROM THEORY TO PARISH: MULTIDISCIPLINARY APPROACHES TO EFFECTIVE MINISTRY

9. Seeking Significant Intervention

LOREN B. MEAD

The transition from the primary disciplines—the basic building blocks of Part II—to the multidisciplinary approaches of Part III is more than a flip of the page. It requires a re-orientation of the mind, a change as dramatic as leaving seminary and entering the pastoral ministry.

In our Alban Institute studies of the boundary between seminary and parish, we found that graduates who were immersed in the culture of the seminary were often unprepared for the shock of entry into the relentless and multifaceted problems of the parish. During seminary the church had been defined by the clarity and consistency of issues that were distributed among the specialists of the seminary faculty: theology, biblical studies, history, preaching, pastoral care, and other elements of preparation. In the parish the problems were not separated into courses. Problems came in unexpected configurations. "Things happened all at once."

In the first section on primary disciplines we took the scholar's approach to working with congregations. Each chapter had a specific set of assumptions that could be clearly and consistently applied to reveal different dimensions of life within Wiltshire Church. It should be noted that these primary approaches are defined and sustained by professional societies and academies of seminary, college, and university. Although Christian in their commitments, and heavy contributors to the work of the institutional church, these scholars are professionally accountable to each other in the application of their methodology and the information that they share among themselves and with their students.

The multidisciplinary approaches place primary emphasis on

significant intervention. Their purpose is not insight but impact in the congregation. They utilize whatever resources are available to motivate whatever change seems appropriate. Because change is their goal, they tend to be eclectic and pragmatic. Their client is the institutional church—the local congregation or the denominational office—not the academy. As "employees" of congregations, they are forced to take local churches seriously, to listen to them carefully, to respect the depth and vision of faith that is found there.

I am not suggesting that the parish is more real than the seminary, or the pastor more Christian than the scholar—or that every congregation that says, "Lord, Lord," is what it ought to be or, I pray, what it may become. But for those of us who have made a commitment to center our work in the life of congregations, the local church is "where the rubber meets the road." We glean the insights of several disciplines as we work to help local churches. We live in the middle between the primary disciplines of the academy and the practical problems of the parish.

There are many people who inhabit the middle ground between theory and practice. The reflective pastor, who puts seminary education to the test, must continually reshape the tools once learned in classes. The sensitive layperson, who tries to understand the interweaving of faith and Christian living, discerns theological patterns as well as answers to particular problems. Others are even more intentional in their efforts to bridge theory and practice: the denominational staff person who provides experience in the clustering of congregations, the architect who helps the congregation shape its liturgy in renewal of the sanctuary, the Christian judge who serves as a lay member of the congregation's committee for social action, and the independent consultant who works under contract to help a congregation to plan or to deal with a problem or conflict.

"Consultant" is the generic term that has come into common use for persons who inhabit the middle ground as professionals, trying to mediate new knowledge to the practice of ministry. Some consultants are on the payroll of the churches; some work for independent agencies or as individual contractors. Church executives, teachers, bishops, pastors, lay leaders, and entrepreneurs of many sorts have all served as consultants to churches. Consulting has become something of a growth industry in religious systems, and deserves special attention.

A consultant tends to be (1) someone outside the decision-making system of the client; (2) someone with skill or insight needed by the client, offering either understanding about the problem faced or a process by which the client can reach a resolution of the problem; (3) someone who agrees to work on the client's agenda, not simply install the agenda of the consultant, bishop, or other outside authority; (4) someone whose continuing relationship is dependent on the client's choice; (5) someone who is trusted by the client.

These guidelines have many implications, but here we can highlight only two: power and relationship. Because of the power dynamics within denominations, it is difficult for administrators to consult within their own organization. For example, a bishop, or one with executive authority, can rarely serve as consultant to a congregation or pastor within his or her jurisdiction. Although he or she may understand the role of consultant, the authority of the office can never be ignored by the congregation or pastor. Under some carefully defined circumstances, staff persons may serve as consultants within their own systems. In general it is clearer if staff persons or executives hold to their regular roles, to better serve their congregations. Payment for services is important in the effective consultant contract. If the consultant is not paid by the client, then the client does not control the relationship. The client must have the power to say yes or no to the consultant. This is rarely possible if the judicatory provides the resource person or pays the fee.

From the consultant's perspective, the relationship between consultant and client is the key to effective consultation. The most critical knowledge for the consultant is knowledge of the helping relationship, the ability to work together in such a way that the client's needs are met.

There is no single source for consultants now working in religious systems. There is no commonly accepted method for training consultants, not even an agreement on definitions for the consultant's task. But the selection of the consultant is always in the hands of the client—if it is a consulting relationship. It is wise to "check the record" of a potential consultant, through academic credentials or through people who have used his or her services previously. It may be important to discover if the person is flexible and can apply more than one set of skills, since most problems turn out to be something different from what is initially diagnosed or identified by the client. "By their fruits ye shall know them."

In the multidiscipline approaches of Part III the three chapters are typical because they are so different. The authors each took different routes to their present vocational choice, and they use different principles in their consulting process. Typically, they did not set out to be consultants. One was a city planner, one a clinical psychologist, and one a local pastor. People like this are frequently among the resources of church membership—people trained in another field of knowledge and expertise whose way of working has led them to acquire the skills of consulting, with or without formal training. There are excellent consultants operating from various positions in denominational offices, in seminaries and universities, in social service agencies, and in other professions and businesses.

The brief history of professional consulting in the church may be seen in the way these three authors have journeyed to their present positions.

Sociological studies of urban issues provide one source for the preparation of many consultants. These studies emphasize, not the changing of individuals, but the training of people to change the organizations within which the individuals exist. The goal-oriented programs of urban causes were adapted for task groups within congregations, and for congregations as a whole. Insightful and charismatic leaders, like Lyle Schaller, have applied the learnings of planning to the needs of congregations.

Psychology provided a second source of consultants, when applied to the problems of the parish. In the previous section Barry Evans and Bruce Reed provide an example of a consistent psychological approach with solid research foundations applied to the problems of Wiltshire Church. As a multidimensional consultant, Newton Malony provides the rationale for a pragmatic combination of resources focused on a particular point of need, in this case on leadership. Organizational psychology, as outlined by Malony, has provided a broad base for the development of consultants.

Perhaps the most influential source for multidimensional consultants is found in the social psychology movement that swept through the churches following World War II. This movement, grounded in interpersonal dynamics ("human relations" and "sensitivity training"), expanded to include the issues and dynamics of organizations ("planned change" and "organization development") and embraced a range of leadership training programs. Although it was frequently introduced through Christian education, the movement more recently has been claimed under the banner of church management and administration. James Anderson reflects a further development of this approach as he incorporates theology and social context into a paradigm that also includes leadership and organizational dynamics.

There are other streams that flow into the preparation of the growing number of consultants for religious systems, which include many wild cards and, unfortunately, a few charlatans. Perhaps the positive examples we offer will help in the selection of effective consultants for local church situations.

Beyond their differences in background and procedure, consultants have a common focus on the congregation as client. They may not agree in their concept of a model congregation, or their understanding of the change process. But their approach is significantly different from the authors of the earlier chapters, who look at Wiltshire through primary disciplines. The multidiscipline approaches are task oriented, seeking to make significant intervention. They are congregation-centered, using (and rejecting) theory to help the congregation deal with its problems.

10. A Practitioner's Perspective

Policy Planning

LYLE E. SCHALLER

An attempt to use the printed word to communicate one's own approach to consultations with congregations resembles the effort to paint a word picture of an individual. Inevitably the word picture will exaggerate certain characteristics, understate others, and perhaps completely miss what some would declare to be the most important features. A photograph may be worth the traditional thousand words, but it too has its shortcomings. Frequently the photograph fails to capture some of the most distinctive personal characteristics of the individual pictured in that photograph. To attempt to present a word picture of oneself is certain to reflect a biased perspective. In other words, this effort to describe what I do in parish consultation does, to some extent, represent reality, but the overlap is less than one hundred percent!

Perhaps the most useful contribution I can make to this discussion is to attempt to identify the seven basic assumptions on which I base my approach to parish consultations and to describe some of the procedures I have found to be useful.

The One Basic Premise

I am overwhelmingly convinced, as the foundation of my approach, that the assumptions, beliefs, prejudices, value system, understanding of contemporary reality, academic preparation, theological stance, age, biases, life experiences, denominational background, and other baggage carried by the consultant constitute the most important single dynamic or variable in determining what happens in a parish consultation. That is the one categorical statement in this chapter.

The concept of a "neutral" or "objective" approach to parish consultation, therefore, ranks somewhere between an illusion and a deception. Everyone carries baggage that influences that person's methodology and style. Likewise, there are no neutral questions. The choice of the subject matter to be questioned represents the application of a value system. The seven operational assumptions identified here not only are of great importance, in my opinion, but also distinguish my approach from that of other practitioners.

SEVEN OPERATIONAL ASSUMPTIONS

The Outside Third Party

Over the past two decades I have become a convert to the value of the "outside third party." The utilization of third parties has been one of the rapidly growing trends in our society during the past four decades. In part, this is a result of our growing affluence. We can now afford the intervention of outsiders. In part this trend reflects the growing specialization of the labor force. Most of all, however, it reflects an appreciation of the potential contributions of the outsider. This pattern can be seen in labor-management relations, in professional sports, in corporate "takeovers," in the practice of medicine, in marriage counseling, in education, in ministerial placement, and in nearly every aspect of American life except, perhaps, the merger of Protestant denominations.

First, and perhaps most important, it means I am very skeptical of the self-study approach in which congregational leaders are expected to analyze their own situation and produce a prescription from their own diagnosis. Self-studies can be useful, but that is a very limited usefulness. The self-study can be a useful beginning point, or a base from which subsequent questions can be derived, but self-study guides suffer an inherent inability to ask the follow-up questions.[1] Self-studies *with a consultant* can be very useful. This also means I have serious reservations about the usefulness of the approach that calls for the congregational leaders

[1] A promising new approach that appears to be pioneering new ground is Robert E. Leach and Erwin G. Somogyi, *The Measure of a Church* (Anaheim, Calif.: Presbytery of Los Ranchos, 1980). Their system may overcome many of the shortcomings of the traditional self-study.

to fill out the self-study "notebook" and mail it in for a diagnosis and prescription. I also believe students who are in the classroom with the teacher learn more than the person who takes the same course from the same teacher by correspondence.

Second, by definition, the outside third-party parish consultant is in a position to read the nonverbal communication, to ask the follow-up questions that are occasioned by the responses to the introductory questions, and to explore issues that otherwise might be overlooked. Those follow-up questions cannot be asked by a self-study.

Third, the on-the-scene presence of the outside third party means that the personality, behavior, values, communication skills, attitudes, credibility, and appearance of the parish consultant become extremely influential factors in determining the outcome of a particular parish consultation. The confidence, or the lack of confidence, displayed by congregational leaders toward the consultant will have a great influence on what happens next. The responses by the parish consultant to the advance preparation; the questions asked by the consultant at the early meetings; the insights offered, the personal style, and the openness of the consultant; and the choice of a planning model all combine to influence the response of the parishioners to the consultant.

Finally, a central variable in the usefulness of any outside third party is the quality of the invitation. We will return to this when the discussion moves to procedures.

Internal Dynamics or Community Context

A second operational assumption of mine is that the internal dynamics of congregational life are far more important than the community context. This is most apparent when the consultation includes the subject of numerical growth or decline. I believe that the dynamics of interpersonal and institutional relationships are more revealing than denominational ties, community context, or general statistical data—which really only provide a base for asking more important questions. This assumption distinguishes my perspective from those who place a far greater emphasis on the influence of the community context or those who use a "data-based" approach to intervention[2] or those who stress the centrality of the denominational affiliation.

At this point it may be necessary to offer an apology to my friends and mentors who stress the importance of external factors, such as the community context or the denominational affiliation, and to inject an autobiographical reflection.

I came into this vocation after several years of graduate training and professional experience in city and community planning. For several years I placed great emphasis on the community context and conducted an extensive analysis of the demographic, economic, and land use factors that might influence the life, ministry, and outreach of a given congregation. Anyone familiar with my work in the early 1960s will find that an analysis of the community context *always* constituted the initial section of any report I prepared for a church or a group of congregations. I was convinced the community context shaped the life of a parish.

In 1961 and 1962 I began to be more heavily involved with black churches in Akron and Cleveland, Ohio. As I worked with these black churches I gradually began to realize that the history of a particular congregation, the impact of the minister's personality and leadership, race, social class, and other internal considerations were far more important that the community context in shaping the life of a particular congregation. As I reflected on this, I also began to realize the community context usually was an influential factor in the life of a new congregation, whether it be in the inner city or in suburbia, but that as the years passed, the impact of internal factors far exceeded the weight of external conditions.

By the late 1960s I was involved with several churches in Dade County, Florida, some of which were affected by the influx of the political refugees from Cuba. Again, however, I observed that the internal dynamics of a congregation, and especially the attitudes and actions of the leaders, were far more influential than what

---

[2] For a contrast between two different approaches see Harry Levinson, *Organizational Diagnosis* (Cambridge: Harvard University Press, 1972), pp. 10–11, and Harvey A. Hornstein, et al., *Social Intervention* (New York: Free Press, 1971), pp. 255–56.

was happening in the community around the meeting place. As a result, today I place relatively modest weight on the impact of changes in the community context.

As part of my pilgrimage I have concluded also that the denominational affiliation or the place of a congregation on the theological spectrum is of less importance that I once assumed to be the case. Most of the parish consultations in which I have been involved since 1960 have been with churches from a broad theological spectrum in over three dozen denominational families. I have become convinced that internal factors such as race, social class, national and ethnic background, the attitudes and actions of the leaders, language, and the age of the congregation are more important variables than the particular denominational affiliation of that congregation.

The Wiltshire Church case study illustrates very clearly the central importance of the internal dynamics, most of which are far more influential than either the community context or the denominational affiliation.

The Behavior Setting

A third operational assumption overlaps the second. I have become convinced that the "behavior setting" has a tremendous impact on what does or does not happen in a congregation.[3] For example, I have become convinced that the organizational structure, the size of the governing board, the frequency of their meetings, the nature of the room in which they meet, and the choice of who will preside at the meetings of the governing body have a significant impact on what happens in the life of a congregation. The design of the building has a great impact on the degree of "friendliness" displayed by the members. In another setting I have argued that the importance of place may be the most neglected factor in church planning.[4] This also separates me from many others who do not place an equivalent emphasis on the concept of

---

[3] See Roger G. Barker, *Ecological Psychology* (Stanford, Calif.: Stanford University Press, 1968), for the summary statement from a pioneer in this field. For suggestions on applications to churches see Lyle E. Schaller, *Effective Church Planning* (Nashville: Abingdon Press, 1979), pp. 65–92.

[4] Schaller, *Effective Church Planning*, pp. 17–64.

behavior setting. It also means I believe the polity is more influential than the denominational affiliation.

The Classification System

The fourth of these operational assumptions is that the classification system used by the parish consultant is an important factor that will influence the outcome of the consultation. What are the categories you use in studying churches?[5]

The most widely used, and one of the least helpful, classification systems is that of denominational affiliation. From my experience I would rank, in order of usefulness, these classification systems: (1) size as measured by the average attendance at worship and membership attendance patterns, (2) the ideological-behavioral dichotomy,[6] (3) the internal dynamics, (4) the tenure of today's members, (5) the contemporary role of that parish and the goals evolving out of that role, (6) the age of that institution and especially the length of time it has been meeting in the present building, (7) the age of the members, (8) the community context, (9) the polity, and (10) the tenure of the current pastor and of the past five pastors. It should be noted that only five or six of those ten can be identified through traditional self-study procedures.

In reflecting on the Wiltshire Church as a case study, I found this to be an excellent and provocative presentation. After reading it I had only two reservations. First, the appropriate name would have been "Legion," for there are many churches that resemble this one very closely. Second, I would like to have seen a tabulation of the worship attendance pattern over a period of four consecutive Sundays, including a frequency distribution between those who joined before the arrival of the present senior minister and those who joined following his arrival.

---

[5]A brief introduction to several classification systems can be found in Lyle E. Schaller, *Activating the Passive Church* (Nashville: Abingdon Press, 1981), pp. 17–39.

[6]For an introduction to the concept that some congregations represent the second of Jesus' two great commandments while others are distinguished by their emphasis on the first of those two commandments, see Roger A. Johnson, *Congregations as Nurturing Communities* (Philadelphia: Division for Parish Services, Lutheran Church in America, 1979).

The Choice of a Planning Model

The fifth of these operational assumptions is that the choice of a planning model is at least as influential in determining the outcome of a parish consultation as the process followed by the consultant.

My own inclinations are that choice of a planning model should be tailored to that particular congregation's unique situation, rather than be standard for all churches. In general, I try to avoid the preoccupation with liabilities that is inherent in the "problem identification and solution" model and try to begin with an emphasis on strengths, resources, and assets by using an "affirm and build" model.[7] This bias can be built into the questions asked by the consultant. I try to use a planning model that *(a)* has a strong future-orientation built into it, *(b)* includes an emphasis on outreach, *(c)* begins by identifying the distinctive resources, strengths, and assets of that particular congregation, *(d)* encourages agreement on the definition of contemporary reality as the beginning point for planning for tomorrow, *(e)* causes people to expand their definition of alternative courses of action, and *(f)* may challenge some stereotypes that no longer are relevant.

It should be added here that although I used it for several years, partly as a result of my training and experience as a city planner, I no longer am an advocate of the "church and community" planning model that has been the most widely used model for developing self-study guides and manuals. The "outcomes" of that planning model, which often include an excessive emphasis on real estate and/or re-creating the past and/or the fact that the private automobile has brought the demise of the walk-in geographical parish, are not compatible with my own values and goals. I strongly believe that mission and ministry, not real estate or the re-creation of yesterday, are high priorities in church planning.

At this point it may be appropriate to classify my approach, as contrasted to other approaches identified elsewhere in this book. Though I draw from these other disciplines in various ways, I would describe my own approach to parish consultations as that

---

[7] For a discussion of these two planning models see Lyle E. Schaller, *Effective Church Planning*, pp. 93–122.

of a "policy planner." I draw heavily from that discipline often described as "policy planning" or "policy formation" and especially from public policy theory.

A Mobilization Opportunity

Over the years I gradually have come to believe my sixth assumption, that in most cases a parish consultation can be a significant rallying point for the members. It can be an occasion for mobilizing the leaders, not only for self-examination, but also to look into the future, and it can be an exciting event. Therefore I intentionally try to design the parish consultation to be a mobilizing event. This includes a requirement for some advance preparation, including asking several leaders to identify issues and concerns. It includes the concept of discovery learning. It includes a structured interview schedule that will involve most or all of the leaders on one or more occasions. It also requires building a strong future-orientation into the questions asked.

The Dangers of Dependency

In my own efforts to comprehend reality, I have come to be a reluctant believer in the old adage "Dependency breeds hostility." This seventh operational assumption helps us to understand the attitudes of many widowed persons, of some people toward the proposed leveling-off in federal expenditures, of many Methodist lay leaders toward their denomination's ministerial appointment system, and of many subsidized congregations toward the denominational home mission staff. Perhaps it even sheds light on the attitudes toward the senior minister at Wiltshire Church in the case study. I also am convinced that the outside third-party consultant can cause the client to become excessively dependent on the consultant.

Although I have not been completely successful, I have attempted to reduce the chances for an excessive postconsultation dependency—and that brings us to the congregation-consultant relationship and another set of assumptions.

THE CONGREGATION-CONSULTANT RELATIONSHIP

There are many assumptions I carry into a parish consultation concerning my relationship with that congregation, and it may be useful to list ten that I have repeatedly utilized.

The first, and by far the most important, is the need for an invitation. I am thoroughly convinced that the chances of an effective and productive relationship will be enhanced if the consultant has a genuine invitation to intervene. There is an ancient adage in adult education circles that applies: "You cannot teach adults anything they do not want to learn."

I seek a five-part invitation consisting of an invitation from the pastor, an invitation from the governing board or congregational planning committee, an "OK" from the denominational executive in the local judicatory, a financial commitment by the congregation that gains the attention of the leaders, and a commitment to do some advance preparation. I want an investment by that parish in thc consultation!

Second, in the vast majority of churches I assume we will have to raise the level of congregational self-esteem before we can do any planning, and that is often the theme of the first few hours.

Third, my skills are not in interpersonal relationships. Therefore I do not intentionally become involved in those situations that reflect severe problems of interpersonal relationships between the minister and the members or among the members. Specifically I try to avoid those situations in which the central issue is the retention or dismissal of the pastor. I believe those require the intervention of a denominational staff person.

Fourth, I tend to be fairly directive. I assume the congregation really is not seeking a nondirective, "objective," and neutral parish consultant. I do not agree with that cliché from the 1960s that "the world sets the agenda for the church." I strongly believe the New Testament sets the agenda. I admit I bring an agenda with me.

Most important, I believe every congregation should have a selfconscious and intentional evangelistic dimension, and I try to lift that up. That is a bias I bring with me.

Fifth, I usually begin with a strong emphasis on statistical data from the congregation as the entry point in identifying other factors, rather than beginning with an examination of the community context.

Sixth, I attempt to identify the strengths, gifts, talents, values, and goals of both the pastor and that congregation and to reinforce them and to build on them. That is my basic approach.

Seventh, I have a strong bias toward long pastorates and seek to encourage long pastorates whenever that appears possible and appropriate—and that includes four out of five consultations.

Eighth, I believe life is increasingly relational and less and less survival goal-oriented. I try to focus on the relational dimensions of parish life rather than to think entirely in functional terms—although the organizational structure of most congregations is designed to encourage an emphasis on functions rather than on relationships.

Ninth, I am inclined to believe most of what I hear in the interviews, and that this information reflects symptoms rather than basic problems or concerns. Therefore, I see myself heavily involved in a diagnostic role. Frequently my major contribution in a parish consultation has been to rewrite the agenda for that parish. This means identifying the "tradeoffs" that many leaders are reluctant to accept. For example, growth usually means change. Or, it is rare to be able to reach and serve all of the youth through a single program.

Tenth, I expect that when I leave I never will return to that congregation. Therefore I try to identify and enlist a group of allies who will feel that they are a part of the consultation and be prepared to take the initiative in the next steps to be taken. I am more concerned with providing those leaders with resources than I am in solving their problems for them. Obviously the pastor will be the chief ally in that coalition on most issues.

The Consultant's Report

I believe a written report or memorandum can be extremely useful. There are many reasons for that. One is that the written word is far more precise than the spoken word. A second is that many oral messages are received that never were sent. A third is that all of us normal people do our best thinking on the way home from the meeting. A fourth is that we all have selective memories. A fifth is that I believe one useful sequence is from symptoms to diagnosis to prescription to action. In many consultations this written report is the new agenda for the deliberations by the leaders of that parish. A sixth is that I believe it is important for the denominational executive in the regional judicatory to be able to read the results. A seventh is that it often helps prevent misunderstandings if everyone receives the same messages in the same words. An eighth is that the written word usually is a more reliable reference point than the oral tradition. A ninth is that if the consultant is invited back to that same congregation, the consultant may want to review the messages left behind from the earlier visit. My standard procedure for parish consultations lasting one day or longer is to provide fifty copies of a written report that usually includes eight to fourteen pages of text. It is hard to lose fifty copies. It also is rare that all fifty will be in use on any given day. I want every person to have access to a copy of that written report. I am opposed to keeping secrets!

Typically the report consists of five sections. The first is a one-page cover letter. The second consists of three to six pages in which I attempt to summarize and interpret the advance preparations—the statistical data—to describe contemporary reality, and to ask questions about what God is calling that congregation to be and to be doing. The third section includes three to perhaps seven or eight policy questions that I have identified. The responses to that new agenda often will determine the future direction and role of that congregation. The fourth section usually consists of two to six pages of specific suggestions and recommendations. Finally, we normally bind into the final report thirty to fifty pages of essays, articles, and other material that elaborate on points raised earlier in the report.

ADVANCE PREPARATION

As was pointed out earlier, we do ask for considerable advance preparation for a parish consultation. This can be summarized in four categories.

First, I ask for a paragraph or two from the minister and from each of several lay leaders in which they identify the most urgent issues and concerns on the agenda. Why do they want an outside third-party parish consultant to intervene?

Second, I ask for considerable statistical data on membership, worship attendance patterns, finances, the age mix and the family and marital distribution of the members, tenure of the members, and similar factual data.

Third, I ask for this to be mailed early enough so that there will be an opportunity to raise follow-up questions.

Finally, I mail to the people who are planning the consultation some suggestions for the interview schedule. In the typical two-day consultation, for example, I will (*a*) interview a half-dozen persons on a one-to-one basis, (*b*) meet with six to eight groups of two or three to seven persons in each group, (*c*) meet with three to seven functional committees, (*d*) interview one or two pastors of nearby or similar congregations, (*e*) spend approximately an hour with professional "outsiders" who are knowledgeable about the community in which the congregation's meeting place is located (planner or realtor or banker, etc.), (*g*) meet with the "core group" or "executive committee" of the planning committee or governing board on the first day, (*h*) meet with a larger group (total planning committee or total governing board) near the end of the second day, (*i*) have a group interview with as many recent new adult members as can be gathered in one group, (*j*) spend a half hour with the minister's spouse if available and interested, and (*k*) meet with two ex-members and (*l*) talk with whoever else is appropriate.

In the typical parish consultation I will meet with thirty-five to fifty individuals, some on two or three or four different occasions, each day that I am on the scene.

DIAGNOSTIC QUESTIONS

In the typical day in a parish consultation, and the day usually runs from 8:15 in the morning until 9:30 or 10:30 at night, I try to ask several sets of questions of many of the members.

One set is used to identify resources, strengths, and assets. This includes questions such as:

"What does this congregation do best?"

"If you were to brag to a neighbor who just moved in next door about this parish, what would you brag about?"

"Can you point out one area or ministry or one program in which your congregation excels?"

"What does your pastor do best as a minister?"

"As you compare this parish with other congregations with which you are acquainted, how does this one stand out in a very positive way?"

A second set of questions is designed to evoke responses that will help me understand what the members view as contemporary reality.

"Let us assume you wanted something to happen here, a change of some sort. You had about given up on that happening, but then you heard that three or four very influential laypersons had come out strongly in favor of that change. When you heard that, you knew the change you wanted would be implemented. What are the names of the members here who have that kind of influence?"

"Let us assume that a change was being proposed that you opposed, but you assumed it would happen despite your opposition. One day you discovered two members had come out strongly against that change. Now you were relieved, because you were reasonably sure that if they opposed it, the change would not occur. What are the names of those two members who have that kind of influence?"

"What do you see as the most urgent issues facing this congregation today? What do you believe God is calling this congregation to be today?"

"What is your understanding of why this congregation brought me here?"

"What do you believe to be the area of ministry or program that is being neglected today?"

"What is the identity or community image of this congregation that distinguishes it from other churches in town?"

A third set of questions concerns the future:

"Everyone has a favorite wish for their church. What is your number one wish for this congregation?"

"How will this congregation be different in 1990 from what it is today? What changes will the passage of five (ten) years bring?"

"Is the Lord calling this parish to a new role in the years ahead?"

"Do you see a fork in the road approaching, so that if this

congregation takes one fork, the future will be different than if the other fork were to be chosen?"

In addition, I ask people when they joined, why they joined, how the congregation of today differs from when they were new members, how far it is from the meeting place to their place of residence, whether or not they have changed their place of residence since they joined, how family members have responded to this congregation's program, and other questions suited to each individual's identity.

When meeting with program committee members, officers, and other leaders, I also focus on the program area that is within that person's area of responsibility and inquire about the details of that program, projections into the future, and related matters.

When meeting with the pastor, and I usually am able to have an hour with the pastor early in the consultation, I ask a series of questions about that minister's background, previous experience, year of birth, family constellation, and expectations on tenure in this parish. In addition, I ask questions designed to secure an understanding of that pastor's vision of the future for this parish and of how that vision informs that minister's work and shapes the policies that direct congregational life.

I also ask the minister, "What do you do best as a pastor? What does this parish do best in ministry?" If it is a multiple-staff church, I ask each program staff member to identify the strengths of other staff members.

A very important part of that hour is devoted to clarifying in my mind the expectations of that pastor for this parish consultation: "What is your agenda? What do you want to be sure we cover? What are the issues you want to be sure we address?"

If the pastor's spouse is available and interested, I also want a half hour to learn what I can from that person's unique perspective. This can be very valuable!

If the consultation is for a day or longer, I usually am able to arrange a 45- to 60-minute interview with one or more pastors of other congregations (preferably on their own turf). In this interview most of my questions are directed at three general subjects:

"How is your ministry here in this community different from where you were before?"

"Tell me about your parish."

"Tell me what you can about the congregation that has brought me in as a consultant."

Usually I will have several follow-up questions to ask on each response, depending on the content of the response.

These are only examples of a few of the questions I ask in a parish consultation, but they do suggest the flavor, the bias, and the nature of the diagnostic process from my perspective.

SUGGESTIONS FOR RELATED READING

These ten volumes have had a profound impact on my thinking and have influenced my approach to parish consultations. I would especially commend the books by Barker, Bender, Greenleaf, and Levitt to anyone who serves as a parish consultant.

Barker, Roger A., and Gump, Paul V. *Big School, Small School.* Stanford, Calif.: Stanford University Press, 1964.

Baird, William. *The Corinthian Church—A Biblical Approach to Urban Culture.* Nashville: Abingdon Press, 1964.

Bender, Thomas. *Community and Social Change in America.* New Brunswick, N.J.: Rutgers University Press, 1978.

Deasy, C. M. *Design for Human Affairs.* New York: Wiley, 1974.

Gabriel, Richard A., and Savage, Paul L. *Crisis in Command.* New York: Hill & Wang, 1978.

Greenleaf, Robert K. *The Servant As Leader.* Cambridge, Mass.: Center for Applied Studies, 1970.

Johnson, Roger A. *Congregations As Nurturing Communities.* Philadelphia: Division for Parish Services, Lutheran Church in America, 1979.

Levitt, Theodore. *Innovation in Marketing.* New York: McGraw-Hill, 1962.

Marty, Martin E., et al. *What Do We Believe?* New York: Meredith Press, 1968.

Veroff, Joseph, et al. *The Inner American.* New York: Basic Books, 1981.

11. A Framework for Understanding and Helping the Church

Organization Development

H. NEWTON MALONY

"Organization Development" is a form of applied organizational psychology. By *applied* is meant that organization development is concerned with changing organizations, not just understanding them. It takes for granted, however, that one has to understand organizations in order to change them. Organizational psychology is different from industrial or business psychology. An organization exists wherever two or more persons act together to meet a human need. Although many organizations are industries or businesses, by no means is this true of the majority of them.

Types of Organizations

There are many types of organizations, yet all involve people acting in concert together to accomplish a task. Amatai Etzioni has provided a helpful model for understanding these differences. Defining organizations in the manner of Talcott Parsons as "social units [for human groupings] deliberately constructed or reconstructed to seek specific goals,"[1] he suggests that all organizations share several components: (1) assignments of tasks and powers in a deliberate effort to accomplish certain objectives, (2) leaders whose task it is to coordinate and control the work of persons in the organization, (3) and a means for rewarding or sanctioning

[1] *Modern Organizations* (Englewood Cliffs, N.J.: Prentice-Hall, 1964), p. 3.

performance in order to enhance the effect of people working together toward a common goal.

Churches share these characteristics with all other organizations, but they differ in the means they use to reinforce or sanction the behavior of their members, as Etzioni's model will illustrate.

He concludes that there are three ways organizations control the behavior of their members: physical, material, or symbolic. Churches use symbolic power. They use persuasion, rather than force, as is typical of armies or prisons. They use encouragement, rather than money, as is typical of factories and businesses. The symbolic means that churches employ to assure that the work gets done are intangible. Persons who participate in the life of the church receive approval, esteem, and status. Others receive criticism, depreciation, and accusation. The church does not forcc or pay its members to participate. Its members are volunteers who give their time because of their interest and who accept approval as their reward for membership. Living up to ideals and principles is the goal. Personal satisfaction and the esteem of others is more important than money or physical comfort.

Thus, the church is a particular type of organization, namely a *symbolic* organization that uses *normative* or *social* power to control its members' behavior. Although it shares other characteristics with armies and industries, it differs from them in the way it enhances individual performance among its members. These differences make individual perceptions and group cohesion of prime importance in the life of the church.

How Organization Development Can Help the Church

Discussion of this issue should begin with the prior question, What is it that organizations need help in doing? The answer is, They need help in accomplishing their goals. For example, currently, American automakers need help because they are having difficulty selling their cars. Organization development would assist them in considering all facets of their organization toward the end that they might better meet their sales objectives.

The same is true of the church; it, also, exists for a purpose. Who is there who would suggest that the church is as effective as it should be? No one in my acquaintance. It needs help in doing what it should have been doing since the time when Jesus, in good organizational terminology, first decided to "build" His church on the basis of Peter's statement that He was the Christ (Matt. 13:13–20). And what is it that the church should be doing? One of the better statements of the goals of the church is found in the United Methodist Book of Worship, which proposes: "The church is of God and will be preserved to the end of time, for the promotion of His worship and the due administration of His word and sacraments, the maintenance of Christian fellowship and discipline, the edification of believers and the conversion of the world."[2]

These, then, are the four goals of the church: worship, fellowship, teaching, and conversion. Organization development can assist the church in accomplishing these goals.

To better understand what it is that organization development can do it needs to be noted that organization development (or OD, as it has been called) is a technical term describing a type of consultation that has come into vogue since the 1960s. Defined as a method wherein organizations are helped to improve all facets of their life in order to produce more efficiently and fulfill their members' lives more fully, OD has been preceded by at least two other developments in this century.

The History of Organization Development

Early in this century, Frederick W. Taylor published his book *Scientific Management*[3] and thereby initiated the *classical* or *formal* approach to managing organizations. Based on the assumption that workers were interested in economic rewards and that what the worker did was of less import than what he or she was paid, this analysis suggested that profits could be maximized by dividing the labor into small parts and having clear lines of authority by which to coordinate these tasks. The underlying assumption here was that organizations could be treated mechanistically by considering their several components and logically relating them into a working machine.

---

[2] 1965, p. 12.

[3] (New York: Harper & Row, 1911).

The *human relations* approach was born out of a reaction to the classical-formal approach. Such writers as John Dewey, Elton Mayo, and Kurt Lewin instigated a reconsideration of the rational approach, suggesting that the amount of work a worker was able to perform depended at least as much on satisfaction with social relationships on the job as it did on the pay received for the work. The pyramid/machine model of the classical-formal approach was less efficient than a group model wherein persons did things together rather than in isolated cubicles. The most significant turning point in this regard came with the publishing of Roethlisberger and Dickson's *Management and the Worker.*[4]

This volume reported the famous studies at the Hawthorne Works of Western Electric Company in Chicago from 1927 to 1932. Women who assembled telephone equipment were subjected to studies, based on the classical-formal model, designed to change their work conditions so that they would be more productive. Working conditions were changed systematically, such as the length of the work day, the number of rest periods, lighting over the work space, and other variables. The women chosen for the study were placed in a special room under one supervisor. With each major change—either for better or for worse—their production increased! The researchers could not understand this from a rational point of view. They concluded that it was not the work conditions as such that accounted for the high morale observed among the women; rather, it was the sense of distinction and camaraderie they experienced at being singled out for the research. Thus, they concluded that the on-the-job satisfaction workers received was just as important as money.

In many ways the classical-formal and the human relations approaches were diametrically opposed. One considered the important variable to be the formal organization, and the other considered it to be the informal relationships beneath the structure. Although both were concerned with increasing production, the classical-formal approach emphasized structure whereas the human relations approach emphasized people.

---

[4](Cambridge: Harvard University Press, 1939).

There was no reason why these two could not be combined, however, and that is just what the *systems* approach did. This was a synthesis of the classical-formal and the human relations approaches that drew on the writing of Max Weber. He suggested that both the work that was done and the fellowship that was experienced were important. Persons should have a sense of being involved in something important and be satisfied with their on-the-job relationships if an organization were to be successful. Therefore, change in organizations was best achieved by looking at them as a system of relationships in which personal as well as organizational goals were being met.

It is out of this third approach, the systems model, that organization development came into being. Organizations were hereby conceived as organic, systemic, and alive entities that could be improved by intentional efforts. The goal is to improve the way they are organized, the jobs they provide, and the relationships they engender, so that they function more efficiently and fulfill their members' lives more fully. It is important to note that organization development consultation assumes that the "fulfilling of the members' lives" is just as important as increasing production. More important, it assumes that participation in the organization is *the* way that the members' lives will become more satisfying. It is a mutually dependent and necessary relationship because nowhere else in modern society is it possible to increase life satisfaction so fully as in organizational life.

When the church is perceived through this systems approach, it is seen as a place where the importance of fulfilling lives is probably *more* important than any program the church may produce or any building it may construct. As I have said in an earlier essay:

> The church most resembles educational institutions whose products are the people they train or graduate. The church produces people. It is not a coincidence that the church has been called the people of God (1 Peter 2:9–10).
>
> So the church, like other organizations, produces things through people. However, unlike other organizations, the church produces people through people. Here the distinction between product and process vanishes. The church tries to produce persons whose lives are filled

> with God's grace THROUGH persons whose lives are being filled with God's grace. This is the church's unique, paradoxical and awesome task.[5]

So organization development consultation, which emphasizes people as well as product, is uniquely appropriate to the life of the church. This type of assistance emphasizes helping the church accomplish its mission through, as well as in addition to, the redemption and sanctification of its members.

This point of view has important theological implications. It puts a radical, if not almost exclusive, emphasis on the group life of the church as opposed to the individual experience of persons apart from the organization. The implication is that the church is the place where the kingdom of God is to be worked out on this earth. The church is not simply a means to an end. In a sense, it is an end in itself. The Christian faith is more social than individual. Theology is less something people bring with them to church than something that is worked out in the relationship *at* church. As the Gestalt psychologist, Fritz Perls, reportedly said, "He who has a *how* to live can live through any *why!*" This was a reversal of Nietzsche's well-known dictum, "He who has a why to live can live through any how"—a maxim that puts the emphasis on individual, as opposed to group, experience. Thus, focusing on social processes, as the organization development consultant does, is not peripheral. It is central and critical because the church is where the kingdom of God is being realized. The Christian faith is unique among the world's faiths in its historical emphasis. The church as an organization is the embodiment of that emphasis. Its "products" are the people of God.

Consulting on the organization life of the church, as OD consultants do, is directed, therefore, toward helping the church become the body of Christ (1 Cor. 12:12–27) and the fellowship of faith (Acts 4). It may be the prime means whereby the Great Commission can be accomplished and the channel par excellence by which Christ can continue to build His church (Matt. 16:18).

---

[5] In "The Christian Church—An Organization to Develop," *Theology News and Notes*, October 1978, p. 23.

How Does Organization Development Consultation Work?

Having established that organization development consultation is uniquely applicable to the church, it remains to detail how it is done. As could be predicted from the above discussion, when they are asked for advice, OD consultants do not simply attend to the formal structure and environmental conditions of the organization nor do they ignore these variables in a focus on member satisfaction and group relationships. They do both. In an effort to consider the experience and feelings of the members, they do not ignore the way in which the organization is organized or the procedures for communicating and exercising authority—and vice versa.

More specifically, the OD consultant believes that every feature of the organization's life is a possible focus for consultation. Among these features are: formal structure or polity, leadership tasks and styles, planning and problem-solving procedures, job definitions, program effectiveness, satisfaction with roles and relationships, methods for reducing conflicts, expectations of leaders and members for each other, program production costs, and marketing procedures. To reiterate, the OD consultant constantly keeps in balance the importance of product, of process, and of people. While attending to any one feature of the organization he or she does not lose sight of this larger perspective.

The assumption that organizations (and churches) can be changed underlies the word *development* in the phrase organization development. Development attests to the importance of time and history in human life. It takes for granted that human organizations, like human beings, can change for the better or for the worse. Development implies change that enhances adaptation. Helping churches become more adept at doing what they were created to do while increasing the inner satisfaction of their members—that is the genius of organization development consultation.

Churches engage an OD consultant because they are experiencing some breakdown in their functioning. For example, a conflict may have arisen between certain groups or they may have become stagnant in their growth or they may have become dissatisfied with their leadership. The OD consultant realizes that the church is an *open* system in the sense that attending to any one of these problems will have its effect throughout all other facets of the organization and, in fact, that the identified difficulty may not be the main problem the church is experiencing. Thus, the presenting problem is seen as merely one way to help the church. However, the consultant takes the matter seriously and works on the identified problem, hoping that these efforts will have their effects throughout the system. Furthermore, the consultant realizes that everything that needs to be done cannot always be done in the time allowed, which is limited by the economics of the situation and the willingness of the church to engage in total re-evaluation. OD consultants never forget that they are outsiders to the system and that they must facilitate a process that can be sustained and incorporated into the ongoing life of the organization long after the consultation is over.

OD Consultation with Wiltshire Church

For example, in considering the situation at Wiltshire Church, it appeared as if there were two areas where an OD consultant could be of help: dissatisfaction with the leadership style of the minister, and lack of agreement on what the minister should be doing. In consultation with the minister, it was decided to focus on these matters, since they seemed to be impeding the work of the church. We felt these were key areas in organizational cohesion.

In an effort to assess perceptions of *what* the minister should be doing, the pastor and a voluntary sample of seventy-one persons completed the Webb Inventory of Religious Activities and Interests—a 240-item scale in which a person indicates how important he or she feels it is for the minister to engage in certain tasks. This scale yields a profile showing the rated importance of the pastor's performing ten roles: counselor teacher, administrator, evangelist, spiritual guide, preacher, priest, reformer, musician, and scholar. The ratings by the pastor and the church members are included in Table 11.1. Roles are listed in order from a rank of 1 (most important) to 10 (least important). This comparison yielded a measure of the extent to which the pastor and his parishioners agreed on how he should be spending his time.

Although there were ties in the pastor's second and third, fourth

Table 11.1 Webb Inventory Results

Rank	*Pastor*		*Parishioners*	
First	Preacher	(2.38)	Counselor	(3.60)
Second	{ Administrator	(2.29)	Spiritual Guide	(3.31)
Third	{ Counselor	(2.29)	Priest	(3.22)
Fourth	{ Teacher	(2.25)	Administrator	(2.87)
Fifth	{ Spiritual Guide	(2.25)	Reformer	(2.67)
Sixth	Priest	(2.17)	Teacher	(2.58)
Seventh	Scholar	(1.79)	Evangelist	(2.41)
Eighth	{ Reformer	(1.62)	Preacher	(2.21)
Ninth	{ Evangelist	(1.62)	Scholar	(2.02)
Tenth	Musician	(1.00)	Musician	(1.48)

and fifth, and eighth and ninth rankings, there is still a marked discrepancy between the judgments of the parishioners and the pastor.

If rated importance relates to how the pastor spends his time, he would be doing much that the parishioners would perceive to be of lesser importance. They agreed with each other on only 18% of the rankings. For example, in spite of the fact that both pastor and parishioners considered counseling to be of great importance, they would prefer that he spend much more time helping them through the crises of their lives than in sermon preparation—a task he rated as most important.

Past studies have suggested that support and participation in churches is based, in part, on the degree to which members agree with what the leaders consider important. This is a crucial matter, since the work of the ministry is always more than can be done in an eight-hour work day. Many individual decisions are involved.

The consultative task with the pastor revolved around how to deal with this lack of agreement on ministerial role priorities. Several means for managing these differences were suggested. First, the differences could be publicly faced and discussed. Wiltshire Church has a history of planning conferences. One of these conferences could be directed toward a discussion of the task of ministry and the priorities for the pastor. Both the pastor and his parishioners would have a chance thereby to express their opinions and to discuss openly why they rated certain roles as they did.

Second, since pastors often do not rate as important those roles they feel they do less well, the pastor might consider some skill training in those roles the parishioners considered important but that he has de-emphasized. He could engage in an effort to learn better how to lead people in community social action and how to carry out better the tasks of routine pastoral care. He might learn to like and to rate as important these new skills. Perhaps his entering into the doctor of ministry program at a local seminary was a step in this direction.

Thirdly, the pastor could put his leadership into a different perspective and decide to accommodate himself to the ratings of the parishioners in order to build up their confidence in him. Hollander's theory of idiosyncrasy credit suggests that leaders serve two functions in organizations: they help organizations do better what they are already doing, and they guide organizations into doing what they are not, but should be, doing.[6] If the pastor assumes that his ratings of role priorities are the "correct" ones, then his job becomes one of how best to lead his parishioners into agreeing with him and supporting his judgment of how he should use his time. In order to lead them toward supporting him he would need to invest himself in doing what they think is important, because this would build up the "credit" he needs to guide them into supporting his priorities. One illustration is the letter of support that a parishioner wrote on behalf of the pastor at the time he was criticized. She noted that the pastor had ministered to her family in a time of crisis, and she supported him in the present because of this experience. He had credit with her.

The second part of the consultation was concerned with leadership style—the *way* a pastor did what he did. In an attempt to understand this, the pastor and several key leaders, as well as his spouse, completed the Life Orientations Survey (LIFO)—a 45-item scale in which a person indicates the way in which the pastor handles a number of leadership events. The pastor rated himself, and we compared his perceptions with those of the leaders. Two basic types of leadership situations were judged: *success* situations,

---

[6] E. P. Hollander, "Conformity, Status and Idiosyncrasy Credit," *Psychological Review* 65 (1958), pp. 117–27.

Table 11.2 LIFO Leadership Style

Situation	*Supporting Giving*	*Controlling Taking*	*Conserving Holding*	*Adapting Dealing*
Success	15	34	21	20
Conflict	14	31	23	22

NOTE: All scores in a given situation add up to 90. The higher the score, the stronger a given leadership style.

in which people follow the leader with little or no resistance, and *conflict* situations, in which people resist and refuse to follow the leader. These comparisons are given in Table 11.2.

The four leadership styles are defined as follows: The supporting/giving style depicts leadership through others and accomplishing goals through encouragement; the controlling/taking style depicts leadership by direct command and accomplishing goals by strong authority; the conserving/holding style depicts leadership by cautious deliberation and accomplishing goals by careful attention to traditional procedures; and the adapting/dealing style depicts leadership by friendliness and accomplishing goals through emphasizing good feelings and group cohesion.

As can be seen, the pastor sees his dominant style in success situations as controlling/taking (high score of 34) and his least preferred style as supporting/giving (score of 15). There is no back-up style because no one of the other two scores is within ten points of the controlling/taking score of 34.

This same pattern emerges in conflict situations, save for the fact that the pastor sees himself as having weak back-ups in the conserving/holding and the adapting/dealing styles.

The ratings of the leaders and the pastor's spouse are presented next (see Table 11.3). Of interest is how much they agree with the pastor's perception of himself.

Differences and similarities among the ratings were analyzed and discussed with the pastor. There is a continuing dialogue among scholars as to whether what persons think about themselves is more, or less, real than what others think about them. However, in leadership in voluntary organizations, such as the church, there is a great need to understand and evaluate one's

Table 11.3 LIFO Leadership Style

Situation	*Supporting Giving*	*Controlling Taking*	*Conserving Holding*	*Adapting Dealing*
Success				
spouse	16	34	22	18
leader 1	22	25	19	24
leader 2	21	28	24	17
leader 3	17	31	17	25
leader 4	27	30	17	16
Gonflict				
spouse	12	38	28	16
leader 1	15	29	24	22
leader 2	17	31	29	13
leader 3	13	30	27	20
leader 4	22	25	23	20

impact on others, because the prime goal of all leadership is influence. Of course, style is only one part of the picture, because even where there is perfect agreement on the style of a given leader there is the further question of whether people approve or disapprove of that style.

The raters were in perfect agreement that in success situations the pastor's dominant style was controlling/taking—a style that leads by direct commands, strong opinions, and clear task demands. However, there was disagreement as to whether the pastor had any back-up styles (scores within 10 points of the highest score) that he used on occasion. One or more of the leaders thought he exhibited the adaptive/dealing style (a style that leads by emphasizing good feelings and group consensus) or the supportive/giving style (a style that leads by staff encouragement and trust).

On his style in *conflict* situations there was much greater consensus between the pastor and the raters. All raters save one agreed that the pastor's dominant style was controlling/taking with a back-up style of conserving/holding (a style that leads by careful analysis and a commitment to well-thought-out procedures).

These issues were discussed with the pastor, and recommendations were made as to how he might become more conscious of his style and manage it more effectively in doing the work of the church and in understanding his impact on those with whom he worked.

No ideal pastoral style was assumed. Five means of managing his leadership style were suggested to the pastor. These procedures were offered to him in an effort to make his leadership more effective. First, he was encouraged to capitalize on his strengths in success situations. This meant that he should intentionally use his dominant style in a self-conscious manner even at times when he had not done so before. Second, he was encouraged to avoid excess use of his dominant style in conflict situations. This meant that he should become more conscious about those times when he became anxious and stressed. Having done this, he was encouraged to change his style and become a more cautious, methodical, and careful, or sociable, gregarious, and friendly leader—qualities characteristic of his back-up styles. This suggestion was based on the finding that persons who persist in using their dominant style in conflict often are at a disadvantage. Third, he was encouraged to develop his least preferred style in success situations. This meant he should identify a low-risk situation in which his leadership was not at stake and intentionally try to be supporting/giving—supportive and collaborative. This procedure would allow him to increase his repertoire of available styles. Fourth, he was encouraged to supplement his dominant style in success situations by agreeing with other leaders in the church to intentionally allow their differing leadership styles to be expressed in organizational meetings. By consciously agreeing that group decisions will include the exercise of different leadership styles by the various persons who are present, the decisions of the group will be enhanced and the leaders will not feel in competition with each other. The fifth suggestion was that he augment his leadership style by agreeing with other leaders in the church. He would moderate his dominant style by intentionally cultivating in himself qualities of their style. By this give-and-take he could reach a better style for himself and for those with whom he worked.

These options were discussed with him, and the importance of working with his style was agreed upon.

Underlying Assumptions of OD Consultation

A word needs to be added concerning the substantive and functional assumptions I make as a consulting organizational psychologist who is a Christian.

Although most organization development consultants have skills that can be applied to a wide range of organizations, they evaluate the purpose of the organizations that request their help and determine whether they can identify with them or not. Personally, as a Christian, I have determined that I can enthusiastically give myself to helping the church. However, I would decline the offer to assist such organizations as the Ku Klux Klan, the CIA, or the Mafia. I have no doubt that most of my colleagues in these endeavors function in much the same manner. Using one's values as a basis for accepting consultations is part of what it means to be professional.

Again, although most OD consultants have knowledge of and skill in administering numerous measures for assessing various dimensions of organizational life, their use of these instruments should not be interpreted simplistically. On the one hand, they know there is no perfect scale, and they utilize their instruments merely to order reality, such as style of leadership, in some manner. The dialogue that is prompted by the administration of such instruments is far more important than the measures themselves. On the other hand, though the issues to which the consultant attends through the use of these scales are strategic, they are not exhaustive. They do not tell us all we need to know, nor were they meant to do so. They do provide an arena for dialogue. The OD consultant is a skilled facilitator of group process—not a technician.

Finally, the OD consultant makes certain presumptions about reality that denote specific psychological as well as theological points of view. In a pervious article entitled "1 Plus 1 = 0 (Organization),"[1] I concluded that reality was social and that personal

[7] *Journal of the American Scientific Affiliation*, March 1978.

identity was acquired through the roles persons play. Most OD consultants agree with this assumption and insist that truth exists in the interaction *between* persons rather than inside them. They resist the temptation to say that truth is private and that change comes by the achievement of rational insight. Instead, they suggest that truth is discovered in the dialogue persons have with one another and that change comes through group action rather than individual insight. I believe this is good psychology and good theology in the sense that it takes seriously the doctrine of creation and the understanding of the church as that arena in which persons become the people of God. The Christian church gives persons status through divine acceptance and gives them roles to play that are significant through time and circumstance. Furthermore, as Jesus said, "Where two or three are gathered in my name, there am I in the midst of them" (Matt. 18:20). I work under the assumption that God is present and active when Christians get together. OD consultants to churches take organizational life and group process seriously and trust them to be revelational in a theological sense and cohesional in a psychological perspective.

The Limits of Organization Development Consultation

No one approach is ideal or exhaustive or perfect. There are limits to all approaches and to all perspectives. By being conscious of their limitations, organization development consultants try to minimize the negative possibilities. For example:

1. Initially there is the problem inherent in approaching organizations as a consulting psychologist who has the "client" perspective. Like attorneys, applied psychologists function on the basis of hourly fees. The importance of time may lead OD consultants to be less relaxed and more impulsive in their evaluations of what is needed. By being aware of the danger, OD consultants attempt to counter this in their professional behavior.

2. OD consultation tends to place more emphasis on inner dynamics as opposed to situational conditions. This may result in an organization that functions well but has no impact on its environment. In response, OD consultants intentionally call the organization's attention to market realities.

3. History assumes less importance in OD consultation than in

some other approaches. This does not mean that tradition and past experience are ignored, but it does mean that present functioning assumes priority. This could limit the impact of the consultation in situations where change appears to be occurring but in which long-term habits or history regain control after the consultant leaves. Once again, the OD consultant hopes to counter this tendency by calling it to the attention of the congregation.

In summary, organization development consultation has much to offer as a framework for understanding and helping the local church. This approach was illustrated through an actual consultation with Wiltshire Church. Some of the underlying assumptions and limitations of the approach were discussed to encourage dialogue and further study in this field.

SUGGESTIONS FOR RELATED READING

Beckhard, R. *Organization Development: Strategies and Models.* Reading, Mass.: Addison-Wesley, 1969.
The unique value of this volume is its emphasis on the importance of people in the organization mix and in its examples of companies that have included personal fulfillment in their statements of purpose. Another feature of the book is the seven case studies of how OD can be applied to organization life.

Bennis, W. G. *Organization Development: Its Nature, Origins and Prospects.* Reading, Mass.: Addison-Wesley, 1969.
The author has written a longer volume, *The Planning of Change*, that develops the theme of this book, namely, that OD is the most appropriate means for dealing with historical change. Another feature of the book is its useful critique of sensitivity training as an OD methodology.

Etzioni, A. *Modern Organizations.* Englewood Cliffs, N.J.: Prentice-Hall, 1964.
This is a seminal volume on the nature of organizations and includes many of the ideas referred to in his longer treatise entitled *A Comparative Analysis of Complex Organizations.* He includes many useful taxonomies for understanding the differences among various types of organizations as well as helpful insights regarding the manner in which organizations control the behavior of their members.

Marguiles, N., and Raia, A. P. *Organizational Development: Values, Process and Technology*. New York: McGraw-Hill, 1972.

This book is one of the most comprehensive texts, covering all the major topics in the field. The book also includes selected readings at the end of each section plus a group of case studies that illustrate the several technological applications of methods in OD. As an encyclopedic text it has no equal.

Schein, E. H. *Organizational Psychology*. 2d ed. Englewood Cliffs, N.J.: Prentice-Hall, 1970.

As compared to the book on organizations by Etzioni (noted above), this volume includes a more general survey of the field and is noteworthy for its coverage of the theories of others more than for any new ideas of its own. It is probably the most quoted text in the field because of its readability and its brevity. It is the best available introduction to the field.

12. Crisis, Communication, and Courage

A Ministry Development Approach

JAMES DESMOND ANDERSON

UNDERSTANDING AND CHANGE

As consultants we are not interested in merely studying the local congregation; we want to find ways to create change. Our interests do not stem from a detached intellectual inquiry. They are motivated by the need to provide help to the clergy and laity of local churches. Basic to this concern is the increase of the love of God and neighbor as it finds expression in the structures and processes of the local church. We focus on understanding the congregation so that change can occur in the direction of a more faithful Christian witness. This dual emphasis on understanding and change is central to all approaches to the local church that are rooted in the field of organization development.

Organization development emerged in the late fifties and early sixties as an applied science dedicated to the process of planned change within organizations and institutions. The basic change mechanism is the involvement of the organization's members in applied research on the covert processes of institutional life. By exposing the gaps between the organization's policies and its actual operating mode, the change process is given energy and direction. Organization development has spawned a broad range of efforts to aid the local church.

Recently the church has evolved the field of congregational development, or better, ministry development, to the point that it has become an important, distinctive, and new discipline in the field of practical theology. The uniqueness of ministry development is its capacity to provide an applied integrative focus for both belief and practice of ministry.

A Model of Ministry

An attempt to understand the ministry of the local church must be comprehensive enough to consider four different perspectives of the church, as well as the relationship or degree of fit between them. Ezra Earl Jones and I made this a main point of *The Management of Ministry* (San Francisco: Harper & Row), published in 1978, and intervening years have only strengthened our conviction. This model of ministry can be diagrammed as follows:

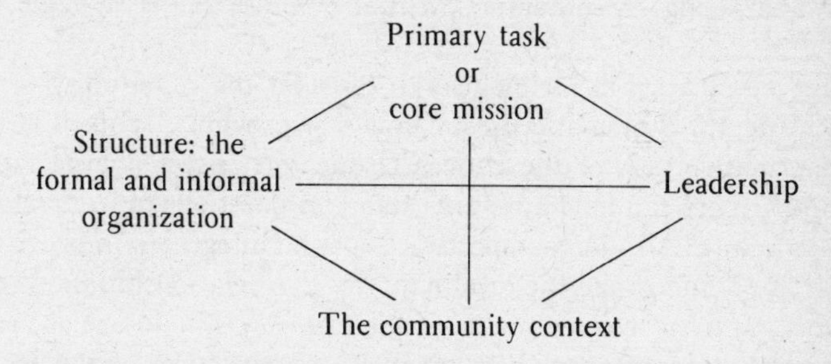

Primary task is significant because it allowed us to compare the ideal and the actual in addressing the mission of the church. The ongoing life of a church—its interaction with the community and interactions among the members—generates an identity or character that in turn shapes the character of its members. This identity transcends any rational planning scheme and will not be captured by a set of goals and objectives. To find the primary task we must observe many things a congregation sees and does to discern its connections by the way it lives. *Community context* is the sociopolitical area that is the mission environment of the congregation. Churches are a part of, and serve, the communities in which they are located. All too often churches lapse into defining themselves by their existing membership—as if they had a life apart from the community. The relationship or fit between primary task and environment is the best criterion for determining the structural forms and styles of leadership needed by the church. *Structure* refers to the formal explicit elements of congregational life such as policies, buildings, creeds, curricula, boards, and committees as well as the hidden, informal structures of cliques, networks, norms, and roles. These invisible, covert structures often function at odds with the visible, formal structures of church life. For example, many congregations adopt official objectives encouraging discipleship in the world while their informal practices endorse only the maintenance of the institutional church. *Leadership* refers to both clergy and laity in the several dimensions of the influence process between leader and participant. Church leaders, both clergy and lay, have the multiple tasks of maintaining a healthy institution, continually re-forming the bonds of voluntary association, and acting as authentic spiritual mentors in the struggle of life.

One might turn to sociologists to consider the community context in depth. Systematic theologians can provide clarification of the normative task of the church. Educators, psychologists, and administrators can lend a helping hand on questions of leadership and structure. All four perspectives must be integrated in order to understand and shape the local church. The relationship between the perspectives or components of the ministry system are as crucial as each component. For instance, the structure of the local church must be suited to the nature of the community context in the light of the primary task of the church. A rapidly transient, highly diverse community requires a different structure from a stable, homogeneous community.

The integration, or linking, of these four perspectives in the local church is not simply a matter of building a composite by fitting the four components together. Each perspective is a view of the whole but from a particular stance, somewhat like four different witnesses to the same event. At the same time, this component creates views and contrasts that highlight decisive linkages and patterns of relationship. For example, the problem will look different if pursued solely from the community context than if investigated from the internal perspective of structure or leadership. Primary task perspective can give full rein to values and vision in a way that the social sciences have difficulty incorporating.

An actual experience of the church can be interpreted in many ways. A neighborhood meeting can be regarded as data telling us of the community context, or as a structure of the church in action; it can be examined in terms of the various leadership processes in the meeting, or in the light of the purposive values being pursued; it can be seen in its relationship to other groups, levels, and processes of community and congregational life. The practice of ministry development provides church leaders with the ability to sort out this experience to achieve a more comprehensive picture of the church in action. When this becomes the congregation's self-understanding, rather than the views of an outside expert, new motivation for action is ensured. By using these four perspectives we believe that the congregation will at least have the option to choose directions that are theologically sound as well as organizationally effective. Our experience suggests that the American church has an entrepreneurial bias that causes an easy choice of methods solely directed toward organizational efficiency and numerical growth. Much of the initial church enthusiasm for methods rooted in organization development appears to stem from its ability to concentrate energy on the marketing problems currently being experienced by church leaders.

The hope for the field of ministry development rests in its increasing ability to help church leaders address the problems that are troubling them in ways that realistically unite parish practice with the standards of Scripture and theology. To understand the problems of a congregation we must feel ourselves to be present with them at the time. For example, we must try to "enter" Wiltshire Church.

WILTSHIRE CHURCH

A Time of Promise

Wiltshire Church seems to be in trouble. The past spirit of harmonious cooperation has evaporated. Financial reports are "depressing." Key leaders have withdrawn their support. A mixed chorus of complaints has swollen in volume. The minister, Sid Carlson, has become a source of concern, to himself and others. A surprising golden era of growth and recognition is ending in discord and confusion. Leaders and members believe that the congregation has fallen onto hard times. My own view is quite to the contrary. For the moment at least, the placid veneer of domesticated fellowship and organizational growth has been broken. Normal assumptions, perceptions, and habitual ways of behaving as members of Wiltshire Church are being put to the test. Anger and anxiety have raised the possibility that the accustomed, seemingly successful modes of operating will be re-examined at a fresh and deeper level. The addiction to success under the controlled leadership of Sid Carlson is failing. In short, Wiltshire Church is face to face with the richest, fullest, best opportunity it has had in a decade to discern its call as a portion of the body of Christ.

All social systems have an inherent tendency to stay frozen and locked into the same patterns of belief and behavior. Like an aerialist on a high wire moving his balance pole in order to remain steady, much of the change in a social system occurs in order to keep basic patterns the same. To those who would help Wiltshire Church in its struggle to become a congregation faithful in its practice to the gospel of its Lord, the present time of inherent instability is welcome. It means that the possibility is present for change in the deep structures that shape and mold the beliefs, attitudes, and behavior of Wiltshire's leaders and members. We can be reasonably certain that without help these deep structures will form even the present seemingly chaotic and disturbed scene—the movements of the balance pole—into stable equilibrium. Just as a canoeist can read the turbulent waves of a raging course of white water so as to "see" the boulders and logs beneath the surface, so the helpers of the Wiltshire Church should expect and must be able to "see" the deep, enduring structures that are asserting their formative power over the current fluid situation.

The town of Wiltshire is a community of managers and business executives. One of the highest compliments paid to the pastor is that he is competent enough to have made it in the business world. This prevalent and highly prized belief in managerial effectiveness and organizational control asserts itself in several fashions. Church troubles are likely to be regarded solely as problems to be solved. Categories such as personnel problem or planning problem are likely to be invoked as the means of understanding the present situation. Without aid, the human and spiritual possibilities of this time of testing and challenge will be overlooked.

However, the built-in receptivity to managerial problem solving does have the advantage of increasing the possible acceptance of outside "expert" consultants. When external consultants come on the scene they will begin to experience pressures to treat the issues of Wiltshire Church solely with rational, analytic approaches.

Subtle and unconscious pressures will be exerted to restore the Church to normalcy—to return to familiar processes that ensure harmony and the sense of well-being that derives from being able to shape and manage a good, successful operation. The consultant will experience the same bind that has enveloped Sid Carlson. Credibility and leverage to influence the congregation will flow from being a "good" problem solver and helping to get things back under control. Wiltshire Church is in a difficult but promising time. Given proper leadership and assistance the opportunity is present for the congregation to emerge from its identification with the cultural values of the community and begin to model a style of life more reflective of the Christian gospel.

Structures of Communication

An examination of the underlying structures of life in Wiltshire Church reveals the patterns of relating regarded as acceptable. These structures or habitual patterns are especially clear, for instance, in the area of interpersonal communication. First, there are indicators that the expression of strong emotions—negative feelings in particular—are not valued in the usual practices of the membership. Thus, a lay leader cites as a reason for dropping the housing proposal that "the issue was too hot at the time." Administrative board minutes reveal a continued emphasis on smoothing disagreement and cooling down discussions by "avoiding direct questions." Member comments suggest that strong negative feelings are more likely to be expressed through phone calls after the board has adjourned than in open, public forums.

Second, indications from several quarters are that it is unusual for members to speak on an issue out of a personal, owned, deeply felt expression of personal perspective. The difference in intensity of feeling and sharpness of expression between private interviews and public comment is dramatic and pronounced. For a congregation that values pastoral responsiveness to its members, the board retreat discussions of purpose are broad and general in character and reveal little of the actual day-to-day dilemmas of board members. Indeed, one can read the entire study and believe that, except for Sid Carlson and those to whom he has been a pastor, the inhabitants of Wiltshire are able to pull up the drawbridge and leave all of the woes of the world on the other side of the moat. In this instance what is not talked about is probably more important than what is. Even, or perhaps especially, in a town like Wiltshire, alcoholism, shattered marriages, adolescent tragedies, and the trauma of sudden death are elemental components of the fabric of life. This level of discussion and personal revelation is missing from the record.

A third important communication pattern is revealed by the realistic anxiety that interpersonal conflict will lead to punitive retribution through the betrayal of personal confidences. This threat has been reinforced by the public symbols of accusation and name calling. Violent, out-of-control verbal exchanges have been allowed to hang in the air—to be resolved, if at all, in private. The uncertainty of this situation can only result in the most cautious and controlled public utterance.

I doubt that any of these communication habits are new or situationally induced by the present crisis. They suggest longstanding normative practice within a congregation that values a warm, comfortable climate of belonging. They suggest habits and ways of relating that confuse caring with protectiveness, acceptance with doormat passivity. The deep structures are less visible when the stream is flowing with a gentle calm. An advantage of the present situation is that the outcomes of these communication habits are becoming more and more apparent. "We are meeting controversy with contempt," said one member, and the chairman of the board resigned with accusations about the pastor. The present lack of trust is quite real. Although this breach of trust is experienced as a loss, the evidence suggests that what has been shattered is the facade of tranquillity, the masks of some of the players in "the best show in town." One of the most hopeful possibilities in the Wiltshire Church situation is that the pain of the present time can lead to a deep level of trust based on a capacity to love where there are differences, to trust because both relationships and faith have been tested, not sheltered.

The late Sam Shoemaker, an Episcopal priest instrumental in the founding of Alcoholics Anonymous, said once that one of the things the church needs to learn from AA is the need for "definite personal dealing with people." The communication patterns of Wiltshire Church may express kindness and good advice, but as Shoemaker points out and AA exemplifies, this is not all that people need. Honest, forthright dealing with one another as we really are, as we are before God and beyond the level of polite appearance, is a necessity of Christian fellowship.

This is a promising time for Wiltshire Church because there is a recognition that it is a congregation being put to the test. Its customary numbing, comforting, soothing ways aren't working. Patterns and habits are beginning to unfreeze and slip out of place. It is a significant opportunity for change and growth in the everyday practices of talking and working together.

Organic Interdependence

When one looks at the dominant task Wiltshire Church is performing, at the ways the organization has been structured, and at the nature of Sid Carlson's leadership, a consistent and self-reinforcing pattern emerges. Sid's leadership is congruent with the cultural values of the town and the congregation's habits of communication. His style should not be considered apart from an examination and clarification of the functional mission of Wiltshire Church.

Wiltshire's sense of task has been described by its minister as helping its members to better cope with the pressures of family and corporate life. The emphasis has been on the pastoral and the pragmatic. As described in a sermon illustration, the congregation is consoled with the thought that although they may not know what they are fighting for, they might at least "think we are winning."

Wiltshire Church has focused its primary energy on a particular kind of care and feeding of its membership and remains unaware of larger issues. Public announcement of the disesteem with which Methodist district affairs are regarded functions to uphold the strength of the closed, enveloping boundaries of the congregation. One suspects that the church maintains its sense of cohesion and strength by seeing itself as so much better than those around it.

Certainly, clear evidence exists to show that the functioning primary task of Wiltshire Church is to be a refuge, a sanctuary, a retreat for its members from the stress and anxiety of the world. The idolization of Sid Carlson, his rapid fall from glory, and the several-years' emphasis on a "one-man show" point to a group cohesiveness, a refuge built around dependency on and idolization of a central authority figure. It is as if the congregation were saying we are strong and secure because our leader is larger than life. His strength is our strength. Such groups have little room for understanding and forgiveness when the leader turns out to be as frail and fallible as the rest of us. Some members may have even wished, at an inarticulate level, to link with the assistant pastor, Stew Collins, to bring to birth a new emphasis to "save" the situation. Such actions would be congruent with the congregation's deepest patterns of life together.

Some members now see the pastor as a "devil personified." This is only the other side of the coin from a god personified in a congregation "built in the pastor's image." Sid's charismatic flair and worldly lifestyle have been charming, attractive, and a source of easy identification for the members. His challenging domination of the lay leadership brought respect, authority, and dependable growth. Undoubtedly this leadership style has contributed to the difficulty the administrative board has in making decisions. There may be, as suggested by Evans and Reed, a collusive quality in the relationship between Sid and the lay leadership.

Ironically, the most significant failure of leadership in Wiltshire Church has been the success of the leadership in building a congregation that, like the town of Wiltshire itself, is so dedicated to hiding from the sharp edges of life. Elsewhere in this volume, James Hopewell has pointed to the themes of joviality and ultimacy as characteristic of the Wiltshire Church ministry. The leadership strives to be warm, engaging, and responsive. They have given their selective attention to those aspects of church life that would seem to free life from temporality, failure, loss, death, and disappointment.

Both the formal and informal structures of Wiltshire Church seem strongly configured to support the leadership in this primary task. The building itself looks special. Worship and Christian education are well supported by staff and utilize large numbers of volunteers. The membership committee is routinely active and blandly concerns itself with gentle, undemanding incorporation of new members into Wiltshire Church. Conspicuously absent, despite their presence in formal Methodist organization, are any mechanics for realistic linkage with the district and with the community of the town of Wiltshire. Despite the fact that this district superintendent has a number of pungent observations to make about Wiltshire Church, the evidence suggests that these have been withheld and that the two-way pattern of communication is guarded and cautious. There are no signs of a recognition of interdependence between district and church or between church and community.

Congregation size does have an impact upon church structure and should affect the intentional design of the organization. Except for the minister, few of the members seem to know each other. Given the public image of the church and the transient nature of the town of Wiltshire, it is realistic to assume a meager understanding of denominational heritage among new members. Aside from the Christian education and music programs, the congregation exists as a large, undifferentiated group with a minimum structure for assimilation, education, continuing spiritual transformation, and peer relatedness. Sunday worship and occasional education programs are almost certain to be inadequate to the transforming and integrating tasks needed to move beyond the basic need for a safe haven toward a clear conviction about God's redemptive power.

Given the size of the congregation, the structure focuses the wishes, hopes, and fears of the congregation on the person of the pastor. Because Sid saw his role as one of building a community of consolation, and because he became the primary instrument through which consolation occurred, he was subject to enormous pressures. Potential relationships with the larger church and with the community could only arouse conflict from differing perspectives and hence detract from congregational cohesiveness.

The Courage to Be Different

The challenge for a consultant working with Wiltshire Church will be to help them see themselves more clearly. The consultant must help them live in the pain of the present long enough to see their darker side, and to know even that can be redeemed. Most congregation members and leaders will expect the restoration of growth. Even those who are asking for adult education and spiritual growth are not likely to make the connection between the spiritual ill of trying always to control life and the patterns of success in the town of Wiltshire.

Whatever a consultant or outside researcher might think to be true of Wiltshire Church, what the congregation thinks and knows is the focus of the consultant's goals in contracting to be of help. The consultant will work within a diagnostic model that determines the focus and nature of the information collected and analyzed. In contracting with Wiltshire, the consultant's model for understanding the mission of the local church will be made explicit and then key leaders and groups helped to develop their own comprehensive model. They will participate and have a stake in their own processes of data collection and analysis. Like the congregation, most of the individuals in the network responsible for the direction and care of Wiltshire Church have been fragmented, unconnected, and unexamined.

Sid's wife and family are mentioned only briefly in this case—the note that they too live in a fishbowl because of the location of the parsonage. An honest, searching exploration of friendship, family, and other support systems within and without Wiltshire Church could be a giant step toward a community of love and trust. The modeling of Sid's relationship-to-his-work role versus his role as husband and father is an important part of the story, especially in a community where success and career achievement have as much primacy as they do in Wiltshire.

Questions of communication, emergent censorship, and minimal trust will be important. Key individuals and groups within the community, the district, and Sid's family should all have a part to play in what happens. As a consultant I believe that it is vital to explore and develop open relationships among the larger network of people who affect the life of this congregation. Wiltshire Church has not been open, even about the refugelike character of the church and community. Since the church has played such a major part in preserving the ideals of Wiltshire, it is doubtful if any change is possible without the involvement of this wider network of individuals and groups.

Deep structures and old habits will re-assert themselves unless the changes are clearly seen and widely discussed. Then is change possible only when members are committed to it, and when the structures of the church embrace the change by a new way of doing business.

FOUR KEY PRINCIPLES

There are principles of ministry development that are important to understanding and helping local congregations. Here are four key elements essential in the task of helping a whole congregation understand itself and make constructive changes.

A Disciplined Relationship

Churches are complex, multifaceted institutions. No reader of this volume could think otherwise. Though the input of one-visit experts through reports, studies, and weekend conferences is helpful, it will not bring about the levels of self-understanding and self-management necessary for a congregation to fundamentally re-examine its ministry. An extended contract between consultant and congregation is a vital step in helping the leadership maintain a careful and continuing attention to the task of ministry development. The discipline of an ongoing process is self-examination, repentance, and reformation taking place at the organizational-systemic level.

A contract for a disciplined examination of ministry is *not* the equivalent of a contract to initiate an outsider's program of renewal. The focus must be on the work of the total ministry of the congregation. Activities and interventions initiated by the consultant are diverting when they suggest alternative focus to the ongoing life of the congregation. The purpose of a disciplined relationship between consultant and client is to help the congregation develop a more comprehensive, articulate model of its ministry and to mobilize itself to live up to that image.

Episodic, short-term programs and consultation can be important in providing a particular array of knowledge and skill. The ministry development consultant, like the family physician, relies instead on a continuing relationship with the entirety of the congregational system. Note that the development of this relationship was prohibited in the instance of Wiltshire Church. The analysis presented earlier would be quite different if it had emerged from interaction with members of the client's church. From my point of view, the real study of Wiltshire Church is not possible without the benefit of this relationship.

The Congregation's Need for a Multiperspective Model

Difficult and mysterious a process as it is, the ministry development consultant must try to help the congregation create a model for self-understanding that attempts to comprehend the levels of theology described in the chapter by Don Browning. Without this effort the congregation will work to resolve its most pressing concerns—usually having to do with the morale of its present membership or with survival issues tied to dollars and membership—and not really address the more fundamental questions of the mission in the light of community needs and gospel imperative. Each of the perspectives represented in this volume has valuable contributions to make toward a richer understanding of the church.

But church leaders need an intelligible map that is close enough to their reality to be reliable and trustworthy. The report of any outsider may be ingenious, detailed, and clear without moving the congregation toward change. Through the use of multiperspectives and continuing relationships with congregations, ministry development has attempted to offer a more adequate theological and intellectual road map for the use of church leaders.

The Whole Is Greater Than the Sum of Its Parts

Early reference was made to structure, community, leadership, and primary task—four perspectives of ministry development. But it should be clear in responding to Wiltshire Church as presented in the case study that I am more concerned with the way these elements related to one another in the function of the whole. Attention to the wholeness of life is one of the strengths of the anthropological approach discussed earlier in this book.

Ministry development is *not* a detached intellectual inquiry that dissects a congregation into its constituent parts. The disadvantage of a written report—like this chapter—is that the writer is tempted to operate only on a rational level. Actually knowing the congregation requires listening with the heart and seeing through the eyes of feelings. Imagination and intuition are requirements, not luxuries. Ministry development is an ideographic science that deals with the uniqueness of the human story of a particular people in an actual setting. As story and history, Wiltshire Church bears many of the marks of American Protestantism in general. But the real vitality and interest of Wiltshire Church will be found in the particularities of its story and in the uniqueness of its personality or character as a human community.

Methods Are Important

The method of inquiry creates legitimacy for the issues it highlights and focuses energy in the directions illuminated. As a result the inquiry itself is a carrier of meaning and a teacher of theology and values.

We have learned, for instance, to be cautious about the use of survey feedback mechanisms for obtaining information on the local church. These questionnaire surveys have an unhappy tendency to suggest that mystery and excitement have no place in the institutional life of the church. An alternative is to train the congregation in skills of interview and participant observation. In a major project on the changing role of women, we found that we were able to train church members to conduct in-depth, reflective interviews. In ways that surprised us, the interview turned out to be an act of ministry in itself. It allowed the interviewee to see more clearly the patterns of meaning in transitional years and critical events. The interview was experienced by both interviewer and interviewee as a time of understanding, caring, and compassion. These interviews made possible the creation of composite case studies that were then utilized in a program of education and change. This approach provides information that has spiritual depth and organizational clarity.

Ministry development is still a youthful enterprise. It is a practical theological discipline that attempts to relate the phenomena of stubborn, shortsighted church boards; the purity of theological ideals; the exciting vision of a charismatic leader; the tragedy of sudden death; the burden of escalating fuel bills and leaky roofs; the mystery of worship; the turbulence of a changing neighborhood. These and the many other untidy aspects of life may be brought within the scope of the intentional ministry of the church and its leaders. It is a way of understanding Wiltshire Church and of emerging with it in repentance and faithful service.

SUGGESTIONS FOR RELATED READING

Anderson, James Desmond, and Jones, Ezra Earl. *The Management of Ministry*. San Francisco: Harper & Row, 1978.
A comprehensive examination and integration of the critical components of ministry in the local church.

Primary Task (clarifying the nature of the actual work and mission of the local church):

Buechner, Frederick. *Telling the Truth: The Gospel as Tragedy, Comedy, and Fairy Tale*. San Francisco: Harper & Row, 1977.
A book that is so slim and well written that you may underestimate its application to the nature and structure of congregational life. The question is the degree to which the patterns of parish life reveal the tragic, comic, and hopeful in the human condition.

Holmes, Urban T. *Turning to Christ*. New York: Seabury Press, 1981.
An Anglican book that offers help to anyone seeking a concrete definition of evangelism.

Structure and Leadership:

Anderson, James Desmond. *To Come Alive! Revitalizing the Local Church*. San Francisco: Harper & Row, Ministers Paperback Library, 1979.

Explanation and example of the formal and informal aspects of the structure and dynamics of congregational life.

Community:

Almost every volume of the recently issued "Into Our Third Century Series" of the Abingdon Press is an examination of some aspect of the relationship of the United Methodist Church to our changing society. The insights are valuable for every denomination.

Dudley, Carl S. *Where Have All Our People Gone?* New York: Pilgrim Press, 1979.

Practical, concise guide to give you some lenses for seeing the community in the framework of the troubling questions of growth and survival.

IV
OVERVIEWS

13. The Practice of Ministry

CARL S. DUDLEY

The practice of ministry is more than any of the various approaches that have been separately presented, and more than all of them combined. Like law and medicine, professional leadership in ministry demands the artistic interweaving of learned perceptions and unconscious responses to constantly changing situations. The social sciences, along with theology and the personal spiritual disciplines of the pastor, are essential to the resources used by the Holy Spirit to shape and strengthen church leadership. The approaches in this book examine the mundane life of the church as a means of revealing the more subtle forces at work. A sensitive pastor already feels much of what has been said.

The strength of these chapters lies in the way they separate and examine the threads of various perspectives woven and matted into the fabric of every congregation—almost lost to consciousness. Mature practice of ministry does not need to examine the assumptions in every step. Such narcissistic behavior would cripple any ministry. But there are times when we need to engage in self-conscious reflection as a means to more effective service.

Conflict is one situation in which this book should prove especially helpful. When conflict is the result of different understandings of the church, the approaches in this book may provide the basis for understanding diversity and developing a stronger congregation. These approaches are useful generally—not only in crisis—to discover the unique character of a congregation found in the routine activities that carry the life and faith of the church. And they are most insightful as a way of examining the patterns of essential church programs, discovering inherent limits in present practices, and offering new options for program effectiveness.

CONFLICT

Wiltshire Church had both strength and problems, and each contributed to our understanding of the congregation. In the previous chapters, sociologists considered the problems in light of the larger social context; psychologists moved from social context to personal relationships; those with an anthropological orientation moved toward an understanding of the corporate character of the congregation; theologians grounded their interpretation in the values commitments of the membership, variously understood; and organizational development specialists utilized several disciplines, with an emphasis on communication and decision making. All of their approaches provided valid interpretations of the conflict in Wiltshire Church. The contributors did not agree with each other, not because they did not understand, but because they saw the situation differently.

Some conflict in the congregation can be relieved by improved communication. Here, however, the conflict between perspectives is based, not on misunderstandings, but on clear differences in the perception of human dynamics. In the practice of ministry, we must differentiate between those who need improved communication and those who perceive events differently.

The perspectives of this book reflect the various viewpoints often found in church conflict situations. In most basic decisions facing a congregation, some people look to community conditions, saying, for example, "What can you expect in such an affluent community?" Others point to the congregation's relationship with the pastor, suggesting that the solution lies in a change in leadership. Still others explore the history and story of the congregation, the depth of commitment to its theological beliefs, or the way in which it is organized and makes decisions. All of the chapters of this book would be represented in a typical church argument. A parish may not need better communication, but appreciation for the differences its members represent. This book helps to identify the sources of pluralism that enliven the controversies of every congregation.

For example, the typical seminary student has a preliminary understanding of the church from the disciplines of theology and sociology and often feels the sharp differences between the demands of the gospel and the behavior of a particular church. Imagine a young seminarian entering the pulpit for a post-Christmas opportunity to preach. The young cleric might preach a prophetic sermon, suggesting to an affluent congregation that its celebration of Christmas is an anemic expression of faith, offensive to the poor and a desecration of the baby Jesus. Some members might respond that their religious culture had been unfairly attacked by someone who did not understand them—and perhaps did not understand the gospel as they did. The conflict might be processed, or ignored. But as long as the young preacher and the irate members remain within their separate approaches, the conflict cannot be understood by either, and each can more easily blame the other. The application of several disciplines, required to show the pluralism of perspectives, enriches the ministry of a congregation.

The use of several approaches may not remove the issues to be reconciled. But it can enrich the congregation with a much wider understanding of the way God is at work in their midst and provide a basis for dialogue to accept their differences and to discover a larger sense of ministry together.

CONGREGATIONAL UNIQUENESS

In the practice of ministry, we discover that congregations have a different feel about them, that they develop a quality and character distinctively their own. Recognition of congregational uniqueness is essential for the pastor who expects to relocate. Two congregations may be demographic twins but opposites in character and commitment to ministry. An awareness of the unique personality of each congregation gives the bishop or denominational executive direct access to the congregation and gives the pastor or consultant the appropriate handles to help the congregation mobilize in ministry.

Many factors contribute to the individuality of a congregation, including the community context and the attitude of the church toward it; the denomination as family and as polity; the history, narrative, and traditions of the congregation; the size, organization, and decision-making patterns of the congregation; the culture, world view, and social worlds of the congregation; the tenure and leadership style of the pastor; and the theology, biblical authority, and commitment of the members to the mission and ministry of the church. Congregations develop unique profiles in the conflict between institution and environment, between current leadership and historical forces, between stated beliefs and cultural commitments, between internal ministry and public witness, between private experience and corporate consciousness. Out of these tensions churches form an identifiable but elusive character.

Without trying to summarize the many insights offered in each approach, let me suggest the ways in which I have found these approaches complementary, and how that complementarity aids congregations in a self-awareness that is the building block of more effective ministry. My comments should be taken as encouragement, not prescription, for congregations and those who work with congregations to discover new ways of expanding their horizons and appreciating the uniqueness of each congregation.

The social context of Chapter 6 provides the framework for understanding the values and lifestyles of the members of a congregation. Since the authors of that chapter take a comprehensive approach, the chapter includes information on the demographic character of the area, changing community values, and the internal structure of the congregation. Perhaps because the authors are most sensitive to the "determinative power of social context," they make a strong appeal for the church to transcend its situation.

The hard empirical data of the sociologists is particularly comforting as a frame of reference for the local church; they describe trends for the area as a whole and provide the basis for long-range decisions. Typically, however, sociology has little to say about the uniqueness of particular congregations within the larger social context. In responding to Wiltshire Church, the sociologists tend to take material from the background statement and from independent sources of community data. They do not find much use for the crisis in Alan Hyatt's narrative, nor do they offer much help in what to say to Alan as he hangs up the phone. Without sociologists we would be floating in space, but the uniqueness of the church remains uninterpreted.

Cultural anthropology (Chapter 4) perceives the congregation as a culture, a subsystem of the larger society. The freshness and apparent immediacy of ethnographic categories has recently attracted increased attention in religious research. Church members enjoy talking about the history and activities of the church, about significant events, leading figures, internal tensions, and sacred space. Like theology, ethnography takes the "sacred" seriously. Ethnography offers new tools for disciplined listening, especially across cultural differences.

Ethnography is so effective in developing the uniqueness of each congregation that the results are difficult to employ for comparisons of one congregation with others. In fact, some researchers are even cautious about anticipating the future of the congregation being studied, providing only a report of the patterns thus far.

The literary symbolism approach of Chapter 5 combines ethnographic analysis with literary exposition in an effort to develop a basis for comparison among congregations, and to interpret their stories as predictable behavior. As a frontier of congregational studies, this approach stimulated the other approaches that are developed in this volume. In its search for the structure of imagination through a synthesis of anthropological technique and literary symbols, this approach brings together diverse disciplines in a way that makes the congregation the central focus of inquiry.

Systems psychology as used by the Grubb Institute (Chapter 3) provides a means to uncover the congregation's primary task, that is, its normative function in the community. Using a broad-based analysis—from psychoanalytic theory to demographic data—this approach seeks to identify the uniqueness of the congregation in its dynamic interaction within the community. When we discover the historical and current role of the church in the community, we understand the appeal of the pastor, the tension of the gospel, and the potential future for this particular church.

Theological ethics (Chapter 7) demonstrates how to find the unique and operative theology of each congregation by looking at the documents of the church and the behavior of its people. The procedure reveals a profile of faith that could provide a basis for discussion in many suburban communities. The chapter demonstrates the weaving of Scripture and theological tradition into an image of the ideal prophetic church, which is then applied to Wiltshire Church with gentle pastoral grace. In its synthesis of social science insights and theological norms, the chapter offers a working example of insights and problems that emerge when general theological norms are brought to focus on a specific congregation.

Philosophical theology (Chapter 8) suggests another function of theological inquiry, that of challenging the class and cultural foundations for assuming the validity of basic concepts about decision making, professional leadership, and the sovereignty of God. It sets Wiltshire Church in a larger context in which metaphors appear to have lost the authority of meaning, interprets the pastor as victim in the breakdown of cultural assumptions, and suggests that Wiltshire Church might find its uniqueness in an unusual willingness to be open to an unpredictable and unmanageable moment of theophany.

Policy planning (Chapter 10) is most pragmatic in the issues raised, and practical in the advice tendered. The questions are sensitive to eliciting the uniqueness of each situation in the complex interweaving of many disciplines. The goal of the consultant is specific: to build stronger congregational organizations through disciplined planning and intentional process. Although assumptions are stated as axioms and complex issues are avoided in the clarity of a chosen goal, the uniqueness of the congregation is protected in the relationship between consultant and congregation.

Organizational development (Chapter 11) defines the history of its approach and consciously selects one dimension (leadership) to serve as an example of the process. Typical of the approach is selecting one area of the client's need and tailoring a response to meet that need. The organizational development approach is not as interested in the conceptual identity of the congregation as it is in enabling the congregation to find identity in action.

The approach of ministry development (Chapter 12) finds the identity of the congregation in the interaction of several elements: leadership, context, organization, and primary task. The immediate crisis of the congregation is an opportunity for rediscovering the need to make decisions openly and finding the unique mission of the congregation in the context of contemporary possibilities.

As a means of discovering congregational identity and uniqueness, the case study itself provides one additional resource. Although many of the other approaches anticipate a third-party participant in the process of self-discovery, when using a case study the learners themselves become third-party observers of the problems in the case. It may be easier for some people to consider the problems of their own congregation when they find those problems happening in another congregation. Case studies provide an arena that gives distance and objectivity to concerns that may be personal and immediate.

Wiltshire Church may have similarities to many other congregations, but it is also unique and cannot be duplicated. The community provides a generally affluent framework, but Reverend Sid Carlson is a particular kind of leader at a vulnerable age. The Methodist setting provides a general example of church polity and connectional ties, but the peculiar conditions of population shift and housing demand give this situation its own individual flavor. The profile of this congregation is enriched by each discipline in turn, whether it focuses on conflicting theologies or the retelling of the stories of the gods. In one sense, Wiltshire Church reflects the crisis in faith of every mainline congregation in affluent America. In another sense, there is no other congregation like it. Together the approaches show in bold relief the generalizations that can be made about, as well as the uniqueness of, this particular group of believers.

PROGRAM DEVELOPMENT

The everyday life of the congregation is not subject to being constantly reflected upon but grows out of the unselfconscious affirmations of belonging together. When we apply the approaches in this volume to the activities of our congregations, we often discover that our programs are grounded in only one or two of them. Using a fuller range of perspectives offers a critique of what we are doing and often provides new options and additional resources for accomplishing the same ends.

Evangelism, for example, is usually represented by a strong theological rationale and organized with a heavy institutional emphasis. Typically committees will use a sociological analysis to identify prospective members. But the effective appeal to new prospects should include the insights about human need offered by psychology, and the promises of God offered in the theological notes. If prospective members are to be assimilated, the insights of cultural anthropology and the literary symbolism approach must be applied in developing programs, and the structures discussed by organizational development must be implemented in practice. As an outreach that demands the fullest explanation and organizational support, evangelism demands the sensitive application of all these approaches.

Adult education as spiritual growth in the congregation is another area about which almost all of the contributors must be consulted. The social worlds of the sociologists, the spiritual communitas of anthropology, the human needs of psychologists, and even the narrative of literary symbolism are vehicles for values that have shaped the congregation. Grist for spiritual growth in small groups is offered in the theologians' discussion of the body of Christ for the congregation and the breakdown of compelling metaphor. Each discipline seems to be begging for mature and unhurried reflection, as if the conversation should have specialists steeped in each approach, or time should be provided when the board is not overwhelmed with planning program details.

Leadership development is another area in which each approach can make a contribution to an enriched understanding of church program. From the LIFO exercise by Malony to the idolized authority in Anderson's review, from the collusion suggested by Evans and Reed to the mythic Zeus described by Hopewell, from the corporate leader described by Williams to the victim of cultural collapse suggested by Pacini: everyone cares about the pivotal figure of Sid Carlson and the way he interacts with church, community, and his own convictions.

Worship suggests yet another area of church program in which the various disciplines could expand present practices with their rich new insights. Worship is a showcase of relationships between pastor and people and a moment of enacting the plot and characterization that the congregation carries from its history. Worship allows values to find expression in preaching and prayers, in liturgy and loaded symbols, in spiritual renewal and management processes.

Pastoral placement receives rough treatment by implication from the perspective of the combined approaches. Many denominations use placement procedures that take no account of the pairing of pastor and people that is suggested by systems psychology. In the interim between pastors, many denominations require congregations to survey the social context and establish institutional goals. But the approaches in this volume are almost unanimous in observing that pastoral effectiveness is more dependent upon internal emotional factors (such as culture, story, psychological bonding, and leadership style) than upon the more objective factors of social trends or organizational goals. Perhaps these objective projects provide therapeutic activity for working through congregational grief, but they seem to offer little aid to the appropriate matching of restless pastors and empty pulpits.

Social action is a program concern at the heart of Wiltshire Church that finds its way into almost every approach. The sociologists make clear the economic privilege of Wiltshire and describe the values that support a sense of separateness. Psychologists distinguish between people with "needs" and people "in need." A theologian urged the "divine human community" to identify with the poor. In fact the Wiltshire congregation had several programs to increase membership participation in social concerns, and the multidisciplinary approaches offered further ways to mobilize the congregation. But the various disciplines also suggested the limited involvement of the congregation. It was part of the creed but not included in the culture; it was an organizational activity but found no place in the mythic structure. The approaches combine to show the strengths and limitations of various programs. Those who seek to establish the congregation's identity with the poor must first change its perception of itself. Change does not happen when the planners propose it, but when the ethnographers discover it.

The various approaches see different realities, and see the same reality differently. They make different contributions to the ministry of the church and are mutually dependent to show the wholeness of the church. They help us critique the congregation, but they do not explain its mystery. They point beyond our knowledge to the manifold ways the Holy Spirit is at work in the church. For building effective ministry we need them all.

14. Integrating the Approaches: A Practical Theology

DON S. BROWNING

Integrating the various perspectives on the study of the congregation is primarily an exercise in practical theological thinking. Most ministers practice practical theological thinking as an art. But like many artists, they have little conscious knowledge of or control over the rules of the art that they intuitively practice. And if their judgments are challenged and they are asked to justify their thinking, they find it difficult to trace their steps, give reasons if required, or put things straight when they go wrong.

Most ministers were not taught how to do practical theological thinking. They were taught some species of systematic or biblical theology and then told to go forth and apply this knowledge to concrete situations. Their professors proudly offered them the meat and potatoes of basic theological thinking and led them to believe that there was nothing more to do but to apply it, and this, they suggested, was the easiest part of all.

If this characterizes most theological education, I hope that theological professors will not take offense if I assert, rather strongly, that this is not enough. Practical theology is not applied biblical or systematic theology. It is not the easiest or most simple-minded branch of theology. It is the most complex, most difficult. Many ministers and laypeople are good practical theologians without having too much conscious knowledge of the actual rules that govern the art. Yet we might be better at it if we knew the basic principles of this discipline. And we certainly would understand and prescribe more ably for this congregation (and for other congregations of our own experience) and better use these various approaches, if we could be more self-conscious about our practical theology.

Imagine that you are someone close to Wiltshire Church but, at the same time, someone with enough distance to think freely about it. Perhaps you are the district superintendent or perhaps the president of the administrative board. You have a job to address the issues facing the church, and you have an opportunity to use some of the interpretative perspectives offered in this book. How do you proceed? Your job is more than just studying the congregation; you must study, interpret, and understand with an end toward action, prescription, decision. You have the task of relating more or less theoretical and scientific frameworks of interpretation toward the end of *praxis*. You furthermore have the task of relating and using perspectives that are clearly partial, that thematize certain aspects of the total situation but neglect others and, for that reason alone, are inevitably reductive. And you do all of this in order to take faithful Christian thought and action. Of course, the kind of thought and action I am recommending should be taken by the congregation as a whole; it should be congregational reflection and congregational action. But nonetheless there will need to be individuals, and you might be one of them, to lead and educate the congregation in the processes of practical theological deliberation.

The interpretative perspectives reviewed in this book can be organized along a continuum from relatively scientific to normative. The two theological positions by Hough and Pacini are clearly normative; even their attempts to describe Wiltshire Church in its is-ness are clearly colored by their normative theological commitments. The approaches of psychology, anthropology, sociology, and literary symbolism are much more nearly scientific and far removed from the task of practical theological thinking. But even with them, we can almost always detect some mild normative commitments lurking in the nooks and crannies of these perspectives. But the multidisciplinary approaches are most nearly a mixed breed, blending scientific analysis with practical and normative recommendations for action. To this extent, they are potential mediators between the more purely objective approaches and the theological perspectives. They approach, although fall short of, genuine practical theological thinking. Because of their mediating position, they receive special attention in Figure 14.1.

They help illustrate the strengths and potential hazards of the church consultant specialist.

Figure 14.1 Levels of Practical Theological Thinking

Interpretative Perspectives on Each Level	*Empirical Approaches (Latent or Manifest)*	*Organization development and planning as interventional*	*Theological*
1. The metaphorical	Anthropological Literary symbolism		Systematic Theology
2. The obligational	Anthropological Literary symbolism		Formal theological ethics
		Organization development and planning	
3. The need-tendency	Psychological		Practical theology
4. The contextual-predictive	Sociological		Practical theology
5. The rule-role-communication	Organization development and planning as descriptive		Practical theology

Relatively scientific ⟶ Relatively theological

NOTE: Solid-line arrows indicate the level at which a particular social science or theological discipline tends to specialize; dotted-line arrows show lines of relevance.

Practical theology, in our time, must be philosophical and critical. Practical theology, like all theology, starts in faith, but to live and communicate in the pluralistic world in which we live, it must be a faith seeking reasons and a faith determined to articulate itself before both believing and nonbelieving publics. Especially must practical theology be seen as philosophical if it is to help us integrate the diverse and sometimes conflicting interpretative perspectives used to study this church. The very fact that we as theologically-minded people are interested in what anthropology, sociology, and psychology have to tell us about the church indicates already that we are in the kind of dialogue that requires mediation by a reflective and philosophical mood.

We return to Wiltshire and the approaches later in this chapter. But let us now look at what practical theology is. Three generalizations can be made about it: (1) practical theology tries to answer the question of what we should do in the face of problems and challenges to faithful action, (2) it consists of several different levels, and (3) it is correlational and critical.[1]

Practical theology is practical because it deals with practice or action and the problems of practice and action. It is one of the three great branches of theology: fundamental or philosophical theology, systematic theology, and practical theology. It is the branch of theology toward which fundamental and systematic theology point; it is their *telos,* for, finally, we seek the truth of fundamental theology and the meaning of systematic theology in order to know how to live and act faithfully, which is the major concern of practical theology.

There are five analytically distinct levels to practical theological thinking. Failure to do work at all these levels, especially the lower ones, keeps our theology abstract and opens it to the charge of irrelevance. Practical theology contains (1) a metaphorical level, (2) an obligational level, (3) a tendency-need level, (4) a contextual-predictive level, and (5) a rule-role-communicational level. Our going academic theologies tend to specialize at one or more levels and ignore others. For instance, our philosophical or fundamental theologies preoccupy themselves with the first level, that is, the question of the truth of our Christian metaphors of ultimacy. Systematic theology concerns itself primarily with the meaning of these metaphors. Contemporary theological ethics concerns itself very much with level two, that is, the implications of our faith for our obligations. And it debates the various ways our Christian theories of obligation are related to our Christian metaphors of ultimacy. All of these theologies—philosophical, systematic, ethical—generally fail to carry their inquiries to the lower levels, that

[1]The tradition of practical theology I am advocating is associated with the names of Daniel Day Williams, Seward Hiltner, and David Tracy. It is a revised correlational perspective in contrast to a Tillichian correlational method. The following are examples of the literature of this tradition. Daniel Day Williams, "Truth in a Theological Perspective," *Journal of Religion* 28, no. 4 (October 1948), and *The Minister and the Care of Souls* (New York: Harpers, 1961); Seward Hiltner, *Preface to Pastoral Theology* (New York: Abingdon Press, 1958); David Tracy, *The Blessed Rage for Order* (New York: Seabury Press, 1975), and *The Analogical Imagination* (New York: Crossroad, 1981). As an example of my own position on this matter, see my "Pastoral Theology in a Pluralistic Age," *Pastoral Psychology* 29, no. 1 (Fall 1980), pp. 24–35.

is, the tendency-need, the contextual-predictive, and the rule-role-communicational levels. If they were to attend to all five levels, they would become genuinely practical theologies. In turn, practical theologies cannot afford to ignore the higher levels, the metaphorical and the obligational. But practical theologies are practical simply because they move further and make statements at the lower three levels. And finally, the lower levels are lower not because they are less important; they are lower only because they depend on certain judgments at the higher levels for their proper positioning. But indeed, some relatively independent judgments are made at the lower levels that complete and give practical meaning to the higher levels of metaphor and obligation.

This framework is not only a guide to thinking practically about theological concerns, it also can be used as a hermeneutical tool to study religious phenomena in general and religious groups in particular. Indeed, I will use it to organize the various interpretative perspectives found in this book. When these approaches are seen in the light of this framework, they emerge as not so much in conflict but as specializing in different aspects of the total structure of religious action. To this extent, they are incomplete yet potentially complementary to one another. But in studying the actual practical theological thinking of real communities, it is important to make a distinction between manifest and latent levels of thinking and action. This opens up the questions: what does the community manifestly say they think and do, and what does the community latently and actually think and do? Many of the differences, and potential contributions, of the various approaches come precisely at the point of providing answers to these questions.

The Metaphorical Level

Not just practical theological thinking, but all practical thinking, has a metaphorical level. By this I mean that all practical thinking necessarily has some way, which is invariably metaphorical, of representing the ultimate context of our experience. To represent anything metaphorically, we do so by taking an aspect of experience with which we are familiar and applying it analogically to aspects of experience that are more foreign or intangible.

In Christian theology we use the metaphors of creator, governor, and redeemer to represent our awareness of the ultimate context of experience as a God who is good, morally serious, and renewing.[2] Other types of practical thinking use other metaphors, such as those of natural harmony to be found in classical capitalism and humanistic psychology, the metaphors of *eros* and *thanatos* that one finds in Freud's psychology, the metaphors of mechanism that one finds behind various forms of behaviorisms, or the metaphors of free variation and selection that one finds in the background of psychologies of adaptation like the one used by Malony in this volume. These metaphors help us see the world in particular ways. They orient us to the world and lead us to see it as trustworthy or capricious, warm or cold, morally serious or indifferent. However, these metaphors of ultimacy influence, but do not dictate, the content of lower levels of practical thinking and experience. And the task of assessing the adequacy of these various metaphors of ultimacy is a correlational philosophical task, which I cannot elaborate in this chapter.

Many of the approaches reviewed in this volume concentrate their analysis at the metaphorical level. Certainly the theological positions of Hough and Pacini do this. They are concerned in their chapters to both uncover the latent and manifest theological metaphors that guide Wiltshire and then measure them against their own understanding of the normative metaphors of the Christian life. Certainly Hopewell's approach through symbolism is concerned with this level. Hopewell's characterization of Wiltshire Church as exemplifying certain aspects of the myth of Zeus is a highly suggestive approach to getting at the latent, if not unconscious, metaphors of ultimacy that operate in the congregation. But other approaches are also interested in uncovering the operative metaphorical level of Wiltshire. For instance, the section of the sociological chapter on the "social world" analyzes the God of Wiltshire Church as one who supports its members' Protestant work ethic and privatism, but the analysis sees this primarily as a function of their membership in the upwardly mobile managerial middle class. Evans and Reed in their psychological analysis also

[2] H. R. Niebuhr, *The Responsible Self* (New York: Harper & Row, 1963).

throw light on Wiltshire's metaphors of ultimacy. They speak about Wiltshire living in a universe of "expectancy" but see this primarily as a function of the church reacting to its circumstances with a particular psychological adaptive strategy, one that now may be breaking down.

The Obligational Level

The obligational level of practical theological thinking is frequently closely related to, but nonetheless analytically distinguishable from, the metaphorical level. The obligational level tells us what it is appropriate to believe and feel about what we should do. Our ultimate metaphors influence, but do not strictly determine, our principles of obligation.[3] For instance we may use the metaphor "love" to refer to God's nature, but we do not know for certain what God's love means in terms of what we should do unless we add a more propositional statement such as "you should be perfect as God," or you should "love your neighbor as yourself" (Matt. 22:4). And even then, we might not be clear about what we are obligated to do unless we go further in interpreting just what the Second Great Commandment means. And then we see that some of our contemporary theologians go toward more utilitarian and situational interpretations, such as Fletcher, and others toward more Kantian and deontological perspectives, such as Outka, Ramsey, and others.[4]

Pacini makes a major point about the relation of the metaphorical to the obligational levels of theological thinking. For the meta-

---

[3] For an excellent discussion of the relation of religion and morality (what I have called the relation of the metaphorical to the obligational levels), see Ernest Wallwork, "Morality, Religion, and Kohlberg's Theory," *Moral Development, Moral Education, and Kohlberg*, ed. Brenda Munsey (Birmingham: Religious Education Press, 1980), pp. 269–98. For excellent discussions of the nature of metaphor, see Ian Barbour, *Myths, Models, and Paradigms* (New York: Harper & Row, 1974), and George Lakoff and Mark Johnson, *Metaphors We Live By* (Chicago: University of Chicago Press, 1980).

[4] Joseph Fletcher, *Situation Ethics* (Philadelphia: Westminister Press, 1966); Gene Outka, *Agape: An Ethical Analysis* (New Haven, Conn.: Yale University Press, 1972); Paul Ramsey, *Basic Christian Ethics* (New York: Scribner, 1950). For an excellent introductory discussion of various theories of obligation, see William Frankena, *Ethics* (Englewood Cliffs, N.J.: Prentice-Hall, 1973), pp. 12–61.

phorical level he also uses the phrase "world view." Along with my term "obligational," he uses the word "legitimation." With this distinction, he makes a major, and very useful, analytical point that will go far in helping us see some of the crucial differences between the various approaches. Following Habermas, he states that it is a signal characteristic of modern societies that they try to answer the question of legitimate action (or what I would call obligatory action) without reference at all to world view (what I would call the metaphorical level). According to this view, legitimation and obligation is determined totally by free and undistorted communication, a view that may be implicit in the strong emphasis on communication in the organization development positions, especially that of Malony. Pacini experiments with looking at the Wiltshire situation from this modern perspective as primarily a breakdown in communication but believes that this explanation alone is not adequate. Pacini believes that the problem of the church, and the problem of Sid Carlson, its minister, is not primarily a matter of bad communication about whether to build new rooms for the church school and whether to help Sid buy a new house. The breakdown really has to do, according to Pacini, with the breakdown of Sid's world view and metaphors of ultimacy—his theology that God and Sid are together in control of history, assuring that both church and the corporation will grow, that the hardworking and self-reliant will be comforted in time of stress, that they finally will be victorious, and that all of this can happen with only cursory interest in the needs of those outside their church and community.

Pacini's chapter is an interesting example of my point that although our metaphors of ultimacy influence our obligations and legitimations, they do not determine them in all respects. For we finally do not find any principles of obligation or legitimation in Pacini's presentation. Nor would Wiltshire Church learn from Pacini such a principle. Neither they nor we will find in his analysis an answer to the question of what should be done or what, in fact, is the permissible range of actions. Pacini wants to replace the controlling and objectifying God of Sid Carlson's theology—the God who removes risks but who also removes responsibility—with a less controlling God, one who persuades, develops partnerships with humans, gives heuristic guidance, but who does not dictate our actions. But Pacini does not tell us what his metaphor might mean, even heuristically, for our actions, our obligations, and that which we might want to legitimate. Pacini goes far in telling us what the problem is but addresses the solution at only the most abstract, albeit fundamental, level.

Hough, like Pacini, attempts to show an intimate relation between our world views (or metaphors of ultimacy) and our obligations but goes further than Pacini in actually developing a principle of obligation. It is through the metaphor of the church as the "body of Christ" that Hough determines both the nature of God and our obligations to our fellow humans. The body of Christ is a metaphor representing the reality of God's presence with us. This presence affirms creation and reveals God's redemptive work for its fulfillment. The metaphor of the body of Christ also reveals for Hough our radical obligation to be with and for the poor and the whole of the natural world. Wiltshire's moralistic, comforting, and success-oriented theology is seen as inadequate from this perspective.

In articulating this principle of obligation, Hough goes further than Pacini toward a truly helpful practical theology, a theology that might really assist Wiltshire to assess its situation. Pacini is interested in getting Wiltshire Church to relinquish control and open itself to real risk and the true grace of God, but he does not give us a more general principle of obligation to guide our actions. Hough does this in his admonition to identify with the poor and to work for the ecological integrity of the world. But even here, a moral philosopher would be quick to tell us just how ambiguous principles like "being with the poor" really are. Does it mean giving directly to the poor, or taking from the rich and giving to the poor? Does it mean the greatest good for the largest number of people, the poor included, as utilitarian definitions of love would suggest? Does it mean acting toward the poor on principles that we could will to be universal laws, as Kantian definitions of love suggest? And does being with the poor mean meeting their needs, and if so, what are their needs?

Pacini and Hough give highly suggestive, but limited, positions on the first two levels of practical theological thinking. They constitute suggestive perspectives from which Wiltshire Church could gain critical understanding of its own preferred metaphors and principles of obligation. Hough and Pacini make crucial but not exhaustive contributions to addressing the problems of Wiltshire Church. They say little if anything about the lower three levels of practical theological thinking. They do acknowledge the impact of the social context—Wiltshire's isolation, its upwardly mobile families, its corporation orientation—but they say little about levels three and five, the tendency-need level and the rule-role-communicational level. What are the real needs of the Wiltshire people, and how do they affect what the church is obligated to do in its ministry? What are the needs of the poor? And finally, what are the effective roles and communication patterns in the church and the rules that cover them? It is doubtless Hough's and Pacini's hope that if Wiltshire gets the right theological metaphors and the right principles of obligation, the right specific roles, rules, and patterns of communication will follow immediately. But is that necessarily true? And what if there is continuing conflict over metaphors and general obligations, are there then more specific roles to be played and rules to be followed until consensus at the higher levels emerges? Clearly, it is at these lower, also crucial, levels that sociology, psychology, and organization development have important contributions to make. It is because of the theologian's lack of attention to these levels and because of the social scientist's expertise at these levels that the church has more and more turned to theoretical and practical specialists in these sciences of human behavior.

Of course, it helps any practical theological analysis of a church to know more about the actual manifest and latent theology (its metaphors of ultimacy and its principles of obligation). This is necessary to be more accurate in commenting on and closing the gap between the actual thought and action of the church and what it ideally should be. Here, as I have already indicated, the social science approaches of anthropology, sociology, and psychology can make a distinct contribution. It is helpful to the practical theologian to know that the latent metaphors and beliefs of that church reflect the structure of the ancient myth of Zeus killing Chronus, overcoming time and tradition and establishing a new rule of efficiency and progress. This might be especially helpful to know the depth of these unconscious themes when planning certain interventions. But except for Hopewell's novel conviction about the mythological depths of the human psyche, his view of the actual theology of the church is analogous to that turned up by several other investigators. His view of the actual meanings operative in the church does not differ essentially from Evans and Reed's emotion of "expectancy" and sections of the sociological analysis that interpreted Wiltshire as privatized and work oriented or a refuge in support of upward mobility. All of these are highly similar pictures of the actual latent and manifest culture or world view of Wiltshire. They differ mainly in seeing this world view as a function of mythical structures (Hopewell), socially conditioned perceptual structures (Carroll/McKinney/Roof and Williams) or psychological responses to perceived threats (Evans and Reed). These anthropological, sociological, and psychological analyses throw light on the actual beliefs, values, and metaphors of ultimacy functioning in Wiltshire Church. But unless these investigators let their own values show forth, and frequently they do, they cannot and should not as scientists argue for what Wiltshire's ultimate commitments ought to be. The practical theologian should make use of their analyses. The knowledge they give us primarily helps make interventions more precise, but such knowledge should not and logically cannot dictate the actual content of our practical theological recommendations.

The Tendency-Need Level

Neither the theologians nor the social scientists say anything clearly systematic about the tendency-need level of practical moral thinking. Yet they all assume and imply a great number of things about this level. Much is said about the more or less culturally shaped needs of the Wiltshire people for success, for affiliation with like-minded people, for weekend rest and renewal, for educating their children, and so on. But little is said by any of these perspectives about the truly human needs of the people of Wiltshire Church. What are their legitimate needs? What are the legitimate needs of other people outside Wiltshire—the inner-city working poor, the working families of Detroit, the peasants of El Salvador? How do the people of Wiltshire Church adjudicate the conflicts between their needs and the needs of others?

Good practical theological thinking requires both theories of obligation and theories of what humans really need. This is true regardless of how a particular principle of obligation is derived.[5] We get our theories of human needs from a variety of sources. Intuitions of our own needs is one source. Our cultural and religious traditions deliver to us indices of human need, some quite authentic and some quite distorted. Finally, in the midst of conflicting claims about what humans need, we turn to the sciences of the human—psychology or sociobiology—to get some idea of our central tendencies or more fundamental needs.[6]

The language of needs is tricky, and we hear a lot of it, especially in the social sciences. But some felt needs are more important than others, and needs conflict with one another, both those internal to ourselves and those between ourselves and other people. That is why we turn to morality and to principles of obligation; we do this to organize, form hierarchies, and resolve conflicts between diverse human tendencies and needs. It is the view of several of these studies that Wiltshire Church has been successful to date in its growth because it has met a variety of needs experienced by the people in that community, some quite authentic needs but most culturally and socially induced by the class, vocation, and geographical location of the families of that community. In addition, it is the moral sensibility of many studies, and the explicit view of Hough, that the people of Wiltshire are meeting their needs unjustly, that is, at considerable cost to those outside their church and community.

But this level of discussion needs further clarification. The lan-

[5] It is commonly accepted in formal moral philosophy that teleological theories of obligation require theories of nonmoral good that in turn generally require theories of what humans want and need. But I take the position that deontological perspectives, even of the Kantian kind, must be supplemented with theories of generic human need once the logic of obligation has been established on logical and formal grounds. I believe this is the position held by John Rawls and his religious interpreter, Ronald Green. See Green's *Religious Reason* (New York: Oxford University Press, 1978).

[6] Three excellent discussions of the relation of nonmoral values or needs to ethics can be found in the following books: Mary Midgely, *Beast and Man* (Ithaca, N.Y.: Cornell University Press, 1978); George Pugh, *The Biological Origin of Human Values* (New York: Basic Books, 1977); and Peter Singer, *The Expanding Circle* (New York: Farrar, Strauss & Giroux, 1981).

guage of needs is everywhere, but seldom systematically discussed. For our purposes, let me distinguish between (1) basic human needs, (2) existential needs, (3) culturally induced needs, (4) technical needs, and (5) moral needs. Basic human needs are those largely biologically grounded needs that include everything from our need for food and clothing to our needs for affiliation and mutual recognition and even our need to care for and educate our children. Our existential needs center around anxiety and loss to our basic needs and are met by assurance, security, love, and presence, both of a finite and an ontological kind. Then we have more culturally induced needs and wants; these are frequently basic needs that take particular, and sometimes overdetermined, forms due to cultural conditioning. Most of our interpreters saw a great deal of cultural conditioning of basic needs among the Wiltshire people. Technical needs refer to our needs to instrumentally organize our resources to satisfy our basic needs. And finally, moral needs refer to the characterological and obligational requirements necessary to mediate justly the conflicts between our basic, existential, technical, and cultural needs. We have moral needs because we need ways to coordinate harmoniously the conflict among all our other needs. Even though ethics and morality are of crucial importance for human life, they are fed by weaker energies than any of our other needs, be they basic existential, cultural, or technical.

Wiltshire Church has specialized its ministry toward meeting existential and culturally induced needs of people within their own congregation. Most basic needs for nourishment and so on are assumed to be met by the general affluence of the community. Other basic needs for affiliation, recognition, and the education of their children are met within the framework of the cultural values of upward mobility, success, and privatism. Existential needs surrounding loss and stress are addressed. The love of God is affirmed. The pastor helps those undergoing stress, grief, or illness. Practical wisdom for handling challenge and loss is offered. But moral needs are largely ignored by the church, and a moral review of how the Wiltshire people meet their basic, technical, and culturally induced needs is also largely overlooked.

But neither the social science analyses offered here by anthropology, psychology, or sociology nor the theological analyses, as far as they go, help to distinguish between the authentic and inauthentic needs being addressed in the Wiltshire situation. This is because of, on the one hand, the aspired-for neutrality of the social sciences and, on the other, the theologian's omission of this necessary level of practical theological thinking. The people of Wiltshire Church need to know how to distinguish their authentic needs from those that are culturally induced or distorted. They need reliable images of their authentic needs to guide their own principles of obligation: which needs are they morally obligated to justly and fairly help actualize, both in themselves and in others outside their community? And, in turn, they need principles of obligation to help them coordinate and adjudicate between conflicting authentic needs, both within their own community and between their community and the rest of the world. For instance, it may well be that even if Wiltshire Church were to forsake its more superficial needs to grow and to support success, it might still conclude that it does have an obligation to meet the basic, existential, and moral needs of the community's children and that, in order to do this, it should expand its facilities. It also might conclude that it has an obligation to meet the basic and existential needs of its pastor through adequate income, housing, and retirement. Because of the immense untapped financial resources of that congregation, one would think that it could simultaneously expand its educational facilities, take care of its minister, and expand its outreach to those outside its own immediate community. But in order to do this, the church must be motivated by commanding vision, a clearer understanding of its own social situation, and better communication between the different role players and actors in the congregation itself. In other words, it needs insight into several other levels of practical theological thought and action.

The Contextual Level

We already have examined to a considerable extent the cultural and social context of Wilshire Church and the way this context establishes certain trends that shape its world view, values, perceptions, and expectations. In fact, much of what is done by Williams, Carroll/McKinney/Roof, and Evans/Reed is to show how the sociological situation of Wiltshire works to condition and shape the dominant metaphors and world views operative in that community.

There are two strictly social-structural ideas that might be usefully highlighted here. The sociological chapter emphasizes the extremely wide gap between home and work that exists in the Wiltshire community. This is typical of many suburban communities, but especially true of Wiltshire because of its physical isolation between two ridges. The second is the structural fact of the influence of corporate life and its accompanying features of bureaucratization and rationalization. In both the structural differentiation between public and private realms (work and home) and in the bureaucratization that marks corporate life, we find dominant characteristics of modern life. Both features of modernity tend to specialize and narrow our lives and make responsible individual or collective action in the public realm all the more difficult for everyone. It has been well known in sociological literature for decades, going back to, and even before, Gibson Winter's *The Suburban Captivity of the Church,*[7] that the church itself has been caught to a considerable degree in these two sets of social forces. This, then, is the major sociological context of the church in advanced industrial countries. Recognizing this has helped give rise to another truth: if the church is to get beyond these privatizing forces and once again address the whole of life, it must develop a higher degree of intentionality than was needed in simpler, more organic societies. It is against the background of this need for heightened intentionality that the substance of level five becomes so important for the modern church. It is against the backdrop of the pluralism and relative isolation of the modern church that there is required more intentional communication, more faithful roles, and more flexible rules.

Roles, Rules, and Communication

This is the level of analysis attended to most by Schaller, Malony, and Anderson, and the final section of the chapter on sociol-

[7] (New York: Macmillan, 1965).

ogy. Although the consultants also attend to the higher levels, they concentrate on the various roles functioning in a given congregation, the rules that govern these roles, and the communication that occurs as roles and rules support goals. This is an absolutely essential level of analysis required to complete the practical theological process. Of course, this level does not stand by itself; we only know what roles, rules, and specific processes of communication must be after we have received our metaphors of ultimacy, determined our principles of obligation, decided which human needs are most deserving of fulfillment, and analyzed our sociocultural context. Nonetheless, our roles, rules, and communication do have some degree of autonomy from these higher areas; there indeed can be subtle confusion about role expectations and subtle distortions of communication even when our higher-level metaphors and moral principles are sound and well understood.

But to study roles and communication patterns too much in isolation from the other levels of practical theology can lead to misunderstanding. Anderson is quite aware of this danger and cautions us against trying to study roles and communication without reference to the higher-level metaphors and obligations that necessarily form the context and content of our ethical decisions.

Schaller, Malony, and Anderson take the stance of consultants conducting studies for the sake of making practical recommendations. To this extent, in ways not typical of the other perspectives, they approach being much more nearly "mixed" thinkers who bring together scientific and practical judgments in ways that begin to merge into practical theological thinking. Malony's chapter is instructive, however, because although genuinely practical, it is isolated from systematic consideration of the metaphorical, obligational, need, and contextual levels. To this extent, his more or less exclusive emphasis upon the clarification of role priorities and the improvement of communication style comes close to exemplifying Habermas's and Pacini's claims about the tendency toward independence of communicative competence from world view in modern societies as a method for establishing legitimation. To Malony, the major problem at Wiltshire Church is not in its metaphors of ultimacy, as it is for Pacini and Hough; it is not in its privatization and its bondage to upper-middle-class values as one might think after reading the sociological analysis. The problem, or at least the only one that he discusses, is that of level five, the level of role conflict and communication problems.

Since Malony is a practicing Christian, he simply assumes the general validity of the faith commitments of the church he studies and advises. But in his chapter he does not tell us how his communication and role analysis approach actually takes account of the higher-level metaphors and principles of obligation that make up the faith of a church. Without more explicit attention to these higher levels, an exclusive attention to roles and communication patterns can take on a marketing orientation. By using a marketing orientation, the consultant conveys the idea that he can market or sell, through the power of better communication and more flexible role enactment, any set of ultimate commitments and moral principles subscribed to by a particular organization. This would be using a technicist approach to consultation. It will work only insofar as the problems of a congregation are totally technical and its larger theological commitments completely sound. This is seldom the case, and if other analyses of Wiltshire Church are reasonably correct, it is not the case with this congregation either. Wiltshire needs consultation at the theological level, although it needs, as Malony rightly sees, consultation at the level of the roles and rules of communication as well.

Schaller, on the other hand, is eclectic in his approach to consultation and works on all of these levels. His preference for internal analyses in contrast to contextual analyses, although not entirely clear, probably puts him closer to Malony's concern with styles of leadership and communication than it does to the sociological perspectives of Carroll/McKinney/Roof. But in spite of his eclecticism, he gives little attention to practical theological thinking at the higher metaphorical or obligational levels. One gains the impression that even though he is eclectic and flexible in choosing his points of entry to a congregation, he too primarily addresses the role-rule-communicational level somewhat in isolation from the higher levels of metaphor and obligation.

The point is that both analysis and consultation need to operate on all of these levels. Theology often seems to fail us in our practical analysis and action because it frequently limits itself, as do

Hough and Pacini, to the highest level of practical theological thinking—the metaphorical—and says little, if anything, about the other four levels. Formal theology seldom actually gets to the level of helping us discern what our metaphors, principles of obligation, needs, and context analyses actually mean for the concrete roles and communicative patterns that life in our congregations demands. Social sciences can help us understand our operative ultimate commitments and, in this way, help us discern the gap between the ideal and actual in the life of congregations. They can help discern the sociological and psychological forces that condition, although do not determine, our ultimate beliefs and the actions that do or do not flow from them. And finally, the communications consultant can help us understand the actual role, rules, and patterns of communication operative in particular congregations. But our analysis will be distorted and our recommendations unbalanced if we do not address, some way or other, both normatively and analytically, all these necessary levels of practical Christian life and thought.[8]

---

[8] For a fuller explanation of these five levels, see my "The Estrangement of Pastoral Care from Ethics," *Concilium* (Summer 1982), and *Religious Ethics and Pastoral Care* (Philadelphia: Fortress Press, 1983).

15. Focus on the Congregation: A Look to the Future

BARBARA G. WHEELER

More than once in the preceding pages, different methods for studying the congregation are referred to as "lenses" through which the local church may be viewed. The word evokes an image for this book: a studio full of photographers, with a live model, the congregation, at the center. Each photographer has portrayed the model using a lens that refracts a distinctive way of perceiving congregational life. The reader has had an opportunity to circumambulate the studio examining the model through the various lenses, each with its different angle of vision, magnification, and points of sharp focus and emphasis.

From this tour a rich, variegated picture of the congregation emerges. The sociologists have shown that there is a two-way movement, full of tension and promise, as the congregation is acted upon by forces in its environment and at the same time moves outward to affect and change its setting. The ethnographic contributors picture the congregation both as a stage for an intense, symbological drama and a unit of culture in which invisible but deep structural forces hold sway. The theologians portray a struggle, never resolved, between the congregation's best theological self-understanding (sometimes adopted from tradition and sometimes strikingly original) and its unthinking daily practice. Other contributors suggest characteristic ways organizations and their leaders behave, and show how an awareness of these patterns can give congregations a new freedom: either to work with, or to resist, the dynamics of organizational life and the forces of personality.

Viewed in these different ways, the congregation looks fuller, more complex, and more varied than it is often perceived in daily experience. The array of methods used to study congregations has broadened in recent years, as this volume testifies. Yet even this composite view does not include many important modes of study and analysis. Aesthetic studies, for instance, could illuminate the meaning of movement, physical space, light, images, color, and sound in the lives of congregations. Historical studies are called for, to show the ways that many of the phenomena of present-day church life are rooted in a dimly remembered past. Congregational studies would also be strengthened by close economic analyses and by studies that focus specifically on social class as it shapes congregational life. Women have been notably absent from the company of congregational researchers. Since women are the majority population of most congregations and continue to encounter obstacles as they seek lay and ordained leadership roles, they have a unique perspective that congregational studies sorely needs. Ecumenical breadth is required as well. Roman Catholic and Jewish researchers and theologians have conducted studies in recent years of congregations in those faith traditions that should be included in any future collection of this kind. In short, both the cast of persons engaged in coordinated efforts in congregational studies and the range of methods employed could profitably be expanded.

The issue of the inclusiveness and range of congregational studies is important but even more important for the future is the question of the use of congregational studies. Of what practical utility are careful research studies and lengthy reflections by consultants, the kinds of chapters gathered into this book? What difference does it make to collect and compare such studies in order to present a richly textured portrait of a single congregation? At the deepest level, how is the faith and witness of the whole church strengthened and renewed by the kind of intense and prolonged attention that these authors have paid to Wiltshire Church?

Some answers to these questions may be found in both what this book achieves and what it does not. Taken together, the chapters show that a local congregation may be viewed in a variety of ways, that some methods of study reveal what others conceal, and that a multiplicity of perspectives gives dimensions to an understanding of congregational life that a single method of study could never offer. The authors succeed in demonstrating that congregations have facets and layers, and that in and among them lie richer resources than most of us expect to find. But just as significant is what these studies do not accomplish. Despite the fact that Wiltshire Church was subjected to scrutiny by over a dozen scholars and consultants, the authors have not succeeded in fully accounting for the church. It was not explainable simply as the product of social, cultural, historical, organizational, or religious forces. No one of the methods alone nor all of them together could "solve" the enigmas of Wiltshire. Nor do they manage to divide congregational life into neat territories, each the province of one of the methods of analysis. Stubbornly, the story of this congregation holds together, unfolding in response to an unprecedented battery of investigatory approaches trained on the case of a single congregation, but never allowing itself to be reduced to simply a social phenomenon, cultural artifact, organizational example, or theological idea.

Different contributors to this volume would suggest different reasons for the sturdy integrity of Wiltshire and of other congregations they have studied closely. Some hold views of the church that ascribe to the congregation a central or even unique role as the locus of ministry and mission. The depth, richness, and wholeness of congregational life, they would argue, is a sign of God's presence. Others would offer a more naturalistic explanation. The congregation is a social institution with unusual characteristics, such as the age range of its members and the fact that major life passages are marked and celebrated there. Thus its powerful quality can be attributed to its complexity as a social and cultural institution. Whichever view is taken, there would be agreement in our group both that the congregation is an extraordinarily fruitful focus for studies of church life and that it has an identity not fully defined or encompassed by the methods of study applied to it, whether singly or in combination.

These two lessons from congregational studies, that the congregation is an abundantly fruitful focus for study and at the same time durable, not easily reduced or explained away, suggest where the significance and promise of congregational studies may lie. The integrity of the congregation, its fullness and wholeness, contrasts strikingly with many of our experiences elsewhere in church life. Much of the literature about the state of the church suggests the opposite: it is rife with divisions—between liberals and conservatives, local churches and denominational offices, and seminaries and church bodies, and among denominations. Its spiritual life, social witness, and theological reflection are criticized for their aridity, rootlessness, and poverty of images. Congregational studies cannot by themselves heal divisions and lend vitality in troubled areas of church life. But they may provide new grounds for conversation among separated or discouraged parties. The study of the congregation might help to restate the issues and improve the quality of discourse in several areas.

First and most critically, congregational studies can help free congregations from their own frequently superficial self-understanding. Both the source of a congregation's unity and power and its resources for outreach and mission are all too often buried under a caricature of itself that it harbors. A symbol or image or explanation of "why this church is the way it is" is chosen because it initially is truthful and powerful. But then the chosen symbol or explanation becomes an emblem, and evidence that contradicts it is excluded, so it becomes empty and finally deceptive. Wiltshire, for example, has reached an easy consensus that its identity is tied to the image of "the best show in town." Yet the studies in this book show that there are other and more meaningful images that bind the congregation together. The freedom to take steps in other directions, the freedom *not* to be the best show, depends on discovering those other images and the relationships and hopes that are also reliably binding forces.

Here congregational studies can help. Of course it is not possible to assemble a multidisciplinary team of scholars under most circumstances. Nor, in most cases, is even a single full-scale research study a possibility. But pastors and lay leaders *can* learn, using more formal studies as examples and guides, to take a careful look at the life and work of their own congregations. Many also have the resources to hire consultants to help in the process of self-study. Whether on their own or with consultants' help, however, two elements are critical. There must be some disciplined research; merely rehashing the ideas, images, and explanations that come readily to hand and mind is *not* congregational study.

And, if the lesson of this larger effort that this book represents is to be taken seriously, the self-study should include multiple methods of investigation, because it is in the clash and complementarity of different "ways of seeing" that both the stubborn power and meaningful richness of congregational life come to light, as well as the deceptiveness of too-easy answers.

A second mission for congregational studies may be to promote understanding between local churches and church executives. Resentments on both sides run deep in this arena. Clergy and laity in local churches tend to view regional, and especially national, staff as privileged idealists, free to take positions on controversial issues without reference to local opinion or political consequences. From the local perspective, executives can also appear self-righteous, judgmental, and even condescending toward the realities of local church life. On their side, executive staff may view local congregations as more concerned for their own comfort and identity than for the larger mission of the church and too often captive to the values that are embedded in the socio-economic location of their members. Congregational studies reveal a much more mixed and complicated image of the congregation than is usually considered on either side of the division between local churches and denominational (or ecumenical) executives. They show how difficult are the distinctions and how permeable the membranes between congregation and community, internal and external concerns, ministry to members and outreach mission, community self-preservation and self-sacrifice—all the classic dichotomies involved in the debate as it is usually carried on. Like leaders of congregations, executives do not have the resources to engage in much formal research themselves. The executives who most frequently work directly with congregations, those in districts, presbyteries, dioceses, and the like, can spend very little time in any one setting. But they can build methods from congregational studies into their pattern of work. They can discipline themselves to ask questions and gather information designed to reveal the pluriform character of the congregations they assist. They can learn to apprehend and take seriously both a congregation's story and its statistics, both its organizational structure and its theological convictions. Proceeding this way, congregations will appear more complex, more "rich and strange," as Shakespeare wrote, and much less easy to stereotype. If church officials who have deepened and expanded their understanding of congregations are joined by congregations who have worked to enrich their self-understanding, the conversations between the two parties are almost certain to improve.

A third arena in which the focus on the congregation may promote understanding is that of the difficult relationship between seminaries and churches. "The great divide" was how one recent magazine article characterized relations between seminaries on the one hand and both local churches and denominational agencies on the other. The critics of seminaries, many of them their own graduates, accuse seminaries of preoccupation with recondite scholarly subject matter and neglect of subjects and issues that pertain to the practice of ministry and the conduct of church life. Seminary faculty have been less openly critical of churches than clergy and laity have been of seminaries, but faculty have held up their side of the estrangement with the conviction that their critics are essentially anti-intellectual and hostile to the scholar's ministry of critical inquiry.

The study of the congregation may help in several ways to create a climate for constructive discussions. Seminary faculty who use the tools of their disciplines to study with local congregations will demonstrate that they take it seriously. Such demonstrations may help to repair the seminary's tattered public relations image with churches and address an even deeper problem: the difficulty that many church people have conceiving of seminaries as important expressions of the church. Even the usual way of naming the problem—"the tensions between seminaries and churches"—suggests how widespread is the notion of the seminary as something-other-than-the-church. Faculty research on the congregation cannot correct this view by itself, but it can create some healthy confusion among those on both sides who believe that scholars and church leaders have such different interests and values that they can never share a common object of study and concern.

The focus on the congregation also holds promise for current efforts to reconceive theological curriculum. Lately some seminary educators have joined church critics in calls for curriculum reform. One of the contributors to this book who teaches in a seminary has written elsewhere[1] about the curiously disembodied quality of much seminary education, about its prudish preference for ecclesiological abstraction over what Clifford Geertz has called "bodied stuff,"[2] in this case, the data of congregational life. Others, such as Edward Farley,[3] have charged that the present organization of the curriculum corresponds to a long-vanished ecclesial reality. The study of the congregation is one response to both these critiques, since it can provide insights about the church's living body significant for both the form and the content of seminary education. If the congregation is in fact a rich expression of the church in which many elements cohere, then perhaps the study of it from a variety of perspectives can serve to re-orient, re-organize and unify what Farley has called the "dispersed disciplines" of theological study.

One can cite other examples of the potential of congregational studies to draw together parties divided on religious issues. *Since congregations are an ecclesiastical form common to all Judeo-Christian faith groups, congregational studies may have a role in ecumenical dialogue.* Comparative studies of congregations in different faith traditions are one way that abstract ideas about religious differences and points of commonality can be tested. In a similar way, congregational studies may promote deeper understanding *within* faith communities divided along theological or ideological lines. As we have noted earlier, the life of actual congregations studied in any depth has a density and variety that confounds the usual partisan dividing lines. Congregations *do* differ from each other in dramatic ways, but rarely are the deepest differences explained to the extent one would expect by denomination, theological position, or political outlook.

In recent years Protestant attitudes toward congregations have changed. Twenty years ago many of those who cared intensely for the mission of the church had given up on the congregation, re-

---

[1] James Hopewell, "Examining the Body," in *Ministry and Mission* 3 and 4 (1981–82).

[2] Clifford Geertz, *The Interpretation of Cultures* (New York: Basic Books, 1973), p. 23.

[3] Edward Farley, *Theological Education* 12, no. 2 (1981).

garding it as fatally committed to its own institutional survival and the preservation of the class and cultural interests of its members. Today most denominational energy is invested in building congregations. The present concern for the physical fitness of the congregation takes different forms. In evangelical and conservative churches the emphasis is on growth in size, especially in membership. More liberal communions tend to focus on effectiveness and organizational strength. But the presuppositions are similar. The congregation is an essentially healthy form of church life. What is required is more of it (church growth) or more effective use of its resources (church management).

Readers with experience of congregational leadership will find neither of these recent views true to their experience; the essays of this book suggest different conclusions as well. The congregation is not bankrupt or irredeemably self-absorbed. Neither is it naturally healthy. The congregation is not automatically either damned or saved simply by being the congregation. Rather, it is a powerful mixture of elements, containing in its culture, tradition, structures, and practices the seeds of its own and the world's undoing or salvation.

This book is an argument for the value of serious analysis of various elements in congregational life. Even more important, it demonstrates the difficulty of isolating or finally defining the limits of those elements. Congregational studies will make significant contributions to the life of local churches and to the healing of deep divisions in the whole church *only* if future studies reflect the integrity and richness found in congregations themselves. There are many methods of analysis, many perceptual lenses, many interpretive conclusions, many members, but "the body is one."

Understanding and Activating Congregations: A Bibliography

CARL S. DUDLEY and JAMES F. HOPEWELL

From a wide assortment of books that have implications for the congregation, we have chosen for this Bibliography those volumes that take the local church as a primary frame of reference. Books on pastoral care by clergy, the work of the laity, or the general purpose of the church in the world were not included unless a major section of their content focused clearly on the life and work of the local congregation. A few unique books were included because they have been widely used to interpret some phase of congregational life, although they were originally written with a larger field in view, for example, H. Richard Niebuhr's *Christ and Culture,* which provides a typology often applied to congregations.

There are three major divisions: Missional Studies, including works that advocate change in the world through the agency of the church, which itself must be changed as a more effective instrument of mission; Studies of Church Functions, works that accept the congregation as basically sound but urge that congregations improve in a particular area of congregational activity; Descriptive Research, reports on the conditions of religiousness within the congregation or the correlations between the congregation and its social context. Each area has several subdivisions. We have made sometimes difficult decisions to place books in a single category although many have implications in several.

MISSIONAL STUDIES

1. Change the Church to Change the World

Berger, Peter. *The Noise of Solemn Assemblies: Christian Commitment and the Religious Establishment in America.* Garden City, N.Y.: Doubleday, 1961.

Berton, Pierre. *The Comfortable Pew: A Critical Look at Christianity and the Religious Establishment in the New Age.* Philadelphia: Lippincott, 1965.

Bordelon, Marvin. *The Parish in a Time of Change.* Notre Dame, Ind.: Fides Publishers, 1967.

Clark, M. Edward, et al. *The Church Creative.* Nashville: Abingdon Press, 1967.

Hadden, Jeffrey K., and Longino, Charles F., Jr. *Gideon's Gang.* New York: Pilgrim Press, 1974.

Hoekendijk, Johannes. *The Church Inside Out.* Philadelphia: Westminster Press, 1966.

Jud, Gerald John. *Pilgrim's Process: How the Local Church Can Respond to the New Age.* Philadelphia: United Church Press, 1967.

Lecky, Robert, and Wright, H. Ellicott. *Can These Bones Live? The Failure of Church Renewal.* New York: Sheed & Ward, 1969.

Neve, Herbert. *Sources for Change: Searching for Flexible Church Structures.* Geneva: World Council of Churches, 1968.

Raines, Robert. *Reshaping the Christian Life.* New York: Harper & Row, 1964.

———. *The Secular Congregation.* New York: Harper & Row, 1968.

Reitz, Rudiger. *The Church in Experiment.* Nashville: Abingdon Press, 1969.

Rose, Stephen. *The Grass Roots Church: A Manifesto for Protestant Renewal.* New York: Holt, Rinehart & Winston, 1966.

Webber, George. *The Congregation in Mission.* New York: Abingdon Press, 1964.

———. *God's Colony in Man's World.* New York: Abingdon Press, 1960.

———. *Today's Church: A Community of Exiles and Pilgrims.* Nashville: Abingdon Press, 1979.

Wieser, Thomas. *Planning for Mission: Working Papers on the New Quest for Missionary Communities.* New York: United States Conference for the World Council of Churches, 1966.

Williams, Colin. *What in the World?* New York: Office of Publishing and Distribution of the National Council of Churches of Christ in the U.S.A., 1964.

———. *Where in the World?* New York: Office of Publishing and Distribution of the National Council of Churches of Christ in the U.S.A., 1963.

Winter, Gibson. *The Suburban Captivity of the Churches.* Garden City, N.Y.: Doubleday, 1961.

World Council of Churches, Department on Studies in Evangelism. Western European Working Group. *The Church for Others and the*

Church for the World. Geneva: The World Council of Churches, 1967.

2. Work with the World As It Is

Bailey, Wilford, and McElvaney, William. *Christ's Suburban Body.* Nashville: Abingdon Press, 1970.

Carroll, Jackson W. *Small Churches Are Beautiful.* San Francisco: Harper & Row, 1977.

Davis, James, and White, Woodie. *Church in the Changing Community.* Nashville: Abingdon Press, 1981.

Desportes, Elisha L. *Congregations in Change.* New York: Seabury Press, 1973.

Frenchak, David, and Keyes, Sharrel. *Metro-Ministry.* Elgin, Ill.: David C. Cook Publishing, 1979.

Goodman, Grace Ann. *Rocking the Ark: Nine Case Studies of Traditional Churches in the Process of Change.* New York: Division of Evangelism, Board of National Missions, UPCUSA, 1968.

Greeley, Andrew. *The Church and the Suburbs.* Glen Rock, N.J.: Paulist Press, 1959; rev. 1963.

Jones, Ezra E., and Wilson, Robert L. *What's Ahead for Old First Church?* New York: Harper & Row, 1974.

Kloetzli, Walter. *The City Church: Death or Renewal.* Philadelphia: Muhlenberg Press, 1961.

Lee, Robert. *Cities and Churches: Readings on the Urban Church.* Philadelphia: Westminster Press, 1962.

Luzbetak, Louis J., S.V.D. *The Church in the Changing City.* Techny, Ill.: Divine Word, 1966.

Marty, Martin. *Death and Birth of the Parish.* St. Louis: Concordia, 1964.

Michonneau, Georges. *Revolution in a City Parish.* Westminster, Md.: Newman Press, 1950.

Moore, Richard E., and Day, Duane L. *Urban Church Breakthrough.* New York: Harper & Row, 1966.

Noyce, Gaylord. *The Responsible Suburban Church.* Philadelphia: Westminster Press, 1970.

———. *Survival and Mission for the City Church.* Philadelphia: Westminster Press, 1975.

Sanderson, Ross W. *The Church Serves the Changing City.* New York: Harper & Brothers, 1955.

Schaller, Lyle. *Planning for Protestantism in Urban America.* New York: Abingdon Press, 1965.

———. *Survival Tactics in the Parish.* New York: Abingdon Press, 1977.

Trexler, Edgar. *Creative Congregations: Tested Strategies for Today's Congregations.* Nashville: Abingdon Press, 1972.

Walrath, Douglas. *Leading Churches Through Change.* Nashville: Abingdon Press, 1979.

Ziegenhals, Walter E. *Urban Churches in Transition.* New York: Pilgrim Press, 1978.

3. Bring the World into the Church

Armstrong, Richard Stoll. *Service Evangelism.* Philadelphia: Westminster Press, 1979.

Belew, M. Wendell. *Churches and How They Grow.* Nashville: Broadman Press, 1971.

Gerber, Vergil. *God's Way to Keep a Church Going and Growing.* Glendale, Calif.: Regal Books, 1973.

Hunter, George G. *The Contagious Congregation: Frontiers in Evangelism and Church Growth.* Nashville: Abingdon Press, 1979.

Jones, Ezra E. *Strategies for New Churches.* New York: Harper & Row, 1976.

MacNair, Donald. *The Birth, Care and Feeding of a Local Church.* Grand Rapids: Baker Book House, 1971.

———. *The Growing Local Church.* Grand Rapids: Baker Book House, 1975.

McGavran, Donald, and Arn, Win C. *How to Grow a Church.* Glendale, Calif.: Regal Books, 1973.

———. *Ten Steps to Church Growth.* San Francisco: Harper & Row, 1977.

McGavran, Donald, and Hunter, George. *Church Growth: Strategies That Work.* Nashville: Abingdon Press, 1980.

Mylander, Charles. *Secrets for Growing Churches.* San Francisco: Harper & Row, 1979.

Porter, Harry Boone. *Growth and Life in the Local Church.* New York: Seabury Press, 1968.

Schaller, Lyle. *Assimilating New Members.* Nashville: Abingdon Press, 1978.

Shenk, Wilbert. *The Challenge of Church Growth.* Scottsdale, Penn.: Herald Press, 1973.

Wagner, C. Peter. *Church Growth and the Whole Gospel.* San Francisco: Harper & Row, 1981.

———. *Our Kind of People.* Atlanta: John Knox Press, 1979.

———. *Your Church Can Be Healthy.* Nashville: Abingdon Press, 1979.

———. *Your Church Can Grow*. Glendale, Calif.: Regal Books, 1976.

Waymire, Bob, and Wagner, C. Peter. *The Church Growth Survey Handbook*. Santa Clara, Calif.: The Global Church Growth Bulletin, 1980.

STUDIES OF CHURCH FUNCTIONS

1. Administration of the Congregation

Allan, Tom. *The Face of My Parish*. London: SCM Press, 1954; New York: Harper & Row, 1957.

Anderson, James D., and Jones, Ezra Earl. *The Management of Ministry*. San Francisco: Harper & Row, 1978.

Black, Samuel Charles. *Building a Working Church*. London: Fleming H. Revell, 1911.

Gilbert, W. Kent. *The Shaping of the Parish for the Future*. Philadelphia: Parish Life Press, 1975.

Glasse, James. *Putting It Together in the Parish*. Nashville: Abingdon Press, 1972.

Judy, Marvin. *The Cooperative Parish in Non-Metropolitan Areas*. Nashville: Abingdon Press, 1967.

Mead, Loren. *New Hope for Congregations*. New York: Seabury Press, 1972.

Pattison, E. Mansell. *Pastor and Parish: A Systems Approach*. Philadelphia: Fortress Press, 1977.

Schaller, Lyle. *Effective Church Planning*. Nashville: Abingdon Press, 1979.

———. *Hey, That's Our Church*. Nashville: Abingdon Press, 1975.

———. *The Local Church Looks to the Future: A Guide to Church Planning*. Nashville: Abingdon Press, 1968.

———. *Parish Planning*. Nashville: Abingdon Press, 1971.

Schaller, Lyle, and Tidwell, Charles A. *Creative Church Administration*. Nashville: Abingdon Press, 1975.

Winter, Michael. *Mission or Maintenance*. London: Darton, Longman & Todd, 1973.

Worley, Robert C. *A Gathering of Strangers: Understanding the Life of Your Church*. Philadelphia: Westminster Press, 1976.

2. Congregational Renewal

Anderson, James. *To Come Alive! A New Proposal for Revitalizing the Local Church*. New York: Harper & Row, 1973.

Broderick, Robert. *Your Parish Comes Alive.* Chicago: Franciscan Herald, 1970.
Dale, Robert D. *To Dream Again: How to Help Your Church Come Alive.* Nashville: Broadman Press, 1981.
De Blank, Joost. *The Parish in Action.* London: A. R. Mowbray, 1954.
Dietterich, Paul, and Wilson, Russell. *A Process of Local Church Vitalization.* Naperville, Ill.: Center for Parish Development, 1976.
Fisher, Wallace E. *Preface to Parish Renewal: Study Guide for Laymen.* Nashville: Abingdon Press, 1968.
Gibbs, Mark, and Morton, T. Ralph. *God's Frozen People: A Book for and About Christian Laymen.* Philadelphia: Westminster Press, 1965.
Gray, Rhea; Lewis, Douglas; Shawchuck, Norman; and Worley, Robert. *Experiences in Activating Congregations.* Chicago: Institute for Ministry Development, 1978.
Greeley, Andrew; Durkin, Mary; Shea, Thomas; Tracy, David; and McCready, William. *Parish, Priest and People: New Leadership for the Local Church.* Chicago: Thomas More Press, 1981.
Howard, Walden. *Nine Roads to Renewal.* Waco, Tex.: Word Books, 1967.
Judy, Marvin. *The Parish Development Process.* Nashville: Abingdon Press, 1973.
Lundin, Jack W. *A Church for an Open Future: Biblical Roots and Parish Renewal.* Philadelphia: Fortress Press, 1977.
Nelson, William, and Lincoln, William. *Journey Toward Renewal: New Routes for Old Churches.* Valley Forge, Penn.: Judson Press, 1971.
O'Connor, Elizabeth. *Call To Commitment.* New York: Harper & Row, 1963.
Raines, Robert. *New Life in the Church.* New York: Harper & Brothers, 1961.
Rose, Stephen, ed. *Who's Killing the Church?* Chicago: Chicago City Mission Society, 1966.
Schaller, Lyle. *Activating the Passive Church.* Nashville: Abingdon Press, 1981.
Schuller, Robert. *Your Church Has Real Possibilities.* Glendale, Calif.: Regal Books, 1974.
Seifert, Harvey. *New Power for the Church.* Philadelphia: Westminster Press, 1976.
Senft, Kenneth. *New Life in the Parish.* Minneapolis: Augsburg, 1970.
Smith, Donald P. *Congregations Alive.* Philadelphia: Westminster Press, 1981.

Southcott, Ernest. *The Parish Comes Alive.* London: A. R. Mowbray, 1956; New York: Morehouse-Gorham, 1957.

Trexler, Edgar. *Ways to Wake Up Your Church.* Philadelphia: Fortress Press, 1969.

Westerhoff, John. *Inner Growth, Outer Change: An Educational Guide to Church Renewal.* New York: Seabury Press, 1979.

Worley, Robert. *Change in the Church: A Source of Hope.* Philadelphia: Westminster, 1971.

———. *Dry Bones Breathe!* Chicago: Center for the Study of Church Organizational Behavior, 1978.

3. Conflict Management

Hadden, Jeffrey E. *The Gathering Storm in the Churches: The Widening Gap Between Clergy and Laymen.* Garden City, N.Y.: Doubleday, 1969.

Harris, John. *Stress, Power and Ministry: An Approach to the Current Dilemmas of Pastors and Congregations.* Washington: Alban Institute, 1977.

Leas, Speed, and Kittlaus, Paul. *Church Fights: Managing Conflict in the Local Church.* Philadelphia: Westminster Press, 1973.

Lee, Robert, and Galloway, Russell. *The Schizophrenic Church: Conflict over Community Organization.* Philadelphia: Westminster Press, 1969.

Lewis, G. Douglass. *Resolving Church Conflicts.* San Francisco: Harper & Row, 1981.

Miller, John Michael. *The Contentious Community: Constructive Conflict in the Church.* Philadelphia: Westminster Press, 1978.

Smith, Donald P. *Clergy in the Cross Fire.* Philadelphia: Westminster Press, 1973.

Sparks, James. *Potshots at the Preacher.* Nashville: Abingdon Press, 1977.

4. Congregation As Pastor

Barr, Browne. *The Well Church Book.* New York: Seabury Press, 1976.

Barr, Browne, and Eakin, Mary. *The Ministering Congregation.* Philadelphia: United Church Press, 1972.

Browning, Don. *The Moral Context of Pastoral Care.* Philadelphia: Westminster Press, 1976.

Clinebell, Howard John. *The Mental Health Ministry of the Local Church.* Nashville: Abingdon Press, 1972.

———. *Mental Health Through Christian Community: The Local*

Church's Ministry of Growth and Healing. New York: Abingdon Press, 1963.

Dittes, James. *The Church in the Way.* New York: Scribner, 1967.

Fenhagen, James. *Mutual Ministry: New Vitality for the Local Church.* New York: Seabury Press, 1977.

Holmes, Urban. *Priest in Community: Exploring the Roots of Ministry.* New York: Seabury Press, 1978.

Johnson, Roger A. *Congregations As Nurturing Communities.* Philadelphia: Division for Parish Services, LCA, 1979.

Lewis, G. Douglass. *Explorations in Ministry.* New York: IDOC, 1971.

Mathieson, Moira B. *The Shepherds of the Delectable Mountains: The Story of the Washington County Mission Program.* Washington: Alban Institute, 1979.

Oates, Wayne Edward. *Protestant Pastoral Counselling.* Philadelphia: Westminster Press, 1962.

Southard, Samuel. *Comprehensive Pastoral Care: Enabling the Laity to Share in Pastoral Ministry.* Valley Forge, Penn.: Judson Press, 1975.

Thornton, Edward. *Theology and Pastoral Counseling.* Englewood Cliffs, N.J.: Prentice-Hall, 1964.

Whitehead, Evelyn E. *The Parish in Community and Ministry.* New York: Paulist Press, 1978.

5. Congregation As Educator

Clarke, Stephen B. *Building Christian Communities.* Notre Dame, Ind.: Ave Maria Press, 1972.

Downs, Thomas. *The Parish As Learning Community: Modeling for Parish and Adult Growth.* New York: Paulist Press, 1979.

Groome, Thomas. *Christian Religious Education.* San Francisco: Harper & Row, 1980.

Moran, Gabriel. *Religious Body: Design for a New Reformation.* New York: Seabury Press, 1974.

Nelson, C. Ellis. *Where Faith Begins.* Richmond, Va.: John Knox Press, 1967.

Slusser, Gerald. *The Local Church in Transition.* Philadelphia: Westminster Press, 1964.

Westerhoff, John. *Will Our Children Have Faith?* New York: Seabury Press, 1976.

Westerhoff, John, and Neville, Gwen. *Generation to Generation: Conversations on Religious Education and Culture.* Philadelphia: United Church Press, 1974.

6. Congregation As Prophet

Gustafson, James M. *The Church As Moral Decision Maker.* Philadelphia: Pilgrim Press, 1970.

Hessel, Dieter T. *A Social Action Primer.* Philadelphia: Westminster Press, 1972.

Huber, Roger. *No Middle Ground.* Nashville: Abingdon Press, 1971.

Hudnut, Robert K. *Arousing the Sleeping Giant.* New York: Harper & Row, 1973.

———. *Church Growth Is Not the Point.* New York: Harper & Row, 1975.

———. *The Sleeping Giant: Arousing Church Power in America.* New York: Harper & Row, 1971.

Moltmann, Jurgen. *The Passion for Life: A Messianic Lifestyle.* Philadelphia: Fortress Press, 1977.

Mouw, Richard J. *Political Evangelism.* Grand Rapids: Eerdmans, 1973.

O'Connor, Elizabeth. *Journey Inward, Journey Outward.* Washington: Church of the Savior, 1968.

Palmer, Parker J. *The Company of Strangers.* New York: Crossroad, 1981.

Spike, Robert W. *In But Not of the World: A Notebook of Theology and Practice in the Local Church.* New York: Association Press, 1957.

7. Congregation As Worshiping Community

Abernathy, William. *A New Look for Sunday Morning.* Nashville: Abingdon Press, 1975.

Brand, Eugene. *Baptism: A Pastoral Perspective.* Minneapolis: Augsburg, 1975.

Kavanagh, Aidan. *The Shape of Baptism: The Rite of Christian Initiation.* New York: Pueblo, 1978.

Neville, Gwen, and Westerhoff, John. *Learning Through Liturgy.* New York: Seabury Press, 1978.

Shands, Alfred R. *The Liturgical Movement and the Local Church.* Naperville, Ill.: Allenson, 1959.

Willimon, William. *Worship As Pastoral Care.* Nashville: Abingdon Press, 1979.

DESCRIPTIVE RESEARCH

1. Internal: Religiousness Within the Congregation

Baker, Wesley. *The Split-Level Fellowship.* Philadelphia: Westminster Press, 1965.

Baumann, Dan. *All Originality Makes a Dull Church.* Santa Ana, Calif.: Vision House, 1976.

Biersdorf, John E. *Hunger for Experience: Vital Religious Communities in America.* New York: Seabury Press, 1975.

Campbell, Thomas, and Fukuyama, Yoshio. *The Fragmented Layman: An Empirical Study of Lay Attitudes.* Philadelphia: Pilgrim Press, 1970.

Dudley, Carl S. *Making the Small Church Effective.* Nashville: Abingdon Press, 1978.

Dulles, Avery Robert. *Models of the Church.* Garden City, N.Y.: Doubleday, 1974.

Fackre, Gabriel, and Fackre, Dorothy. *Under the Steeple.* New York: Abingdon Press, 1957.

Glock, Charles; Ringer, Benjamin; and Babbie, Earl. *To Comfort and to Challenge.* Berkeley: University of California, 1967.

Gustafson, James M. *Treasure in Earthen Vessels: The Churches As a Human Community.* New York: Harper & Row, 1961.

Heilmann, Samuel. *Synagogue Life.* Chicago: University of Chicago Press, 1976.

Johnson, Douglas, and Cornell, George W. *Punctured Preconceptions: What North American Christians Think About the Church.* New York: Friendship Press, 1972.

Kelly, Dean M. *Why Conservative Churches Are Growing.* New York: Harper & Row, 1972.

King, Morton B., and Hunt, Richard. *Measuring Religious Dimensions: Studies of Congregational Involvement.* Dallas, Tex.: Southern Methodist University, 1972.

Metz, Donald. *New Congregations: Security and Mission in Conflict.* Philadelphia: Westminster Press, 1967.

Moberg, David O. *The Church as a Social Institution.* Englewood Cliffs, N.J.: Prentice-Hall, 1962.

Quinn, Bernard. *The Small Rural Parish.* New York: Parish Project, National Conference of Catholic Bishops, 1980.

Reed, Bruce. *The Dynamics of Religion: Process and Movement in Christian Churches.* London: Darton, Longman and Todd, 1978.

Sweetser, Thomas. *The Catholic Parish: Shifting Membership in a Changing Church.* Chicago: Center for the Scientific Study of Religion, 1974.

Williams, Melvin D. *Community in a Black Pentecostal Church: An Anthropological Study.* Pittsburgh: University of Pittsburgh Press, 1974.

Wilson, Robert L. *Shaping the Congregation.* Nashville: Abingdon Press, 1981.

2. External: Relationship Between the Congregation and Its Community

Anderson, Arthur L. *Divided We Stand: Institutional Religion as a Reflection of Pluralism and Integration in America.* Dubuque: Kendall-Hunt, 1978.

Brewer, Earl, et al. *Protestant Parish: A Case Study of Rural and Urban Parish Patterns.* Atlanta: Communicative Arts Press, 1967.

Douglass, H. Paul. *The Church in the Changing City.* New York: George H. Doran, 1927.

———. *1000 City Churches.* New York: George H. Doran, 1926.

Ducey, Michael H. *Sunday Morning: Aspects of Urban Ritual.* New York: Free Press, 1977.

Dudley, Carl S. *Where Have All Our People Gone?* New York: Pilgrim Press, 1979.

Fichter, Joseph H., S.J. *Dynamics of a City Church.* Chicago: University of Chicago Press, 1951.

———. *Social Relations in the Urban Parish.* Chicago: University of Chicago Press, 1954.

Hoge, Dean R. *Converts, Dropouts, Returnees.* New York: Pilgrim Press, 1981.

Hoge, Dean R., and Roozen, David A. *Understanding Church Growth and Decline, 1950–1978.* New York: Pilgrim Press, 1979.

Leiffer, Murry H. *City and Church in Transition.* Chicago: Willet, Clark, 1938.

McGavran. Donald. *Understanding Church Growth.* Grand Rapids: Eerdmans, 1970.

Niebuhr, H. Richard. *Christ and Culture.* New York: Harper, 1951.

Nuesse, Celestine, and Harte, Thomas. *The Sociology of the Parish.* Milwaukee: Bruce, 1951.

Rauff, Edward A. *Why People Join the Church.* New York: Pilgrim Press, 1979.

Roof, Wade C. *Community and Commitment: Religious Plausibility in a Liberal Protestant Church.* New York: Elsevier, 1978.

Sanderson, Ross W. *The Strategy of City Church Planning.* New York: Institute of Social and Religious Research, 1932.

Schroeder, Widick, and Obenhaus, Victor. *Religion in American Culture: Unity and Diversity in a Midwestern County.* New York: Free Press of Glencoe, 1964.

Schroeder, Widick, et al. *Suburban Religion: Churches and Synagogues in the American Experience.* Chicago: Center for the Scientific Study of Religion, 1974.

Index

I burst out of the chair, discard the blanket on the floor in my haste to leave, push the mug of tea into her waiting hands, and hurry back to the car. In the lowering light I see that despite everything, she still waves and mouths to me to look after myself.